LIFE SCIENCES *before the* TWENTIETH CENTURY

BIOGRAPHICAL PORTRAITS

Editor

Professor Everett Mendelsohn teaches the history of science at Harvard University, where he has been on the faculty since 1960. He founded the *Journal of the History of Biology* in 1968 and served as its editor for the first 31 years. He has specialized his research in the history of the modern life sciences and the relations between science and society. His first book, *Heat and Life: The Theory of Animal Heat,* was published in 1964. His most recent book is an edited collection titled *The Practices of Human Genetics* (1999).

THE SCRIBNER SCIENCE REFERENCE SERIES

VOLUME 3

LIFE SCIENCES *before the* TWENTIETH CENTURY

BIOGRAPHICAL PORTRAITS

Everett Mendelsohn, *Editor*

Charles Scribner's Sons
an imprint of the Gale Group
New York • Detroit • San Francisco • London • Boston • Woodbridge, CT

Developed for Charles Scribner's Sons by Visual Education Corporation, Princeton, N.J.

For Scribners
PUBLISHER: Frank Menchaca
ASSOCIATE PUBLISHER: Timothy J. DeWerff
COVER DESIGN: Pamela Galbreath

For Visual Education Corporation
EDITORIAL DIRECTOR: Darryl Kestler
PROJECT DIRECTOR: Meera Vaidyanathan
WRITERS: John Haley, Charles Roebuck, Rebecca Stefoff
COPYEDITING MANAGER: Helen Castro
INDEXER: Stephen R. Ingle
PHOTO RESEARCH: Susan Buschhorn
INTERIOR DESIGN: Maxson Crandall, Rob Ehlers, Lisa Evans-Skopas
ELECTRONIC PREPARATION: Fiona Torphy

Library of Congress Cataloging-in-Publication Data

Life sciences before the twentieth century : biographical portraits / Everett Mendelsohn, editor.
     p.cm. - (The Scribner science reference series ; v. 3)
    Includes bibliographical references (p.).
    Summary: A collection of biographical profiles of famous anatomists, biologists, bacteriologists, biochemists, and others involved in the life sciences from ancient times through the nineteenth century.
    ISBN 0-684-80661-4
    1. Life scientists-Biography. 2. Life sciences-History. [Life scientists.] I. Mendelsohn, Everett. II Series.
    QH26.L52. 2001
    570'.92'2-dc21
    [B]   2001032045

TABLE OF CONTENTS

Table of Contents

INTRODUCTION

BY EVERETT MENDELSOHN

The study of living things, an activity that ultimately became biology and the life sciences, has a long and complicated history. But the reason for this is relatively simple—defining and identifying life and the living was often uncertain and contested. The plants and animals that are visible around us could easily be identified and classified, but it was the minute, often invisible forms that both eluded classification and gave rise to some of the most interesting scientific questions.

Debates over "What is life?" began in ancient times and continue today. The ancient Greek philosopher ARISTOTLE (384 B.C.–322 B.C.) wrote that life was best understood when observed within a framework in which each organism was part of a larger whole and had a purpose in that system. He believed that life was something that involved special living forces, special forms, and special ways of study. From Aristotle's time well into the early sixteenth and seventeenth centuries, the study of living things was closely linked to, and often embedded in, the writing of philosophers, although their major interests lay in broader philosophical questions rather than in the detailed look at life itself.

If one tradition in the early study of life developed among the philosophers, a second source can be found among the medical writers, such as the ancient Greek physician HIPPOCRATES (460 B.C.–ca. 370 B.C.), his associates, and their disciples. Hippocrates and his colleagues examined the fundamental questions of the nature of life and the living within the context of medicine. They studied the human body in its healthy and diseased states and attempted to understand the relationship between the two. They explored many biological topics within the context of the human as the living organism and as the subject of direct examination through theory, therapy, and surgery.

As medicine became more closely linked to the sciences, and biology more available to medicine for theory and explanation, the life sciences and the medical sciences became inextricably linked to one another and even necessary for each other's explanations and practices. Physicians from the time of Hippocrates well into the nineteenth century were among the major observers, experimenters, and authors of texts and treatises in biology and the life sciences. They developed ideas not only in their own area of study, but also transcended those boundaries to work in other areas of biology, sometimes as amateurs, other times as professional experimenters and theorists.

Because biology consisted of so many things, its modes of study also differed widely. The study of the functions of living organisms, particularly animals and humans, occurred within the context of medicine, where the primary focus was the organs of the body (the heart, the liver, the lungs, the urinary tract, the brain, and the kidneys). Physicians and surgeons examined the way in which each of these organs operated, measured and studied their physical structures, determined what went in and what came out, and compared their normal and abnormal functions.

Beyond these studies of animal function and locomotion there was a different tradition in the study of living things—natural history. In this tradition, unlike medicine, the text was not nearly as important as observation. Natural historians conducted field identification, sorting, collecting, and classifying plants and animals. They pondered the questions of which rules to use in relating the organisms they collected to others in the plant or animal kingdom.

During the sixteenth and seventeenth centuries the thirst for the knowledge of animal and plant forms increased and scientists began to launch expeditions around the globe. They established communities in South and North America and developed contacts with China, the Asian mainland, and South Asia. The variety of forms found in North and South America, Africa, and Asia provided challenges to the "settled" knowledge of European natural philosophers. Soon new methods of examination and understanding nature emerged, bringing with them new challenges. During the seventeenth century there was an increasing focus on the direct observation of nature as the source of knowledge, and on experimentation as a powerful way of interrogating nature and gaining new understandings of both plant and animal functions.

In the seventeenth century there was also a shift toward a mechanistic view of the world, the point at which the major challenge to the life sciences became apparent, giving rise to the following questions: Were living things fundamentally different from nonliving things? Could organisms be understood satisfactorily as mechanical, chemical, or physical systems? The implications of the mechanistic view set the stage for scientific debates in the centuries that followed. René Descartes (1596–1650), the great French philosopher, claimed that living systems obeyed the same fundamental mechanical rules as nonliving matter. William HARVEY (1578–1657), the great English experimenter whose classic work on the motion of the heart and blood set a new model and standard for experimentation, disagreed with Descartes. Harvey claimed that he was not seeking philosophical answers but was only observing and reporting what he found in nature itself, and that based on his observations, living things were fundamentally different from nonliving matter.

Another advance that occurred during the second half of the seventeenth century was the invention of the microscope, an achievement that enabled scientists to observe things that lay beyond normal vision. The works of the Dutch natural scientist Antoni van LEEUWENHOEK (1632–1723), the Dutch biologist Jan Swammerdam (1637–1680), and the English physicist Robert Hooke (1635–1702) disclosed the existence of active life at the microscopic level. This finding soon gave rise the questions: Where do these microorganisms fit in the order of nature? Were they just at the bottom of a continuous scale or were they something different? What function did they have in the larger scheme of living things? Was there a level of organization even smaller than these microorganisms?

The reproduction of living things was a focus of the students of nature from the time of Aristotle to the sixteenth century, when anatomists finally provided detailed observations of the formation of the fetus. Later William Harvey provided a new explanation in which he claimed that living structures were formed from undifferentiated (unspecialized) living matter that always originated in the egg. Harvey's explanation involved a continuity of life from generation to generation, but his opponents, the materialists, argued that life could be spontaneously generated from nonliving matter.

During the eighteenth century—a period of intense experimentation in all fields of science, and notably in the life sciences—the questions of reproduction took on the qualities of both scientific and philosophical debate. Were the structures of life formed anew in each succeeding generation (epigenesis)? Or were there preformed organisms derived from the male sperm or female egg that developed into the juvenile and later adult form (preformationism)? The problems surrounding reproduction and generation were not satisfactorily resolved in the eighteenth century. The issue of reproduction and generation reemerged in the nineteenth and early twentieth centuries when embryologists attempted to explain how simple cell division could lead to complex differentiated tissues, organs, and organisms. A recast of the debate resurfaced in the late twentieth century when the understanding of the structures and functions of life were taken to the molecular level and the problems of differentiation and organized structure became important again.

It is hard to imagine how the structure of living organisms was understood before scientists discovered that all the tissues of plants and animals consisted of cells. Although scientists had observed cells through their microscopes as early as the seventeenth century, they did not fully understand the role of cells in the structure of organisms until the third and fourth decades of the nineteenth century. The German botanist Matthias SCHLEIDEN (1804–1881), the German zoologist Theodor SCHWANN (1810–1882), and several other microscopists, morphologists, and physiologists were responsible for the development of a comprehensive cell theory. The new theory included Harvey's theme of the continuity of life when the German physician Rudolf VIRCHOW (1821–1902) proclaimed that all cells were derived from previous cells, and that by extension all life came from previous life. The debates surrounding this claim not only affected cell theory but also the controversial questions about spontaneous generation (the emergence of living microorganisms from nonliving material) and ultimately, the origin of life. In the 1850s Louis PASTEUR (1822–1895) demonstrated that almost every case of spontaneous generation was explainable by the existence of spores (single-celled body capable of development into a new individual), which are invisible to the naked eye but visible under the microscope.

Even as Pasteur was disproving spontaneous generation the parallel movement of a biological chemistry emerged to provide a solid link between the sciences of life and the sciences of matter—between biology and chemistry. Biochemists were demonstrating that all living matter and living processes involved chemical elements and molecules and chemical reactions. They began to explain function after function of living organisms at the level of chemical activity. In the process they uncovered new forms of chemical matter, most notably the large molecules found naturally only in living substances, and always found in living material, called proteins. As one nineteenth-century chemist put it, "Proteins are the natural form of existence of life."

Although the emergence of biochemistry showed the close link between living things and nonliving matter, the development in the mid-nineteenth century of the theory of evolution provided a very forceful explanation of the emergence of the great diversity of living forms. The English naturalist Charles DARWIN (1809–1882) argued in his 1859 treatise, *On the Origin of Species,* that change (evolution) came from the interaction of the organism with its environment, in which natural selection played the role of providing for the survival of the best-adapted organisms and their ability to reproduce their kind. The theory of evolution, which separated biological things from the nonbiological, became a powerful unifying theory in biology, replacing Aristotle's goal-driven framework and seeming to introduce chance as a key theme in understanding how life takes its forms and undergoes continuing change. Not surprisingly, evolution by natural selection was controversial at the time that it was first proposed and it was challenged largely because it undermined religious explanations of the origin and nature of life. While scientific debates about the processes of evolution continued, they occurred within the general acceptance of the belief that evolution itself did occur in a natural manner. Periodically, in the years since Darwin's 1859 publication, religious reaction aimed at reintroducing a role for a deity, a guiding hand, or an intelligent designer, has resurfaced but it has operated on the margins of science rather than within it.

One of the scientific criticisms of Darwinian evolution was that it left vague the explanation of how heredity actually occurs, of how traits are passed from one generation to the next, and what it is that natural selection acts upon in organisms. One of the ironies of the history of biology is that the answers to these questions, which were provided in the early decades of the twentieth century, actually came from the rediscovery of the scientific work of the Austrian monk Gregor MENDEL, who published his papers on heredity in 1865. Although historians have argued about why Mendel was overlooked, it seems to many observers that his theories, although clear, were insufficient. More experimentation on heredity and the processes of cellular division and reproduction had to occur before the fundamental laws of heredity, which Mendel had stated, could be readapted and firmly linked to the processes of evolution by natural selection.

The term *biology* itself was an invention that occurred around 1800 in the works of several scientists who were looking for a term that would bring together the variety of activities that focused on the structures and the functions of living things. The beginning of the nineteenth century was a time when scientists attempted to unify the sciences and seized the chance to bring together the disparate parts of the life sciences.

The history of biology and the life sciences is a history of continuing integration and specialization, bringing together the many separate parts and at the same time spawning new, strong, separate projects and proposals. The lives noted in the entries that follow give very good indication of this history, of the attempts, the successes, the failures, and the new challenges in understanding what living things are and how they behave.

TIME LINE

460 B.C.	HIPPOCRATES, the "father of medicine," is born.
ca. 430–380 B.C.	Hippocrates and members of the Coan and Cnidus schools produce the medical works that are later published in the *Collection*.
335 B.C.	ARISTOTLE establishes the Lyceum, a school.
322 B.C.	THEOPHRASTUS succeeds Aristotle as leader of the Lyceum.
A.D. 161	GALEN establishes a medical practice in Rome.
1153–1169	IBN RUSHD composes his major medical work, *Generalities,* drawn mostly from the works of Galen.
ca. 1240	ALBERTUS MAGNUS begins translations of Aristotle's works.
1528	PARACELSUS publishes his manual of surgery.
1530	Girolamo FRACASTORO publishes a narrative poem on the sexually transmitted disease syphilis.
1539	Jerome BOCK's *Neu Kreütterbuch* marks a new beginning in the field of botany.
1543	Andreas VESALIUS's *Fabrica* revolutionizes human anatomy.
1545	Ambroise PARÉ publishes a work on the treatment of gunshot wounds.
1546	Fracastoro states his view on infections and epidemic diseases and publishes a work describing many contagious diseases.
1551–1571	Konrad GESNER publishes *Opera botanica,* a botanical treatise, and *Historia animalium,* a zoological work.
1553	Michael SERVETUS publishes *Christianismi restitutio,* proposing the pulmonary circulation of blood; later executed for heresy.
1559	Realdo COLOMBO's *De re anatomica* describes human anatomy and Colombo's rich experiences in dissection, vivisection, autopsy, and surgery.
1565	Royal College of Physicians, London, empowered to carry out human dissections.
1603	Girolamo FABRICI publishes *De venarum ostiolis,* describing the valves that regulate the flow of blood.
1604	Fabrici's *De formato foetu* explains fetal development in birds, animals, and humans.
1614	Santorio SANTORIO announces the results of his study of metabolism and perspiration in *De statica medicina*.

Time Line

1831	Charles Robert DARWIN begins his five-year voyage aboard HMS *Beagle*.
1831	Brown discovers the cell nucleus in plants.
1831	Justus von LIEBIG and American scientist Samuel Guthrie simultaneously invent chloroform, an anesthetic.
1832	Liebig founds the *Annals of Chemistry and Pharmacology,* the leading journal in those fields.
1832	Jan Evangelista PURKYNE acquires a new microscope, which accelerates his histological work.
1833	Johannes Peter MÜLLER's *Handbuch der Physiologie* links physiological research to medical treatment.
1838–1843	In *Flora of North America,* Asa GRAY proposes a shift from the Linnean classification system.
1839	Theodor SCHWANN announces his cell formation theory.
1840	Liebig discovers the fundamentals of artificial fertilizer.
1847	Ignaz SEMMELWEIS discovers a connection between puerperal fever and contamination from cadavers.
1849	Claude BERNARD publishes a paper on the role of the pancreas in digestion.
1849–1856	Rudolf Carl VIRCHOW develops the concept of cellular pathology at the University of Würzburg.
1851	Hermann von HELMHOLTZ invents the ophthalmoscope.
1854–1862	Alfred Russel WALLACE independently formulates a theory of evolution based on natural selection.
1857	Louis PASTEUR publishes his findings on lactic fermentation; proves that living organisms cause fermentation.
1858	Joseph LISTER studies coagulation of blood.
1859	Charles Darwin publishes *On the Origin of Species by Means of Natural Selection.*
1860	Pasteur publishes his findings on alcoholic fermentation.
1861	Henry Walter BATES is the first to offer a scientific theory to explain why certain animals mimic others.
1863	Thomas Henry HUXLEY publishes *Evidence as to Man's Place in Nature.*
	Pasteur invents pasteurization (heat treatment) for wine.
1865	Lister initiates antiseptic surgery using carbolic acid on a compound wound.
	Johann Gregor MENDEL enunciates his laws of heredity based on plant hybridization experiments.
	Pasteur cures silkworm disease, saving the French silk industry.
1867	Lister announces the results of his antiseptic surgeries in the prestigious journal *The Lancet.*
1868	Graceanna LEWIS publishes *Natural History of Birds.*
1876	Robert KOCH discovers anthrax bacillus.
1877	Koch develops techniques to isolate, cultivate, and stain disease-causing bacteria.

Time Line

1880 Pasteur creates vaccines for anthrax and fowl cholera.

Josef BREUER uses hypnosis to treat hysteria.

1882 Élie METCHNIKOFF discovers the role of phagocytes in the defense against disease microorganisms.

1883 Francis GALTON coins the term *eugenics*.

1885 Theodor BOVERI begins his chromosome studies.

Pasteur performs his first successful rabies treatment on a nine-year-old boy.

1890 Emil von BEHRING announces the discovery of antitoxins.

Koch announces his discovery of a substance capable of preventing the growth of the tubercle bacillus.

1899–1906 Paul EHRLICH develops and elaborates on the side-chain theory.

1901 Behring is the first recipient of the Nobel Prize for physiology or medicine for his work in serology.

1905 Koch receives the Nobel Prize for physiology or medicine for his work on tuberculosis.

1906 Camillo GOLGI receives the Nobel Prize for his investigations of the anatomy and functioning of the nervous system.

1906 August Paul von WASSERMANN develops the Wassermann test, a method to diagnose syphilis in humans.

1908 Ehrlich and Metchnikoff share the Nobel Prize for physiology or medicine for their work on immunity.

1910 Ehrlich announces that his experiments with Salvarsan have shown curative properties in rabbit syphilis and in clinical trials on syphilitic patients.

THE AGASSIZES

Jean Louis Rodolphe Agassiz
1807–1873
NATURAL HISTORY,
GEOLOGY, PALEONTOLOGY

Elizabeth Cabot Cary Agassiz
1822–1907
NATURAL HISTORY

Alexander Agassiz
1835–1910
ZOOLOGY, OCEANOGRAPHY

*naturalist one who studies objects in their natural settings

The Swiss scientist Louis Agassiz was one of the leading naturalists* of the nineteenth century. He is best known for his study of glaciers and his work on fossil fishes. He worked closely with his wife Elizabeth, who wrote natural history and travel books and championed women's education; and his son, Alexander, a distinguished zoologist and oceanographer. Together, the Agassizes were instrumental in establishing new institutions and in popularizing the study of natural history in the United States.

Lives and Careers. Born into a wealthy family in Motier-en-Vuly, Switzerland, Louis Agassiz studied natural history and medicine in Europe. His early work on the fishes of Brazil stimulated greater interest in natural history and brought him to the attention of the French naturalist Georges CUVIER. In 1830, after Agassiz earned his doctorates in philosophy and medicine, he moved to Paris, where he studied under Cuvier. Two years later, he accepted a professorship at the College of Neuchâtel in Switzerland. The same year he married Cécile Braun and the couple had three children, including Alexander. Agassiz then turned his attention to the study of glaciers, the large rivers of ice that covered much of the Swiss Alps. In 1847, when Cécile Braun died, Agassiz decided to move to the United States and to accept a professorship at Harvard University's Lawrence Scientific School.

In Boston, Agassiz met Elizabeth Cabot Cary, the daughter of one of Boston's prominent families. Although Cary had little formal education, she shared Agassiz's enthusiasm for teaching and popularizing natural history and science. The couple was married three years later and they formed a successful scientific team. Elizabeth kept notes of her husband's lectures, and these formed the basis of his publications. They traveled together on scientific journeys throughout the Americas, many of which Elizabeth organized and managed.

Alexander Agassiz was born in 1835 in Neuchâtel. During his youth, he was greatly influenced by his uncle, Alexander Braun, a famous botanist. In 1849, Alexander joined his father and stepmother in the United States. He attended Harvard College and the Lawrence Scientific School, graduating with degrees in engineering and zoology. In 1859, after a short career in the United States Coast Survey, Alexander became his father's assistant at Harvard University's Museum of Comparative Zoology. Alexander also worked closely with Elizabeth, with whom he had formed a lasting bond.

Scientific Accomplishments. Louis Agassiz first gained recognition for *Poissons fossiles* (Fossil Fishes), which he wrote in the tradition of his mentor Cuvier. Agassiz used principles of comparative anatomy to reconstruct, illustrate, and classify more than 1,700 extinct species of Brazilian fishes. This effort provided future students with primary data relating zoology to the fields of geology and paleontology*.

Agassiz is also well known for his study of glaciers, which he conducted during his tenure as professor at Neuchâtel. He examined the glacial formations of Switzerland and compared them with the geology

*paleontology study of extinct or prehistoric life, usually through the examination of fossils

1

of England and central Europe. By examining rock deposits and measuring ice formations, Agassiz found widespread evidence of past glacial activity in Europe. In 1840, he published *Études sur les glaciers* (Studies on the Glaciers), in which he concluded that massive sheets of ice once covered much of northern Europe and that the recession of ice was responsible for modern geological formations.

Agassiz's assertions were sufficient to convince the English naturalist Charles DARWIN and his supporters that glacial movement explained how genetically related species of animals and plants came to inhabit lands widely separated from one another. Agassiz, however, believed that the Ice Age was one of many catastrophes sent by God that separated ancient species from those of modern times. He argued that creation occurred about 20 separate times during the earth's history, with God introducing new species in each successive creation. For Agassiz there was no continuity of development or evolution* of earlier species into later ones. He became the most prominent American opponent of Darwin's theory of evolution by natural selection* and engaged in a series of debates with a fellow Harvard professor, the botanist Asa GRAY, who was Darwin's most prominent defender in North America.

Campaign for Education. Louis and Elizabeth Agassiz were pioneers of education. At Harvard, Agassiz introduced a new style of instruction that emphasized gathering and examining data from the real world instead of relying on the information in textbooks. In 1859 Agassiz founded the Museum of Comparative Zoology at Harvard, and some years later he and Elizabeth founded a marine laboratory in Buzzards Bay, Massachusetts, that had a major influence on biological research in the United States. The institution later became the Marine Biological Laboratory at Woods Hole.

Elizabeth Agassiz also ran a school for girls out of the couple's home. She published several books, including *Seaside Studies in Natural History* and *A Journey in Brazil,* which were based on the field notes she kept during the couple's many scientific expeditions. Her writings were widely read and helped popularize the study of natural history in the United States.

Elizabeth continued to promote women's education after Agassiz's death from a stroke in 1873. Her efforts led to the founding of a college for women taught by the faculty of Harvard. In 1893, this institution became Radcliffe College and Elizabeth was its first president. She retired some years before she died of a stroke in 1907.

After Agassiz's death, Alexander became the director of the museum at Harvard, a position he retained for the rest of his life. From about 1860 to the late 1870s, Alexander was largely concerned with the study of zoology, beginning with the animals of the New England shore. During this time his theories on the geographical distribution of animals coincided more with his father's than with those proposed by Darwin, which were then sweeping through the American scientific community. He later explored the waters of

*evolution historical development of a biological group such as a species

*natural selection theory that within a given species, individuals with characteristics best adapted to the environment survive and successfully produce more offspring than other individuals, resulting in changes in the species over time

the Pacific from the Galápagos Islands to the Gulf of California to make a comparative study of marine life on both sides of the Isthmus of Panama.

Also interested in coral reefs, Alexander Agassiz explored the Barrier and Bermuda Islands, the Great Barrier Reef, Fiji, Maldives, and several islands in the central Pacific during the mid- to late 1890s. He wrote and published reports on his voyages but never finished a general work on the coral reefs. By the time of his death in 1910 during a voyage across the Atlantic, from England to America, Alexander had become a well-known zoologist and oceanographer.

Saint Albertus Magnus, also known as Albert the Great, is best known for his translation of the works of the Greek philosopher ARISTOTLE, whose ideas formed the basis of much of medieval* science. Albert, however, was an accomplished scientist in his own right; his work incorporated principles that were useful to later generations of scientists.

Albert was born into a wealthy and powerful family in Lauingen, Bavaria (a state in present-day Germany). He was educated in Italy, where he joined the Dominican religious order despite his parents' objections, studied theology*, and was ordained a priest. Around 1241, he was sent to teach at the University of Paris, where he remained for seven years. He then went to Cologne, where he founded his own school; among his students was the famous Catholic theologian Thomas Aquinas. Albert died in Cologne in 1280.

An early champion of the direct study of nature using observation and forms of experiment, Albert urged scientists not to rely solely on previous authority, but to conduct their own investigations and formulate conclusions based on the evidence they collected. Although his theories of nature were basically Aristotelian, he did undertake new empirical* studies. Albert's most important contributions to life sciences are his masterful treatises on plants and animals. He carried out a comparative study of the anatomy of plants and made observations on new plant species. In his animal studies he identified four different types of reproduction and outlined the basic principles of sexual reproduction. He dissected embryos* to study their development and understood some aspects of fetal nutrition. He also acquired a thorough knowledge of insects, particularly insect mating.

In addition to his work in life sciences, Albert made contributions to veterinary medicine, dentistry, astronomy, cosmology*, physics, meteorology*, and theology. Many of these subjects were previously studied by Aristotle, and Albert provided commentaries and new evidence. His efforts earned him the titles "Albert the Great" and the "Universal Doctor." In 1931 Pope Pius XI named him a saint, and ten years later Pope Pius XII declared him the patron of all who explore the natural sciences.

Saint
ALBERTUS MAGNUS
ca. 1200–1280
LIFE SCIENCE

medieval relating to the Middle Ages in Europe, a period from about 500 to 1500

theology study of religion

empirical based on or derived from observation and experiment

embryo organism from the first division of the fertilized egg through the early stages of development until birth or hatching

cosmology study of the origin, history, and structure of the universe

meteorology science that deals with the atmosphere, especially the weather and weather predictions; also known as atmospheric science

ARISTOTLE

384 B.C.–322 B.C.

SCIENTIFIC METHODOLOGY,
BIOLOGY, PSYCHOLOGY,
PHYSICAL SCIENCES

The philosopher and scientist Aristotle was one of the most influential thinkers of ancient Greek culture. Embracing the entire realm of human knowledge as his field, Aristotle studied and wrote about such diverse topics as poetry, politics, physics, astronomy, and the purpose of life. He defined the scope of the sciences, helped establish principles of scientific investigation, and developed a formal system of logic that became a foundation of Western intellectual activity.

Unlike his teacher Plato, the other leading philosopher of the ancient Greeks, Aristotle did not regard the soul as something separate from the body. He believed that the divine and the earthly were mingled in physical existence, and his approach to philosophy and science was grounded in the material world. Aristotle was a skilled observer of both human society and nature. Among his major contributions were works in zoology, human biology, and psychology.

Life and Work

Aristotle lived in a time and place that produced many famous and noteworthy people, and during his lifetime he encountered many of them. At the same time, his own accomplishments and writings earned him a place as one of the foremost philosophers of the time.

Four Phases. Aristotle's life falls into four general phases. The first phase, his childhood and early education, began with his birth in the Greek community of Stagira, located in Chalcidice, a peninsula in Macedon, the kingdom north of Greece. Aristotle's father, a physician, served the Macedonian king. During his childhood, Aristotle was probably exposed to the widely used Greek medical thought and practice.

The second phase of Aristotle's life began after the deaths of his parents. At the age of 17, he was sent to Athens, one of the leading Greek cities, to complete his education. He entered the Academy, a school run by the renowned philosopher Plato, where he remained for 20 years, studying, teaching, and writing. His large family estates provided him with sufficient income to support him in comfortable style, and he was known for dressing well and for his large book collection.

Plato's death in 347 B.C. ushered in the third phase of Aristotle's life. Aristotle left Athens, either because he disapproved of Plato's nephew, who had inherited the Academy, or because his own connections with Macedonia made him politically unpopular in Athens, where feeling against the conquering Macedonians was on the rise. Accompanied by several close friends and fellow scholars, Aristotle spent 12 years traveling. He went first to a Greek city on the coast of present-day Turkey, where he befriended the local ruler. There he wrote works on politics and kingship and married the ruler's niece. Three years later Aristotle and his group moved to the island of Lesbos, where he carried out much of his biological research. In 342 B.C., Aristotle returned to Macedon and spent the next three years tutoring a young prince who later became the ruler Alexander the Great. Thereafter Aristotle settled on the property in Stagira that he had inherited from his father.

Pzobleumata Areſtote
lis determinantia multas
queſtiones de varijs corpozuz humanoz diſpoſitionibus
valde audientibus ſuaues Cum eiuſdem Areſtotelis vita
et mozte metrice deſcripta Subiunctis metrozum cum in
terlineali gloſa ſententialibus expoſitionibus.

In 335 B.C., Aristotle founded the Lyceum, a school located just outside Athens. He lectured to students while walking along a covered walkway in the school. Because of this, the school and its students were called Peripatetics, from the Greek "to walk around." In this 15th-century woodcut, however, Aristotle is seen seated at a lectern before two admiring and attentive students.

By 335 B.C., Athens had come under Macedonian rule, and for the fourth phase of his life, Aristotle returned to that city. On the grounds of a school called the Lyceum, he gave lectures on many subjects. With the support of his philosophical associates and some distinguished students and disciples, he established a natural history* museum and a library for maps and manuscripts. Aristotle also developed a research plan that influenced various authors' histories of Greek mathematics, astronomy, medicine, and natural philosophy*.

*natural history systematic study of animals and plants, especially in their natural settings

*natural philosophy set of theories or ideas about the natural world; theoretical basis for research in the natural sciences

5

After Alexander's death in 323 B.C., the anti-Macedonian mood again gained strength in Athens. Aristotle, a friend of the Macedonian rulers, came under criticism and he again withdrew from the city. He resettled on his mother's estate in Chalcis on the Greek island of Euboea, but died shortly thereafter.

Achievements and Writings. Aristotle produced several works on literary and philosophical topics. His literary works include *On Rhetoric,* which deals with the art of using language persuasively, and *Poetics,* which analyzes the elements and purposes of literature. Aristotle's philosophical work *On Philosophy* defines the role of the philosopher and sets forth his belief that the development of philosophy—the intellectual exploration of the natural and eventually the divine realms—is the highest expression of civilization. The six works containing Aristotle's system of logic are together known as the *Organon.*

Scholars believe that most of Aristotle's work in biology dates from his years abroad, after he left Athens for the first time. The groundwork for his scientific studies, however, was laid during the years he spent studying under Plato at the Academy. One aspect of the Academy that Aristotle came to regard highly was the institute's emphasis on mathematics, which he believed was the model for any well-organized science. Aristotle felt that it was important to establish clear-cut borders for the various sciences, and he was greatly concerned with the issue of pairing questions with their appropriate branch of inquiry. His approach to knowledge was to sort things into categories, whether he was mapping all understanding into the particular sciences or attempting to develop a system for classifying animals according to their similarities and differences.

Aristotle outlined the kinds of questions scientists ought to ask. He recognized that the nature and behavior of things called for forms of explanation beyond those that mathematics could offer. Faced with a person, a tree, or a flame, a scientist could ask what is it made of (its matter), what is its essential character (its form), what produced it (its cause), and what is its purpose (its end). Aristotle believed that one could ask these questions of almost everything in the universe.

One of Aristotle's main contributions to science was his concern with methodology, or the way in which science is done. In his view, science begins with observations of the way things are in the physical world. The scientist forms theories to explain those observations, but if new knowledge refutes a theory, the theory should be able to change to accommodate the facts. Aristotle clarifies this important point in a discussion of bees, saying, "This, then, appears to be the method of reproduction of bees, according to theory together with the apparent facts. But the facts have not been satisfactorily ascertained, and if ever they are, then credence must be given to observation rather than to theory, and to theory only in so far as it agrees with what is observed." However, his empirical* approach to the study of biological forms stood in contrast to his methods in some other fields where he deemed theory more important.

***empirical** based on or derived from observation and experiment

The ancient Roman writer Cicero compared Aristotle's smooth writing style to a "river of gold." Unfortunately, however, modern readers cannot float down that river. All of the writings that Aristotle produced have been lost in the centuries after his death. What remains is a collection of texts assembled between 100 and 1 B.C., long after Aristotle's death. Most are working documents that Aristotle produced during his research and teaching, notes and essays not intended for publication. In addition, the scholars who edited or interpreted Aristotle's work in ancient times rearranged and added to this material, so that what remains is probably not always in Aristotle's original words.

Aristotle on the Life Sciences
Today Aristotle's philosophical works are read more than his scientific ones because science has changed greatly since his time. His zoological writings, which consist of observations and theories, comprise one-fourth of his entire known output, and for many centuries after his death, they provided a guide for explanations and observation.

Zoology. Aristotle's fullest collection of writings about animal biology is a text called *Historia animalium* (History of Animals), in which he describes or at least mentions 555 species. This text, which some scholars believe may have been partly written by others, was meant as a reference volume. People studying Aristotle's shorter zoological works, such as *De partibus animalium* (Parts of Animals) and *De incessu animalium* (Movement of Animals), both of which were theoretical in nature, could consult the *Historia* for more information about the animals mentioned in them.

Aristotle wrestled with the problem of how best to sort animals into categories but was never able to develop a fully satisfactory system of classification. For practical purposes he created some major groupings, such as animals that give birth to live young, animals that lay eggs, fishes, insects, and so on. He realized, however, that before he could devise a satisfactory system of classification, he needed more information. In the *Historia,* he tried to organize information not by individual species but under such general headings as "Parts of the Body." Information about elephants, for example, could appear under many different headings.

Familiar animals, such as horses, dogs, sheep, and pigs, received much attention in Aristotle's zoological writings, as did creatures not native to Greece, such as elephants, camels, monkeys, and lions. Although Aristotle's main sources of information were fishermen, farmers, stockbreeders, and hunters, he also gathered material from travelers and from the operators of traveling animal shows. For instance, his discussion of the lion's appearance and manner of walking suggests that he probably observed a live lion in such a show.

Many of Aristotle's reports are based on his own observations, including careful dissections of chameleons, lobsters, and several species of fishes and birds. (Some of his reports, however, are based on reports of animals seen by others during Alexander's travels to the East.) In his writings, he complains often that the smallness of some insects made it impossible for him to make out their structures, especially the insides of their bodies (the microscope was many centuries in the future). Some of the obvious mistakes in his works are in his references to human beings, where dissection was not possible, or to rarer animals, where he might not have had a chance to study and dissect a dead body and had to rely on others' accounts. Often, however, his careful observations enabled him to correct old misconceptions. By describing a viper that he had seen shedding its skin, for example, he corrected an earlier statement that this type of snake does not shed its skin.

Under the main heading "Parts of the Body" in the *Historia animalium,* Aristotle discusses the external and internal structures of animals, noting the significant differences between various animal types. Under "Lives and Activities," he addresses such topics as reproduction, feeding, migration, hibernation, and habitat. Under "Characters," he discusses animal psychology and intelligence, comparing such habits as nesting, care of the young, and rivalry. When Aristotle began working on the *Historia,* the work was an orderly arrangement of information under headings, but complete reports of particular animals were later inserted into the *Historia* as if into a filing cabinet, waiting for their information to be properly assigned to the headings. This change of plan and the lack of revision and editing make the *Historia* seem bewildering. Nevertheless, its wide range and Aristotle's high degree of insight made it the outstanding work of zoological description in the ancient world.

Anatomy and Physiology. In his study of animals, Aristotle devoted some attention to their anatomy and physiology*, giving great importance to the heart, blood vessels, and blood. Aristotle divided animals into two great classes, those with blood and those without. Modern classifications place the major division between vertebrates (animals with spinal columns) and invertebrates (animals without spinal columns), and although there is some overlap between the two systems, the Aristotelian classification has not survived.

Aristotle provided a fairly accurate description of the blood vessels as a system extending throughout the body, with its center in the heart. Earlier writers had focused only on the blood vessels near the body's surface, such as the ones visible just under the skin in very thin people. Aristotle's more detailed account of the internal arrangement of the blood vessels was of use to later anatomists. He achieved this success by examining animals that had been strangled, allowing the blood to remain in their vessels.

Aristotle's understanding of the blood system left some important discoveries to be made by others. He did not distinguish between the arteries, vessels that carry blood away from the heart, and the veins, which carry blood toward it, but he traced the main branches of both. He interpreted the pumping of the heart as a reaction to an innate beat in the heart that caused a kind of boiling movement in the blood, which in turn caused the blood to become thin (rarified), pour into the

*physiology science that deals with the functions of living organisms and their parts

blood vessels, and create heat in the body. Breathing, in Aristotle's view, helped cool the heat produced in the blood and in the heart. He considered the brain a cold organ as compared to the heart. The brain's purpose was to cool the body, balancing the warmth of the heart. Unaware of the nervous system and its relation to the brain, Aristotle considered the warm heart as the center of the body.

Psychology. Aristotle believed that the source of movement in plants and animals was their souls but he did not regard the souls as separate entities that inhabit bodies. In both his biological writings and his other works, Aristotle argued that soul is not an independent substance but is the essence that gives life and form to bodies. In plants the soul causes growth and reproduction. In animals it also causes feeling, hearing, taste, sight, smell, and movement. In humans the soul has an additional aspect—the intellect.

In a series of short works later grouped together under the title *Parva Naturalia* (Short Treatises on Natural Science), Aristotle turned his attention to various aspects of physical and mental life. Some of these works, such as Aristotle's treatments of memory, sleep, and dreams, are concerned with topics now considered part of the field of human psychology. Other writings in this group briefly discuss breathing, youth and old age, and the length or brevity of life.

Influence on Science

Aristotle's influence on later philosophical and scientific thought has been vast. By A.D. 200, Aristotle's texts were popular in most of the Mediterranean world. Roman scholars translated his works into Latin, and manuscripts translated into the languages of Syria and of Armenia in western Asia also survive. Arab scholars were among the main translators of Aristotle's works, and some of the Arabic texts were in turn translated into Latin after 1100, especially when the original Greek texts had been lost.

Aristotle's writings became increasingly available to educated Europeans from about the 1200s. They were often linked to the rebirth of scientific activity that took place in Europe around that time, led by such pioneers as the English philosopher Roger Bacon and the German-born Saint ALBERTUS MAGNUS. The *Historia animalium* played a key role in biology. Combined with Aristotle's other zoological works, the *Historia* became the major ingredient in a work titled *de animalibus* (On Animals), written in the 1200s by Albertus Magnus, which dominated zoological science until the 1500s.

Perhaps Aristotle's greatest influence on the development of science was his insistence that the necessary beginning of science was the observation of nature and natural phenomena. Another sign of his lasting legacy is the number of scientific terms that come directly from his Greek writings or from their Latin translations. Of particular use in the life sciences are *genus** and *species,* two terms that form the basis of the modern system of classifying animals and plants.

Aristotle the Observer

Aristotle made mistakes in his accounts of animals, but he also reported things that had remained unknown to other scientists for centuries. He wrote that the eggs of sea urchins are larger during the full moon, which was recently corroborated by studies conducted in the Red Sea. His observation that some partridges cackle and others whistle helped lead to the 1962 discovery of two species of these birds living side by side in northern Greece. Aristotle also described a species of river catfish that was rediscovered in modern times and named *Parasilurus aristotelis* in his honor.

***genus** category of biological classification; class, kind, or group of organisms that share common characteristics; *pl.* genera

John James
AUDUBON

1785–1851

ORNITHOLOGY

---

*naturalist one who studies objects in their natural settings

John James Audubon's extensive collection of sketches and drawings of birds has made him famous among bird lovers and naturalists* around the world. Although he had no formal training in either field, his name is forever linked to art and to ornithology, the scientific study of birds.

Life and Work. Audubon was born on the Caribbean island of Santo Domingo (present-day Haiti), the illegitimate son of a French sea captain and a Creole woman. In 1791 Audubon and his half sister went to live in France with Audubon's father, who legally adopted the children three years later. At age 18 Audubon was sent to live on a farm in Pennsylvania run by friends of his father. Five years later he married and moved to Louisville, Kentucky, where he was a partner in running a store. Although unsuccessful as a merchant, he was a skilled hunter and artist who roamed the countryside hunting birds and painting those that he shot. He often mounted the dead birds on wires to draw them in natural poses. After going bankrupt in 1820, Audubon set out for Louisiana, hoping to find a publisher for his bird pictures. For the next four years he lived in Mississippi and Louisiana, during which time he created his best works.

In 1826, having failed to find a publisher in the United States, Audubon left for England, where he found supporters. During the next 12 years, he published his masterwork, *The Birds of North America,* which contains 435 magnificent copperplate prints of his paintings. This multivolume work immediately established his reputation as an American naturalist and led to his election as a fellow of the Royal Society of London. Audubon returned to the United States several times in an attempt to include all of the birds of North America in his work. His travels took him from the Florida Keys to Canada, southeast Texas, and as far as present-day North Dakota. During his later years, he produced another work called *Viviparous Quadrupeds* that discussed and illustrated North American mammals. It was his last major work. Audubon died in New York in 1851.

Evaluation of Audubon's Work. Audubon's reputation rests on his abilities as an artist, not as a scientist. His drawings were dramatic and colorful, and they expressed a sense of birds in their natural environment. This approach was revolutionary at the time and has been rarely duplicated since. His pictures contained many technical errors, however, but these were apparent only to specialists and did nothing to diminish the popularity of his work. Like other naturalists of his day, Audubon accompanied his drawings with notes on the habits and habitats of his subjects. His observations were unsystematic and lacking in detail, precision, and consistency, and they were no match for the quality of his illustrations.

Audubon did however engage in many original experiments that showed his originality of mind. In one experiment, he tied colored thread to several birds and recovered them a year later, demonstrating their return to nesting places. This was the first attempt to band birds, a practice that was adopted by scientists more than 50 years later. Although he did not pursue his talent for experiment with much vigor, his work influenced many later American naturalists and remains overwhelmingly popular more than 150 years after his death.

Karl Ernst von
BAER

1792–1876

BIOLOGY, ANTHROPOLOGY

Karl Ernst von Baer's greatest contributions to science came from the study of embryos* and their development into adult organisms. His efforts in this field were important in shaping scientific thinking about the processes of animal development. In addition to the study of embryos, von Baer was also interested in anthropology*, entomology*, geology, and geography.

Life and Career. Born in Piep, Estonia, into a family of nobles, von Baer was sent to live with his uncle on a neighboring estate where he acquired an early love for plants and natural history. Although his uncle had hoped he would follow a military career, von Baer enrolled as a medical student at the University of Dorpat. After receiving his M.D. in 1814, he continued his medical studies at the Universities of Berlin, Vienna, and Würzburg. At Würzburg he studied comparative anatomy under Ignaz Döllinger, the famous German physiologist who tried to persuade him to study chick embryos using advanced scientific methods. At the time, von Baer was unwilling to spend the time or money necessary to do so, but he later returned to this line of inquiry.

In 1817 von Baer moved to Königsberg, East Prussia, to teach anatomy at the university there and later became professor of zoology. He also served as dean of the medical school, rector (priest) of the university, and director of the city's botanical gardens. He made his most important discoveries in embryology while working in Königsberg, and after spending 11 years in that city, he moved to St. Petersburg, Russia. He had been appointed a member of the Russian Academy of Sciences in St. Petersburg two years earlier. His work included acting as director of the academy's anatomical museum and teaching comparative anatomy and physiology at the Medico-Chirurgical Academy. He also undertook scientific expeditions in Europe and Asia, which enabled him to contribute to natural history, geology, geography, and anthropology.

During his time in St. Petersburg, von Baer also helped found the Russian Geographical Society, the Russian Entomological Society, and the German Anthropological Society. He retired from active membership in the Academy of Sciences in 1862 but continued to work as an honorary member for five more years. Thereafter he returned to Dorpat, Estonia, where he lived until his death in 1876. By that time, von Baer was one of Europe's most widely accomplished and recognized scientists.

Scientific Accomplishments. In his early work with embryos, von Baer made several discoveries relating to the development of organs

Von Baer began more writings than he completed. For instance, he never completely described his collections from his 1828 scientific expedition to Novaya Zemlya. Nevertheless, many of his writings were published—perhaps a testament of his importance to science.

embryo organism from the first division of the fertilized egg through the early stages of development until birth or hatching

anthropology study of human beings, especially in relation to origins and physical and cultural characteristics

entomology scientific study of insects

11

Baer, Karl Ernst von

*neural of or relating to the nerves or nervous system

*vesicle fluid-filled cavity in the body

*vertebrate animal with a backbone

*undifferentiated not specialized

*differentiated referring to differentiation, the process whereby cells, tissues, and structures are specialized to perform certain functions

*evolutionist one who studies evolution, the historical development of a biological group such as a species

*cranial of or relating to the skull (cranium)

and organ systems. He discovered the notochord in the embryo, the structure from which the spine develops, and was the first to observe that neural* folds in the embryo develop into the central nervous system. However, he was puzzled by the exact mechanism by which these embryonic transformations occurred. Von Baer was also the first to describe the five primary brain vesicles* and to advance the understanding of the various membranes that surround the embryo in chicks and mammals.

He made perhaps his most important discovery in 1826 when he became the first to identify an egg in the ovary of a dog. He later found eggs in the ovaries of many other mammals, proving that all animals that reproduce sexually begin life as an egg. This breakthrough in the understanding of the origins of animal life was followed by other significant contributions to the study of the development of vertebrates*. Based on his own work and that of the Russian embryologist Christian Heinrich Pander, von Baer next observed the formation of embryonic germ layers (early undifferentiated* tissue). He described the way in which the layers underwent the changes that result in the formation of various organs. He also knew that this process was more or less similar in all vertebrates and that the change that living organisms undergo throughout their lives could be directly observed by studying the embryo.

Von Baer emphasized that development proceeds from the general (undifferentiated tissue) to the specific (differentiated* tissues and organs), and that all the tissues and organs of an organism develop from what are originally very similar cells in the embryo. His observations contradicted and replaced an older idea that the various parts of an organism existed in a preformed state in the egg. Additionally, von Baer disagreed with the notion that embryos resemble their adult forms. Instead, he stated that embryos resemble each other more than adults do.

Based on his embryological observations, von Baer concluded that animals could be classified in four fundamental types. He felt that some types of animals might be transformed into other types over time, but never accepted the English naturalist Charles DARWIN's theory that all animals evolved from a common ancestor(s). Interestingly, early evolutionists* supported the idea that embryos resemble adults of other species, but later development of evolutionary theory was based on von Baer's rejection of this notion.

Von Baer's other contributions ranged from establishing a collection of skulls to standardizing cranial* measurements in anthropology. He also conducted research in entomology and geography and wrote on such unlikely subjects as the source of tin found in ancient bronze and the location of the biblical region of Ophir that was famous for its fine gold. By the time of his death, he had published more than 300 works in various fields of science and had earned election to and medals from many international scientific societies. The esteem in which he was held was evident in the fact that the eminent German natural scientist Alexander von HUMBOLDT personally delivered to von Baer a medal from the Académie des Sciences in Paris.

A naturalist* and explorer, John Bartram is often considered a founder of American botany. During his lifetime, Bartram undertook many scientific expeditions in eastern North America including trips into the Appalachian Mountains and other wild regions to discover and collect trees, flowers, and other plant species. The first North American to hybridize* flowering plants, Bartram also introduced more than 100 American plant species into Europe.

Born on a farm near Darby, Pennsylvania, Bartram was the eldest child of Quaker parents. Educated at a small country school, he took an early interest in botany and natural history*. On reaching adulthood, Bartram inherited a farm from an uncle. He sold that farm in 1728 and bought yet another farm (which is now a museum) on the banks of the Schuylkill River at Kingsessing, a few miles from Philadelphia. Bartram converted the marshy areas of his Kingsessing farm into productive meadows by draining them, and by using fertilizer and crop rotation he soon had more abundant harvests than most of his neighbors. By 1730 he had laid out a small garden where he grew plants, shrubs, and trees from different parts of America. Bartram received encouragement in his botanical studies from a provincial justice, who loaned him money and books.

Around 1734 Bartram met Peter Collinson, an English merchant, who arranged for Bartram to sell American plant specimens in England. Soon Bartram had a thriving career providing seeds and plants for the gardens and greenhouses of some of the most influential people in England. Collinson also introduced Bartram by letter to Carl LINNAEUS, George-Louis BUFFON, and other European naturalists, as well as to other Americans who shared his interests.

As the market for his plants became well established, Bartram began to undertake several botanical journeys. He traveled to Virginia and the Blue Ridge Mountains, the coast and Pine Barrens of New Jersey, the Catskill Mountains, and other areas. He collected so many plant specimens on his travels that Benjamin Franklin and other prominent members of Philadelphia's society tried to arrange it so that Bartram could devote all of his time to discovering and collecting plants. By 1750 Bartram had become famous throughout America and Europe. Copies of his journals circulated widely, and American naturalists and philosophers sought him out for his expertise.

Bartram's observations were not limited to plants. He also collected shells, insects, hummingbirds, turtles, and wild pigeons, and he described mussels, rattlesnakes, wasps, and locusts. He became interested in every scheme to promote scientific inquiry in America and promoted some ideas of his own, including the formation of a society or college for the study of natural science. In 1756 he proposed a kind of geological survey of the mineral resources of the North American continent.

In 1765 Bartram was named "king's botanist" and given a small annual allowance. Soon afterward he set out with his son William to collect specimens in South Carolina, Georgia, and especially Florida. He visited plantations, noted the quality of soils, and recorded trees,

John
BARTRAM

1699–1777

BOTANY

*naturalist one who studies objects in their natural settings

*hybridize to produce an offspring by crossing two or more varieties or species of plants or animals

*natural history systematic study of animals and plants, especially in their natural settings

plants, and fossils. This was Bartram's last trip. Aging and plagued with failing eyesight, he spent his remaining years at his farm at Kingsessing, tending his garden and welcoming visitors. Bartram received many honors, and his friends and fellow citizens ranked him along with Benjamin Franklin and David Rittenhouse as one of the country's great natural geniuses.

Bartram's third son, William, followed in his father's footsteps and became a famous naturalist. During a four-year journey through South Carolina, Georgia, and Florida, William made notes on animals, plants, and Indian life. Published in 1791 as *Travels,* these notes and sketches with their flowery language would capture the imagination of famous romantic poets such as Coleridge and Wordsworth.

Henry Walter
BATES

1825–1892

NATURAL HISTORY

*evolution historical development of a biological group such as a species

*natural selection theory that within a given species, individuals with characteristics best adapted to the environment survive and successfully produce more offspring than other individuals, resulting in changes in the species over time

Henry Walter Bates is best known for his extensive work in entomology (the study of insects), particularly for recognizing the ability of some insects to protect themselves by mimicking other species. His work also offered evidence to support Charles DARWIN's theory of evolution* by natural selection*.

Early Life and Studies. Bates was the eldest son of a hosiery manufacturer in Leicester, England. He attended schools in Leicester and in a nearby village until age 13 when his father apprenticed him to a colleague. Bates worked 13 hours a day and took night classes at the local Mechanic's Institute, where he learned Greek, Latin, and French and became an outstanding draftsman and writer. In later life he taught himself German and Portuguese. He also developed a fondness for reading and music, both of which remained strong interests throughout his life. Bates was also an avid entomologist, and with his brother, he spent long hours in the woods collecting specimens. Bates's first scientific paper was a work on beetles that was published in the first issue of *The Zoologist* when he was just 18 years old.

When his supervisor died, Bates ended his apprenticeship and became a clerk in a nearby town, a job he greatly disliked. Consequently, he spent most of his time writing detailed accounts of his entomological expeditions and the specimens he had gathered. Around 1844, Bates befriended the Welsh natural historian Alfred Russel WALLACE, who would later propose a theory of evolution very similar to Darwin's and at about the same time as Darwin. Bates interested Wallace in entomology, and in 1847 the two made plans to travel to the Amazon jungle to collect specimens. They also hoped to gather information "towards solving the problem of the origin of species," a frequent topic of their conversations and correspondence.

Insects of the Amazon. Bates and Wallace arrived in the Amazon the following year and embarked on many expeditions into the interior of the jungle. They explored and collected specimens within four degrees of the equator, often traveling miles deep into the wilderness. Wallace returned to England in 1852, but Bates stayed in the region for another seven years. Bates estimated that he had collected 14,000 species of animals, largely insects, more than 8,000 of which were new to science.

During the time he spent in the Amazon, Bates became a recognized expert on butterflies, which he studied in particular depth. These studies led him to his ideas on mimicry among animals. After returning to England in 1859, Bates began his work on this subject. It proved to be important not only for entomology, but for evolutionary theory as well.

Bates was not the first scientist to note that certain animals mimicked others, but he was the first to offer a scientific theory to explain the phenomenon. In an 1861 paper, he showed that insects favored as food by certain predators often mimic the looks and behavior of species that predators avoid because those species taste bad or are poisonous. He proceeded to attempt to answer the question of what mechanism produced these different forms of the same general type of insect. The accepted notion at the time was that God created each species separately. Some scientists also suggested that the different types were due to mutations*.

*mutation genetic change, which when transmitted to offspring, results in heritable variations

Mimicry and Natural Selection. Bates showed, however, that it was the process of natural selection that produced the variations that he had observed. Because different varieties of mimics existed in the same physical environment, he ruled out environmental conditions as a cause. Since the predators did not eat those insects that best mimicked bad tasting or poisonous species, he concluded that the mimicry was a natural form of adaptation that helped ensure the survival of that species. By observing the various forms of a particular mimic, Bates argued that he could trace how it had changed from its original form. He concluded that the mimics offered a way to see natural selection at work.

Darwin was delighted with Bates's paper because it so forcefully supported his own ideas on evolution by natural selection. The paper successfully challenged the position of creationists* by proving that some mimics were clearly variations of existing species, while others represented distinct species or varieties. This challenged the creationist views that all animal species had been specially created. The paper went a long way toward legitimizing Darwin's and Wallace's views.

*creationist one who believes that the world and all living things were created by God as described in the Bible

Other Accomplishments. In 1863 Bates published *The Naturalist on the River Amazon,* a two-volume account of his journeys in South America. One of the best scientific travel books of the 1800s, *The Naturalist* was a popular and financial success, but Bates remarked that he would rather spend another 11 years in the jungle than write another book. He received the traditional honors in recognition of his work, including assistant secretaryship of the Royal Geographic Society; three-time presidency of the Entomological Society of London; election to the Linnean Society and the Zoological Society; and Fellowship in the Royal Society. The emperor of Brazil also awarded him the Order of the Rose, an honor rarely given to any foreigner. Bates died in London in 1892.

William BATESON

1861–1926

GENETICS

*genetics branch of biology that deals with heredity

*chromosome threadlike structure in the cell that contains the DNA (genes) that transmit unique genetic information

William Bateson helped popularize the concepts of heredity and natural variation that were first proposed by the Austrian monk Gregor MENDEL. Born in Whitby, England, Bateson was dismissed as a "vague and aimless boy" in school, but he earned his bachelor's degree with first-class honors in natural sciences at Cambridge University in 1883. The rest of his scientific knowledge was slight, however; he had little training in physics and chemistry and virtually none in mathematics.

After graduating from Cambridge, Bateson began to study heredity and natural variation, disagreeing vigorously with established ideas in evolutionary theory. He searched the literature and began to conduct experiments to understand the transmission of traits from parent to offspring. His work was not fully appreciated until 1900, when he read Mendel's 1866 papers on breeding experiments with peas. Bateson translated Mendel's text into English and wrote a classic text on Mendelian heredity. This marked a turning point in Bateson's career. During the 15 years that followed, he performed experiments that proved that Mendel's theories applied to plants and animals. Bateson soon became a leading spokesperson for the science of genetics*, coining the term itself and becoming England's first professor of genetics.

After 1915 Bateson fell out of favor with the scientific establishment because he did not agree with the popular belief that an organism's genetic makeup was determined by its chromosomes*. He demanded to see direct links between chromosomes and bodily features, but the science of the day could not provide a demonstration. As genetics turned increasingly toward chromosomes and genes, Bateson became isolated and his work disappeared from leading journals of genetics.

Emil von BEHRING

1854–1917

BACTERIOLOGY, MEDICINE

*physiology science that deals with the functions of living organisms and their parts

*serology study of the properties and reactions of serums, clear watery fluids in the blood that carry the substances that provide immunity against diseases

*diphtheria infectious disease caused by a bacterium, characterized by inflammation of the heart and nervous system

*immunology science that deals with the immune system, which protects the body from foreign substances, cells, and tissue by causing the body to produce substances to counteract the infectious materials

*theology study of religion

In 1901 the German scientist Emil von Behring became the first recipient of the Nobel Prize in physiology* or medicine. He received the award for his work in serology*. Perhaps best known for his role in developing a serum that could be used as a vaccine against diphtheria*, Behring is considered the founder of immunology*.

Behring was born in the small German town of Hansdorf. His father, a teacher, wanted Emil to become a teacher or a minister. During his school years, the young Behring discovered an interest in medicine, but he saw little hope of pursuing that dream because his family was too poor. Instead, he planned to study theology*. Fortunately, one of his teachers arranged for Behring to study at the Friedrich Wilhelms Institute in Berlin, where he could get a free medical education in return for promising to serve in the army.

While studying in Berlin, Behring became interested in the possibility of fighting infectious diseases through the use of disinfectants. His first paper on the subject, published in 1881, raised the question of whether an entire organism could be disinfected internally. In experiments, however, he discovered that disinfectants often had a toxic effect on the organism that was stronger than its effect on the bacteria for which it was intended.

Behring began his military service in 1881 and was promoted to captain six years later and sent to the Pharmacological Institute in Bonn for further training. There he gained the knowledge and learned the techniques necessary for conducting accurate animal experiments and research in toxicology*. Between 1889 and 1895 he worked at the Institute of Hygiene in Berlin, where he developed his pioneering ideas on serum therapy and a theory of antitoxins—substances in the body that counteract specific toxins, or poisons.

toxicology science that deals with the effects, detection, and antidotes of poisons

In Berlin, Behring worked with a Japanese scientist named Shibasaburo Kitasato, and the two men experimented with different agents that could fight infection. In 1890 they published a paper on blood-serum therapy—the use of serum in the blood to counteract infection—and Behring later proposed using such a therapy to treat tetanus* and diphtheria. Behring's findings revealed a new principle concerning an organism's defense against infection—that an organism can produce antitoxins in its blood to counteract specific toxins and provide immunity against them. A year later the German immunologist Paul EHRLICH discovered that even vegetable poisons led to the formation of antitoxins in an organism, confirming Behring's theory.

tetanus infectious disease marked by contractions of the voluntary muscles; also known as lockjaw

In 1893 Behring and other scientists began conducting more extensive experiments in serum therapy on animals. They showed that it is possible to provide an animal with immunity against a disease by injecting it with a vaccine made from the blood of another animal infected with the same disease. Behring soon realized that to obtain the best results in humans, it was necessary to standardize the serums. His colleague Ehrlich developed methods to do so in 1897.

Beginning in 1889, Behring focused on a new task, the fight against tuberculosis. Competing with a former colleague, the German bacteriologist* Robert KOCH, Behring attempted to find a substance that could be used as a vaccine against the disease. Although Behring failed in his attempts to find a tuberculosis vaccine, he made important discoveries about the spread of the disease that brought about vital changes in public health policies.

bacteriologist specialist who studies microscopic organisms called bacteria that can cause infection and disease

During World War I, Behring caught pneumonia. Already weak from other illnesses, he was unable to withstand the strain and died in 1917. For the discovery of antitoxins and the development of vaccines against diphtheria and tetanus, Behring was honored as the "Children's Savior" because the vaccines saved the lives of so many children. He was also awarded the Iron Cross, an unusual decoration for a civilian, because his tetanus vaccine helped save the lives of millions of German soldiers during World War I.

Claude Bernard was one of the most highly regarded scientists in nineteenth-century France. His work was the foundation for modern experimental physiology*, a branch of research that he helped define through his ideas and discoveries. Bernard conducted experiments on animals to study digestion, circulation of blood, the nervous system, and the integration of functions in the organism. His work led

Claude
BERNARD

1813–1878

PHYSIOLOGY

*physiology science that deals with the functions of living organisms and their parts

*apothecary individual trained to make up the drugs necessary to fill prescriptions; also called pharmacist or druggist

*gastric of or relating to the digestive system

*bile substance produced by the liver

*pancreatic of or relating to the pancreas, the gland that produces the juices (chemicals) that enable the body to digest and absorb fats

to a new understanding of metabolism (the set of chemical reactions through which bodies convert food into energy) and how the nervous system acts to coordinate bodily functions.

Life and Career

Bernard was born in the village of St.-Julien in the Beaujolais region of France. His parents were vineyard workers who lived in very modest circumstances. All his life Bernard remained attached to his birthplace, returning home every fall to relax and help with the grape harvest.

Education and Early Life. After an education that did not emphasize science, at age 19 Bernard went to the city of Lyons to serve as an apprentice to an apothecary*. The apprenticeship, instead of leading to a career in pharmacy, turned Bernard toward the theater and writing. He enjoyed some local success when a comic play he wrote was produced. In 1834 he went to Paris to make a name for himself in literature, but a well-known literary critic discouraged Bernard, advising him instead to learn a profession that would help him make a living.

That same year, with great difficulty, Bernard qualified to enter the Faculty of Medicine in Paris. Hardworking rather than brilliant, Bernard was an average student. In 1839 he passed the examination for internship and went to work on the staff of a physician and experimentalist named François MAGENDIE. In Magendie's laboratory Bernard discovered his passion for conducting experiments in physiology. From 1841 to 1844 Bernard worked with Magendie on the study of the working of nerves. Bernard also learned the techniques of vivisection, or performing experiments on living animals, such as horses, rabbits, and dogs.

Bernard received his medical degree in 1843 but wanted to conduct research, not practice as a physician. However, he failed to obtain a teaching position and was on the verge of abandoning his research and returning to St.-Julien to become a country doctor when a friend suggested another way out of his difficulties—marriage. Following his friend's advice, Bernard married the daughter of a Paris physician and used her dowry to fund his research. The marriage was not a happy one, however, and would soon end in a legal separation.

In 1847, two years after his marriage, Bernard obtained a teaching position at the Collège de France, where he was to substitute teach for his friend and mentor Magendie. Five years later Magendie retired, and Bernard replaced him. He also became the first vice president of the newly founded Société de Biologie and earned his advanced doctorate in zoology from the Sorbonne University in Paris.

Later Career. Bernard made most of his major scientific discoveries between 1843 and 1853. During this period, he investigated the chemistry of gastric* juices and demonstrated that bile* is involved in the digestion of proteins. He also conducted research on the digestive properties of gastric and pancreatic* juices and studied the ner-

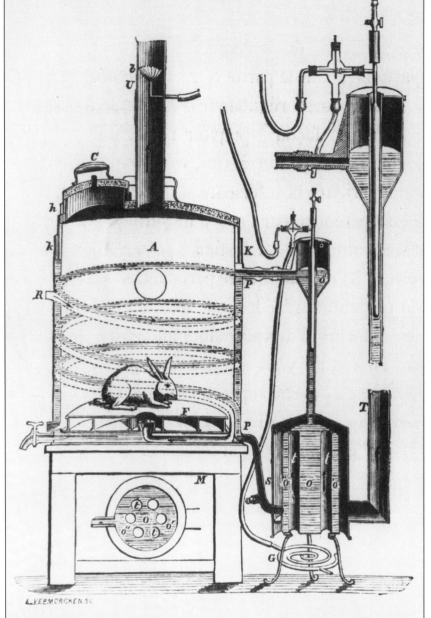

FIG. 8. — Appareil (étuve) pour l'étude du mécanisme de la mort par la chaleur.

One of Claude Bernard's contributions to physiology was his research on the way animals react to varying temperatures. This 19th-century wood engraving shows an apparatus that Bernard used to study the effects of heat on animals.

vous system. In the years that followed, he made additional important discoveries and also began to develop a framework of concepts and theories to explain the results of his experiments. His research notebooks compiled during the 1850s show a change of emphasis from the pursuit of facts to a concentration on research methods and general scientific principles.

During those years, Bernard's reputation grew and he received many honors, including membership in two respected scientific organizations in France, the Académie des Sciences and the Académie de

The Power of Poison

Bernard was a true innovator in the study of the effects of poisons (toxins) and drugs. No one before him had so well understood drug metabolism, the processes by which the body uses drugs. He began his investigations into the metabolism of poisons when he first used curare in physiological experiments. Sometimes called arrow poison, curare is a plant extract that paralyzes muscles. Bernard pioneered and advocated the use of some toxins in physiological research because they helped him destroy specific structures or functions selectively and furthered his research.

Médecine. He continued to lecture at the Collège de France, teach at the Sorbonne, and conduct experiments at the Muséum d'Histoire Naturelle (Museum of Natural History) in Paris, impressing his lecture audiences with his vivid and original arguments and experiments. Many of the members of these audiences were not students but were visiting scholars and members of the public.

From about 1860, Bernard spent his vacations in St.-Julien, where he bought the manor house of the landlord on whose farm he had been born. He received many new honors including the presidency of France's elite learned society, the Académie Française. Bernard's later years were marked by a series of illnesses, but he continued working until the end, preparing his final publication on his deathbed. He died in Paris in 1878, probably of a kidney disease, and was given a state funeral, an honor that had formerly been reserved for military and political leaders.

Contributions to Physiology

During much of the 1840s, Bernard studied the processes of digestion. The horizon of his research kept widening, and he progressed from studying digestion to nutrition to metabolism. He also made the revolutionary discovery that the liver produces sugar and deposits it into the blood.

Work on Digestion. Among Bernard's impressive discoveries in the field of digestion was the functioning of an organ called the pancreas, which produces the juices that enable the body to digest and absorb fats. He had noted differences in the chemical content of the urine of carnivores, or meat-eating animals, and herbivores, or plant-eating ones. By designing experiments to trace the process of digestion in a dog (carnivore) and a rabbit (herbivore), he found that the metabolism of fat is affected by pancreatic juices. He also understood that metabolism is not simply the physical movement of substances absorbed by the animals but a complex series of chemical processes governed by the organs.

Bernard then became interested in how food is converted into heat and life in an animal as well as how animals produce and regulate heat. His research included experiments in which he slowed down the animal's bodily functions by lowering its body temperature. He also studied how exposure to high temperature causes death, examined the causes of fever, and conducted pathbreaking experiments on the chemical properties of muscles after death and on rigor mortis*.

rigor mortis stiffness of the body after death

While carrying out a series of experiments to study the sugar contained in animal blood and organs, Bernard found that an animal's liver continued to produce sugar even though the animal had been deprived of solid foods for several days. Surprised, he turned his research in a new direction and found that the liver is involved in the production of glycogen, the molecular form in which carbohydrates (sugars and starches) are stored in animal tissues. His work was not only fundamentally important but also improved scientists' understanding of diabetes, a disease in which the body does not properly regulate its production of glycogen.

Research on the Nervous System. When Bernard discovered that the organs involved in the processes of metabolism and digestion are governed by the nervous system, he began to study the functions of nerves. His greatest success in this field was his discovery of the vasomotor nerves, which regulate the size of blood vessels, causing them to shrink or expand. Many scientists shared in the discovery of the vasoconstrictor nerves that shrink blood vessels, but Bernard alone discovered the vasodilator nerves that enlarge the vessels and the principle of the opposing sets of nerves working together in balance. This understanding of how nerves regulate blood flow forms the basis for modern understanding of heart disease and other related medical conditions.

Fermentation. Bernard's last experiments were concerned with fermentation, the process within an organic substance that produces alcohol. Around the same time, many scientists, including Louis PASTEUR, were attempting to explain this process. Bernard's notes on the subject were published after his death but they provoked an angry reply from Pasteur. Later research showed that both men's understanding of fermentation was incomplete.

Methods and Philosophy of Science. In works such as the *Introduction à l'étude de la médecine experimental* (Introduction to the Study of Experimental Medicine), published in 1865, which Bernard wrote as he recovered from a nervous breakdown, he expressed his philosophy of science. He believed that the scholar's duty was to study phenomena as they exist in nature and that questions about the origins of or ultimate reasons for things lay beyond science.

Bernard was a man of the laboratory, interested less in general theories of knowledge than in the logic and methods of scientific research. The experimental method, as he described it, has three stages: observation, hypothesis, and experimentation. Having observed a fact or a phenomenon, the scientist forms a hypothesis or theory to explain it. The hypothesis is the essential part of every discovery but is worthless if it is not tested and confirmed by experimentation. Bernard cautioned, however, that a scientist must avoid fixed ideas and keep an open mind. He wrote, "A skilled hand without the head to direct it is a blind instrument; the head without the hand to carry out an idea remains impotent."

Bernard also developed a concept he called the *milieu intérieur,* which can be translated as "internal environment" and which came to occupy a central place in his thought. He believed that the internal environment was the sum of all the mechanisms that govern an organism's internal conditions. A stable or constant *milieu intérieur,* Bernard declared, is essential to the free and independent life of an organism and is characteristic of all higher animals.

Bernard's view of life was broad and all-embracing. Unlike some scientists, he did not focus on the differences among species but concentrated on features and processes, such as nutrition, that all living things have in common. His final work, which he completed while on his deathbed, dealt with features common to plant and animal life, for him a statement of the underlying unity of all organisms.

Daniel
BERNOULLI
1700–1782

PHYSIOLOGY, PHYSICS, STATISTICS

*mechanics science that studies how energy and force affect objects

Daniel Bernoulli was a multitalented scientist who published important papers in subjects as diverse as the mechanics of breathing and the expected duration of the average marriage. Bernoulli made his earliest scientific contributions in the fields of medicine and anatomy, but his chief interests were always mechanics* and physics. His accomplishments resulted in the development of devices that solved many practical problems of his time.

Life and Career. Bernoulli was born into a respected family in Basel, Switzerland. His father, Johann, was professor of mathematics at the University of Basel and his older brother, Nikolaus II, was a mathematician. As a young man, Bernoulli received instruction in mathematics from his father and brother. He studied philosophy and logic in college and earned his master's degree at age 16. His father tried to find him a position as a commercial apprentice, but when that venture proved unsuccessful he allowed his son to study medicine at Basel. Bernoulli continued his medical education at universities in Heidelberg and Strasbourg. He later returned to Basel, where he earned his doctorate in 1721 and applied for the position of professor of anatomy and botany. However, he failed in his effort to win that position, as well as in a later attempt to obtain a professorship in logic. Unsuccessful in landing a teaching position in Basel, Bernoulli left for Venice, Italy, to continue his studies in medicine. He hoped to stay in Italy to work, but he contracted a serious illness that ended those plans.

In 1724, Bernoulli published a book on mathematics and physics that brought him widespread recognition and an invitation to teach at the St. Petersburg Academy in Russia. The following year, the Académie des Sciences in Paris awarded Bernoulli the first of ten prizes he would receive from that institution. In his winning paper, he discussed the best shape for hourglasses filled with sand and water, as well as the best way to install them.

In 1725, after his return to Basel from Venice, Bernoulli left for Russia with his brother Nikolaus. His time in St. Petersburg was perhaps the most creative period of his life, but it was not altogether a happy one. The climate was severely cold and his brother died suddenly. While still in Russia, Bernoulli applied three times for a professorship at Basel, but was turned down each time. In 1732, he was finally awarded the chair of botany and anatomy, and he returned to Switzerland the following year. On his trip home he toured much of Europe with his younger brother Johann II and was warmly received by scholars throughout the continent.

At Basel, Bernoulli lectured in medicine and botany but continued to publish papers in mathematics and mechanics. He eventually traded his lectures in botany for those in physiology*, and in 1750, was appointed the chair in physics. He occupied that position for almost 30 years, presenting lectures on his impressive experiments to packed audiences. Bernoulli died in 1782 and was buried near his home.

physiology science that deals with the functions of living organisms and their parts

Anatomy and Medicine. Bernoulli's dissertation, titled *De respiratione* (On Respiration), was a comprehensive review of the mechanics of breathing. In 1728, while in St. Petersburg, he published a mechanical theory of muscular contraction. Bernoulli's position challenged the view of many scientists, including his father and the Italian anatomist Giovanni BORELLI, that muscular contraction was caused by chemical reactions in the blood corpuscles (blood cells) and muscle cells. The same year, Bernoulli also helped identify where the optic nerve enters the eye's blind spot, and its shape at that location.

After returning to Basel, Bernoulli gave an important lecture discussing the mechanical work done by the heart. He later developed a method to correctly calculate the amount of work performed by the heart. Because of its lasting significance, this lecture was published in 1941. Bernoulli also made significant contributions to understanding the physiology of work and determining the maximum amount of work a person can perform over a specified period, such as a working day.

Mechanics and Physics. Bernoulli's most important work was in the disciplines of physics and mechanics. In 1738, he founded the modern science of hydrodynamics* with the publication of *Hydrodynamica*. The book explored the reactions of fluids under varying conditions and the properties and motions of liquids and gases. He showed that as the velocity of fluid flow increases, its pressure decreases; this is called Bernoulli's principle and remains in use today. His work on gases anticipated major discoveries in this field by 100 years.

hydrodynamics scientific study of the motion of liquids

Mathematics and Statistics. Early in his career, Bernoulli published a paper on the probabilities involved in the card game called faro. He later produced some original works that were useful to economists and the insurance industry. Bernoulli later looked at two other interesting statistical problems. In 1760, he published a paper in which he calculated the probability of dying from smallpox for different age groups. Based on this work, Bernoulli argued that if a person took an inoculation* against smallpox, his or her average life expectancy would increase by three years. In another paper, he attempted to determine the expected average duration of marriage for people of various ages.

inoculation introduction of a disease agent into an animal or plant to produce a mild form of the disease and render the organism immune

Evaluating Bernoulli's Work. Bernoulli's work in statistics highlights his gift for finding practical applications of his studies. His gift

23

is also evident in the many prizes he won from the academy in Paris. These included the best practical design for an anchor, the best way to reduce sources of error in constructing a compass, a method for determining the time of day at sea when the horizon is not visible, the effects of forces other than wind on a ship's movement, and how to reduce the pitch and roll of ships at sea. Because he explored so many disciplines, he was often unable to complete projects he started. Still, his contributions and his ability to apply his findings to practical problems make Bernoulli an outstanding figure in the history of science.

Jerome BOCK

1498–1554

BOTANY

theology study of religion

At a time when botanists tried to classify plants based on descriptions in ancient Greek texts, Jerome Bock based his descriptions and classifications of plants on observations from nature. By challenging the authority of ancient writers and developing new ways to study and describe plants, Bock helped lead the way to the modern science of botany. He is considered one of the three German founders of botany.

Jerome Bock was born in either Heidesbach or Heidelsheim, Germany, and spent his adult life in the Saar region. He may have attended the University of Heidelberg, but because there is no record that he ever received a degree, it is unknown whether he studied medicine, philosophy, or theology*. In 1523 he accepted a position in the city of Zweibrücken, where he married and remained for a time before taking a position at the church of St. Fabian in the nearby town of Hornbach. He was forced to leave Hornbach in 1550 for following the religious views of the German Reformation leader Martin Luther. Bock served for a short time as the personal physician for Philipp II, a member of the nobility in the German region of Nassau, before returning to Hornbach the following year. He died there three years later, probably from tuberculosis.

During his years in Hornbach, Bock spent a great deal of time taking botanical excursions. From these travels, Bock published his first botanical work in the early 1530s. Titled *De herbarum quarundam nomenclatures* (Nomenclature of Selected Plants), the work dealt with Greek and Latin names of local plants. Bock's next work, a book about medicinal plants and herbs, was published in 1539. The first edition, which was written in German and contained no illustrations, was initially overshadowed by the better-known writings of the German botanists Otto Brunfels and Leonhart FUCHS. It was only after the publications of a second illustrated edition and a Latin translation that Bock's work gained fame. The book contained descriptions of plants he encountered on his travels and was considered innovative because it was the first to contain descriptions of local plants based on their physical details, such as height, foliage, shape, texture, odor, and color.

Bock was also the first to emphasize the importance of structural differences in distinguishing between different types of plants. He provided complete and accurate descriptions of the flowering portions of plants, as well as their various forms of seeds and fruit. To confirm one of his ideas he planted particular parts of a willow that later germinated, proving that the parts were seeds as he suspected. Such an experimental, hands-on approach was a complete break with the tradition of accepting the statements presented in classical sources.

Bock's work helped lay the foundations for future botanical investigations, and his emphasis on naturalistic observation and description became the model for later botanists. By freeing botany from its dependence on ancient books, Bock helped to introduce a new age in which investigators would overturn long-established ideas about plant anatomy and biology.

Hermann
BOERHAAVE
1668–1738
MEDICINE, BOTANY, CHEMISTRY

Hermann Boerhaave was not only one of the greatest medical teachers of his day, but also one of the pioneers of the field of physical chemistry. In addition, Boerhaave earned acclaim for his attempts to build a universal doctrine of medicine by combining the ideas of the ancient Greek physicians with new discoveries made during the 1600s, the period of the Scientific Revolution.

Early Life and Studies. Boerhaave was born in Voorhaut, Netherlands. His mother died when he was just five years old and his father, a clergyman, who personally supervised his upbringing and education, died ten years later. In 1683, in accordance with his father's wishes, Boerhaave took up the study of theology* and philosophy. An outstanding student, he won a gold medal for an oration based on the ideas of the Greek philosopher Epicurus. He graduated with a degree in philosophy in 1690, but soon turned to the study of medicine. He attended public dissections and studied the writings of ancient and modern physicians such as HIPPOCRATES and Thomas SYDENHAM. In 1693 he earned a medical degree from the academy of Harderwijk and began a medical career.

theology study of religion

Medical Teaching. In 1701 Boerhaave was named lecturer in medicine at the University of Leiden. He also lectured in chemistry at this time, but was best known for his work in medicine. Boerhaave's presence helped restore the declining prestige of the university's medical faculty, and within two years, the University of Groningen offered him a professorship in medicine. However, he decided to remain at Leiden in exchange for a promise that he would be chosen to fill the first professional chair that became vacant. That occurred in 1709, when Boerhaave became the chair of botany and medicine.

Boerhaave's lectures were extremely popular and the hall was typically crowded with students from several countries. These lectures became the basis for many popular textbooks that helped spread Boerhaave's reputation throughout Europe. In his lectures and texts, Boerhaave outlined a course of study that became the basis for the new medical school curriculum. One of the most important principles he championed was clinical training. He emphasized the importance of bedside observation and the systematic examination of patients. Medical faculties at many of Europe's leading universities reformed their curriculum and teaching methods following Boerhaave's system.

Medical Synthesis. In the early 1700s, medical science was in a state of transition, struggling to incorporate the many new ideas and discoveries of the sixteenth and seventeenth centuries into long-accepted medical doctrines. Boerhaave set out to create a comprehensive medical system that would combine the new with the old. For instance, following the successes of the physical and mechanical sciences, he developed mechanical explanations for the workings of the body and used mechanical theories to develop a theory of the human body as a self-regulating machine.

Boerhaave rejected the attempts of some scientists who argued that the workings of the body could be explained primarily by chemical theories. Instead he explained circulation in terms of the velocity of blood flow, the angle and diameter of the blood vessels, the shape and size of blood particles, and the viscosity (thickness) of the blood. Although his ideas found broad acceptance, they were not adequate to explain all the workings of the human body. Interestingly, his medical experiments would lead him to discoveries in the field of chemistry, which he felt was still an undeveloped field of science.

Achievements in Chemistry. Boerhaave's investigations led him to the question of how animals generate internal heat and respond to stimuli. This in turn inspired the chemical investigations that produced some of his most important scientific findings. For example, Boerhaave was the first to obtain the bodily acid urea and to demonstrate its diuretic* properties and its cooling effects when dissolved in water. He also showed that water could be condensed from burning alcohol, and discovered a rapid way of making vinegar.

The secret to Boerhaave's success in chemistry was the same as that for his medical career. He introduced exact methods of measurement, used the most accurate equipment he could obtain, and showed amazing rigor and perseverance in his work. His critical investigations of alchemy* provide an example of his thoroughness. Boerhaave conducted many experiments to test the alchemical claim that it was possible to turn base metals such as mercury into gold. He used an apparatus to shake a specimen of mercury for 81/2 months before distilling it 61 times. He heated another specimen of mercury for more than 15 years, boiled it 511 times, mixed it with gold, then distilled it 877 times. No matter what he did, mercury remained mercury and gold remained gold.

Other Achievements. In addition to medicine and chemistry, Boerhaave served as supervisor of Leiden's botanical garden. Despite little

diuretic tending to increase the discharge of urine

alchemy medieval form of chemical science, especially one that sought to turn base metals into gold or silver or transform something common into something special

HERMANNI BOERHAAVE
SERMO ACADEMICUS
DE COMPARANDO CERTO
IN PHYSICIS
☞
LUGDUNI BATAVORUM,
Apud PETRUM VANDER Aa, Bibliopolam.
· MDCCXV.

Students crowded into classrooms to hear Boerhaave's lectures, which the scientist delivered with unmatched energy and zeal. Many students were forced to listen while standing, as seen in this engraving, and some even hired men to get to class early to reserve their seats.

formal training in botany, he drew up a catalog of plants in the garden and added more than 2,000 new plants. When Leiden's professor of chemistry died in 1718, Boerhaave succeeded him. For ten years he held three of the five chairs of the university's medical faculty. His lectures in chemistry formed the basis for a textbook that became the standard work in the field for years.

In 1722 Boerhaave suffered an attack of lumbago (severe backache) that confined him to bed for five months. He recovered the following year and his return to the university was celebrated by the entire city of Leiden. Six years later he resigned his chairs in botany and chemistry and concentrated on his medical teaching. In 1737 he began to experience heart failure, and he died the following year after a prolonged illness. By the time of his death, he had been named a member of Europe's most prestigious scientific societies and was considered one of the most influential scientists in Europe.

Charles
BONNET
1720–1793
NATURAL HISTORY, BIOLOGY

naturalist one who studies objects in their natural settings

entomology scientific study of insects

Charles Bonnet is among the scientists who established the foundations of modern biology. His theories and experimental research were influential on the work of scientists in the eighteenth century. Most remarkably, Bonnet achieved his many successes despite suffering from serious physical disabilities since his childhood.

Early Studies. Bonnet was born in Geneva, Switzerland. An average student, his progress in school was further hampered by his increasing deafness. Because his schoolmates teased him for his deafness, his father hired a private tutor who stimulated Bonnet's early interest in natural science. At age 16 he read *The Spectacle of Nature* by the French scientist Noël-Antoine Pluche. The following year Bonnet read the memoirs of René Réaumur, a prominent physicist and naturalist* of the early 1700s, and began a correspondence with him. When he was 18, Bonnet submitted a paper on entomology* to the Académie des Sciences in Paris.

Bonnet's father, however, did not approve of a scientific career for his son, who then agreed to study law. In 1744 he received his law degree and later settled in Geneva. All that time, Bonnet contended with his worsening health, becoming almost completely blind and suffering from severe attacks of asthma.

Bonnet's early scientific career focused on animal life. At age 26 he discovered that aphids (small sluggish insects that suck the juices of plants) can reproduce without mating, a phenomenon known as parthenogenesis. His paper on the subject led to his election to the Académie des Sciences in Paris. Thereafter Bonnet took up research on regeneration using rainwater worms of the species *lumbriculus*. He demonstrated that when the worm is cut into pieces, each piece develops into a whole worm. He followed this work with experiments on the regeneration of a snail's head. From this he went on to examine the breathing of caterpillars and the locomotion of ants. In 1745 he published his findings in *Traité d'insectologie* (Treatise on Insects), an important work in experimental entomology.

The Study of Plants. As his eyesight worsened, Bonnet could no longer continue his entomological investigations and turned instead to the study of plants. He discovered that green leaves exposed to light produced and absorbed gases. This was one of the first steps toward recognizing photosynthesis—the process by which plants, in the presence of light, convert carbon dioxide into oxygen and carbon and produce energy. In other experiments, Bonnet studied the movement of leaves, their position on the stalk, and the movement of sap within plants.

Because of his poor eyesight, Bonnet surrounded himself with able students who carried out the actual observations. Many of his assistants, such as François Huber, went on to important careers as scientists. Bonnet and his associates also performed many plant breeding experiments in which they produced hybrid* varieties of corn, wheat, and darnel (weedy grasses).

hybrid offspring produced by crossing two or more varieties or species of plants or animals

Theory and Method. Bonnet's discovery of parthenogenesis in aphids reinforced his belief in the theory of preformation. According to this theory, a miniature version of a fully formed animal exists before birth in the germ cell, or egg. He rejected the notion that the embryo* developed over time from a mass of undifferentiated (unspecialized) cells, a theory called epigenesis.

Although best remembered for his theories and experiments, Bonnet was always concerned with methodology, or how an experiment was carried out. Every fact he collected or phenomenon he observed gave him an opportunity to suggest the best method to use to find a solution to the problem at hand. He stressed the importance of observation in the scientific process.

*embryo organism from the first division of the fertilized egg through the early stages of development until birth or hatching

Giovanni Alfonso Borelli was an Italian scientist and professor whose enthusiastic mind led him through several fields of study. Although his work was often interrupted by political and religious conflicts, he made important advances in astronomy, physics, and animal physiology*, with fascinating side projects to study epidemics and volcanoes.

Giovanni Alfonso
BORELLI
1608–1679
ASTRONOMY, PHYSICS, ANATOMY

*physiology science that deals with the functions of living organisms and their parts

Born into Conflict. The Italy of Borelli's childhood was not yet a nation but a group of independent provinces ruled by aristocrats. The region was a stronghold of Catholicism, and dissent was viewed with suspicion. For instance, the astronomer Galileo Galilei was condemned for defending his theory that the earth is in motion because it contradicted Catholic doctrine.

At the time, Naples was occupied by Catholic Spain, and a Spanish guard named Miguel Alonso married a local woman; the couple's son, born in Naples in 1608, was Giovanni Borelli. In 1614 Alonso was stationed at the castle where a friar named Tommaso Campanella was imprisoned for defending humanist* ideas and for attempting to reconcile Christianity with Renaissance* science. The young Borelli came to know Campanella, who may have introduced Borelli to Benedetto Castelli, an astronomer in Rome who became Borelli's first professional mentor.

*humanist referring to humanism, a cultural and philosophical movement to revive ancient Greek and Roman works and to value individuals' capacity for reason and dignity during their earthly life

*Renaissance period that marked the beginnings of modern science and the rebirth of interest in classical art and literature that occurred in Europe from the late 1300s through the 1500s

Making a Name in Sicily. Borelli studied astronomy and other sciences with Castelli in Rome. In about 1635 Castelli recommended Borelli for a position teaching mathematics in Messina, Sicily. Borelli got the job. He quickly fell in with a group of nobles and merchants who were agitating to improve Sicily's political and intellectual life, despite Spanish rule. They formed an academy, where Borelli gained respect and admiration. He was sent to other cities to recruit teachers, and he made a reputation for himself throughout Italy. Meanwhile, he published a work on the epidemic outbreak of fevers in Sicily, proposing that the fevers were caused not by the weather or by astrological influences but rather by a chemical that entered the body.

toxicologist one who specializes in toxicology, the science that deals with the effects, detection, and antidotes of poisons

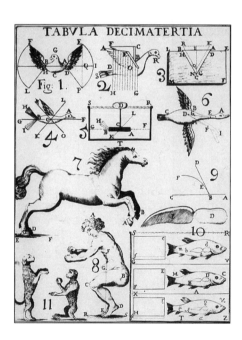

This page from *De motu animalium,* a treatise on the movement of animals, contains illustrations depicting Borelli's mechanical approach to living organisms. He explains muscular action, the movement of bones, and the workings of internal organs in mechanical terms.

Professorship in Pisa. In 1656, in his late 40s, Borelli was selected as chair of mathematics at the University of Pisa. He was not greeted kindly at first; students shouted catcalls to interrupt his first few lectures, which were long-winded, dull, and lacking in grace or eloquence. He was also a difficult man to get along with, but he soon won a dazzling reputation for his knowledge and skill as a scientist.

One of his first projects at Pisa, a rewrite of Euclid's *Elements* in a clear and concise form, was very well received. Borelli's pursuit of ancient Greek mathematics also involved him in a collaboration to revive the works of Apollonius of Perga, several of whose books existed only in Arabic versions. With the help of a scholar who knew Arabic, Borelli translated the Arabic version into Latin and published it.

Borelli also helped establish a new academy, which grew out of an informal circle of scientists at the courts of Prince Leopold and Grand Duke Ferdinand II, two powerful Tuscan nobles. The new academy, the Accademia del Cimento, included many distinguished scientists, such as the Italian toxicologist* Francesco REDI and the Danish anatomist Niels Stensen. The group soon became known for publishing its reports collectively, without acknowledging individual members.

Another project presented itself in 1664, when a comet blazed prominently in the sky. Borelli took up detailed astronomical observations for more than two months. Some of his conclusions about the solar system went against the accepted doctrine, so he published his report under a fictitious name. The following year Borelli established an observatory on a nearby hill and studied the moons of Jupiter. He noted that Jupiter exerts a gravitational pull on its satellites, acting on its moons the way the sun acts on the planets. Like Galileo, Borelli viewed Jupiter and its satellites as a possible model for the solar system with the sun at its center. However, Borelli had to hide this implication by pretending to focus solely on Jupiter.

Borelli's Physiology. All these projects sometimes seemed like mere distractions from his favored endeavor—a laboratory in his own home for the study of animal anatomy, founded almost immediately after he arrived in Pisa. Together with many talented students, including Marcello MALPIGHI, Borelli studied the movements of animals in relation to many other topics in physics and chemistry. Borelli explained muscular action and the movement of bones in terms of levers. He extended these mechanical explanations to the internal organs, such as the heart, stomach, and lungs, helping establish an outlook called iatromechanics. His treatise on the movement of animals—*De motu animalium* (On the Movement of Animals)—is a model of this mechanical approach to living organisms. The approach was later challenged and supplemented by chemical explanations of animal functions.

Politics and Poverty. Nearing the age of 60, Borelli returned to Messina, where he soon found a new area of inquiry. The volcano Mount Etna erupted in 1669, and he made a close study, even climbing to the volcano's rim. Borelli also returned to local politics, which was reaching a boiling point. The meetinghouse for his old academy was burned down in 1672, and he was declared a rebel by the Spanish authorities. Borelli fled to Rome two years before Messina broke into open revolt against the Spanish.

In Rome, Borelli renewed his many professional relations and for a time enjoyed the patronage of Queen Christina. But this arrangement did not provide a sufficient salary, and Borelli wrote to an old colleague named Gian Domenico Cassini, who was flourishing in the royal court of Paris. Borelli hoped to join Cassini there but soon felt too old to travel. A robbery left him without any possessions, and he was forced to take shelter with a local church. Borelli earned his keep by teaching mathematics in the church's elementary school. Late in 1679 Christina at last agreed to finance the publication of *De motu animalium*. Sadly, Borelli died on December 31, and a priest at the church carried out the publication over the next two years.

THE BOVERIS

Theodor Boveri
1862–1915
BIOLOGY

Marcella Imelda O'Grady Boveri
1863–1950
BIOLOGY

Theodor and Marcella Imelda O'Grady Boveri are famous for their collaborative investigations that revealed the central role chromosomes play in heredity, as well as their effects on the development of malignant* tumors. Marcella was also an accomplished teacher who introduced her North American students to the revolutionary scientific work that was in progress in Europe in the late 1800s and early 1900s.

Lives and Careers. The son of a physician, Theodor Boveri was born in Bamberg, Germany. He attended the University of Munich where he first studied history and philosophy but later switched to natural science, a subject in which he showed outstanding abilities. Boveri was a gifted scientist as well as an accomplished musician and a talented artist. He graduated in 1885 and received a fellowship to transfer to the Zoological Institute in Munich. Boveri spent the next eight years in Munich, after which he accepted an appointment as professor of zoology and comparative anatomy at the University of Würzburg. He also became director of the school's Zoological-Zootomical Institute. He remained at Würzburg until his death in 1915.

Marcella Imelda O'Grady was born in Boston and was educated at the Massachusetts Institute of Technology. During her studies, she met the famous American cell biologist Edmund Beecher Wilson, who recommended her for advanced graduate study and a teaching position at Bryn Mawr College in Pennsylvania. In 1890, after three years at Bryn Mawr, she accepted an offer to teach biology at Vassar College. She upgraded the school's curriculum by teaching Darwinian evolution* (the theories proposed by the English naturalist* Charles DARWIN), new theories of heredity, and embryology*. She also established a summer research center for students at the Marine Biological Laboratory in Woods Hole, Massachusetts. Six years later she traveled to Würzburg to do research on chromosomes. There she met Boveri, and the two worked together and within a short time they were married.

*malignant showing abnormal growth and a tendency to spread throughout the body

*evolution historical development of a biological group such as a species

*naturalist one who studies objects in their natural settings

*embryology branch of biology that deals with embryos, organisms from the first division of the fertilized egg through the early stages of development before birth or hatching

Chromosome Research.

In 1885, two years after he arrived at the University of Würzburg, Boveri began the chromosome studies that led to his greatest discoveries. At this time scientists believed that the nuclei of sperm and egg cells carry the physical basis of heredity and their fusion was an essential feature of fertilization. They also knew that part of the substance in the nucleus forms rodlike bodies called chromosomes, but were unaware of the role that these bodies play in heredity.

Inspired by these earlier studies, Boveri conducted a series of experiments with the eggs of the roundworm *Ascaris megalocephala*. He demonstrated conclusively that chromosomes are organized structures that exist independently of the matter in the rest of the cell. This discovery was fundamental to theories concerning the role of chromosomes in inheritance. He later confirmed earlier work that showed that the sperm and egg contribute equal numbers of chromosomes to the offspring. Together, these studies produced a radical change in attitudes toward heredity. Previously, scientists had believed that the cell nucleus was responsible for heredity, but Boveri showed that the chromosomes inside the nucleus were actually the agents of inheritance.

In later experiments with sea urchins, Boveri proved that different chromosomes were responsible for different hereditary features. He studied eggs that had been fertilized by more than one sperm. The eggs split into several cells, and the chromosomes divided unequally among the cells. Boveri showed that these cells developed abnormally, which he attributed to the unequal distribution of chromosomes. He demonstrated that it was not the number of chromosomes present in an offspring that influences development, but the distribution of specific chromosomes. This was the first experiment to establish a physical basis for the laws of heredity that had been worked out in 1865 by the Austrian monk Gregor MENDEL.

Boveri's work on chromosomes led to several other important discoveries. In one of his studies he put the eggs of *Ascaris* in a centrifuge* to change the position of the nuclei within the cytoplasm (the part of the cell that surrounds the nucleus). He showed that such eggs developed differently from normal eggs, suggesting that both the cytoplasm and the nucleus affect development.

In 1914, one year before he died, Boveri developed the theory that tumor cells containing an abnormal number of chromosomes may become malignant, becoming one of the earliest scientists to view tumors as a cell problem. Although his later contributions were significant, Boveri's primary influence on biology rests on his demonstration of the individuality of the chromosome.

Marcella's Later Life.

From the time she arrived in Würzburg, Marcella Boveri collaborated closely with her husband on many of his projects, but published only one independent paper on chromosome mitosis*. She also worked on his last book, which outlined his theory of tumor development. When he died shortly thereafter, she was cut off from active research, but she remained in Germany. In 1926, she accepted an offer to develop the biology program at Albertus Magnus

centrifuge device used to separate materials of different density by spinning them at high speeds

mitosis separation and replication of chromosomes that takes place prior to cell division

College in Connecticut. Three years later, she translated into English her husband's last book on tumors. During 15 successful years at the school, she organized the laboratories, gave exciting lectures on biology, and persuaded many top German scientists to speak and teach in the United States. She retired from teaching at the age of 80 and died seven years later in Wickatunk, New Jersey.

The Austrian physician Josef Breuer maintained a busy private practice and conducted experiments on the physiology* of mammals. His research advanced scientific knowledge about breathing and about the structure and function of the inner ear. In addition, Breuer's use of hypnosis in treatment helped establish the practice of psychoanalysis, a discipline that was further developed by his colleague Sigmund Freud.

Josef
BREUER
1842–1925
MEDICINE, PHYSIOLOGY

Life and Career. Josef Breuer was born in Vienna, Austria. Although his father was a religious teacher employed by the city's Jewish community, Breuer did not develop an interest in religion. His mother died when he was about four years old. Thereafter he was raised by his maternal grandmother. He was tutored by his father until he started school at the age of eight.

In 1859 Breuer entered the medical school of the University of Vienna. He completed his medical studies eight years later and became an assistant to an internist*. Several years later he entered private practice. In 1875 Breuer qualified as a private lecturer in internal medicine but he resigned the position after ten years because he felt that he had been unfairly denied access to patients for teaching purposes. He also refused to be nominated for the title of professor extraordinarius (assistant professor). Despite his strained and weak relationship with the medical faculty, Breuer was considered one of the best physicians in Vienna. Many of the medical professors at the university were his patients, including Freud, himself a physician. The prime minister of Hungary was also among his patients. In 1894 the Viennese Academy of Science elected Breuer to membership. Throughout his career, his private medical practice remained his chief interest. Breuer died in Vienna in 1925.

Scientific Achievements. Although Breuer was a respected scientist, his fame today is less than his achievements suggest, perhaps because he had no pupils, held no lasting connection with a university or institute, and published a limited number of (about 20) papers on physiology in a 40-year career. Breuer conducted his first major scientific study at the military medical school of Vienna, along with Ewald Hering, the professor of physiology. Together they discovered a feature known as the reflex regulation of breathing. They showed that the lung contains receptors that detect how far it is stretched. When the lung is full, these receptors send a message to the brain via the vagus nerve* to begin exhalation. When the lung is empty, other receptors transmit the signal to inhale. The whole system, called the Hering-Breuer reflex, was one

*physiology science that deals with the functions of living organisms and their parts

*internist physician specializing in internal medicine

*vagus nerve either of a pair of nerves that arise in the brain and supply the organs with nerve fibers

of the first "feedback" mechanisms demonstrated in mammals. Breuer and Hering published their results in 1868.

Breuer next conducted a long series of researches into the function of the labyrinth, the canals and other structures of the inner ear. These experiments were remarkable for their importance and even more because Breuer conducted them privately—working in his home and supported by the fees he earned in his private practice. Experimenting on animals, humans, and even birds, he proved that the inner ear is a double organ, part of which is involved in hearing and part of which detects the movement of the head and its position in space. Breuer showed that the otolith system, a group of hair cells and a tiny hard body in the inner ear, is another set of receptors. By sensing the head's position in the gravitational field and its movement, these receptors help control the animal's posture and balance. Although Breuer's work was not generally recognized until about 1900, it laid the foundation for modern knowledge of receptors for sensations of posture and movement.

Breuer's other main contribution to science arose out of his efforts to treat a female patient's psychological disturbances through hypnosis. In the course of working with this woman, known in the history of psychology as "Anna O.," Breuer arrived at two conclusions—that her symptoms were caused by pressure from ideas and emotions held in her unconscious mind and that her symptoms disappeared when she brought these ideas and emotions into her conscious awareness by talking about them.

Breuer shared these discoveries with Freud, who then began treating his own patients using Breuer's method. The two men worked together and published an article on psychotherapy, or the treatment of psychological symptoms, in 1893 and a book—*Studien über Hysterie* (Studies on Hysteria)—in 1895. The following year, Breuer withdrew from psychological research, claiming that he was too busy with his general practice to continue. His friendship with Freud ended abruptly, but Freud went on to develop new forms of "talk therapy" that became the basis for his school of psychological treatment, psychoanalysis*.

*psychoanalysis method of treating emotional disorders in which the patient is encouraged to talk freely about personal experiences

Robert
BROWN

1773–1858

BOTANY

*taxonomy orderly classification of plants and animals into groups and subgroups according to their relationships

*naturalist one who studies objects in their natural settings

Robert Brown was regarded by his peers as one of the most learned botanists of his time. He pioneered the scientific description of many plant species, made important contributions to botanical taxonomy*, and brought into existence Britain's first national plant collection.

Early Travels. Brown was born in Montrose, Scotland. He attended Marischal College in Aberdeen and completed medical studies at the University of Edinburgh. In 1795 he joined the military and was sent to Ireland with the duties of a surgeon's mate. Those duties were not too demanding; Brown's journal reveals that he had plenty of time to pursue private studies in German and in botany.

In 1798 when Brown was in London on a recruiting mission, he was introduced to Joseph Banks, a well-known British naturalist*.

Brown's interest in botany earned him an invitation to Banks's home in Soho Square, which with its rich library and herbarium was the botanical center of Britain. Banks approved of young Brown's zeal and ability. Several years later he recommended that the British Admiralty offer Brown the post of naturalist with an expedition that was about to survey the coast of New Holland (present-day Australia) under the command of the explorer Matthew Flinders. Brown accepted the offer at once and spent some time before the voyage at Banks's house, studying what was then known about New Holland plants.

During the voyage, which lasted from 1801 to 1805, Brown visited South Africa, various points along the Australian coast, and the nearby island of Tasmania. He returned to England with nearly 4,000 plant specimens as well as many drawings and zoological specimens. On Banks's recommendation, Brown received a government salary during the five years he spent writing a description of his specimens and selecting examples for display in the British Museum.

By 1810 Brown had described nearly 2,200 plant species, more than 1,700 of which were new to botanists. The same year Banks's librarian died, and Banks hired Brown to tend his library and natural history collections. When Banks died in 1820, he left Brown an annual income, lifetime use of his house in Soho Square, and his extensive library and collections, which were to go to the British Museum on Brown's death. Brown turned the materials over to the museum in 1827, however, on the agreement that the museum would create a new botanical department with Brown as its head. In this way, Brown created, for the first time in Britain, a nationally owned botanical collection available to the public. For more than 30 years, until his death in 1858, he remained in charge of the collection, which became an important research center.

Scientific Achievements. The years from 1806 to 1820, after his return from Australia, were Brown's most creative and productive. He not only published works dealing with the flora of Australia but also on other scientific matters. Brown tended to pursue an investigation from one problem to another, examining each in detail.

In 1810 Brown published several important scientific papers. One proposed a new classification for the Proteaceae, a family of evergreen shrubs. That same year he published the first volume of what was intended to be a multivolume book on the flora of New Holland. The volume covered 2,000 species in 464 genera* and remains a work of fundamental importance in Australian botany. Brown was disappointed by the book's sales, however, and stopped working on the second volume. Fortunately for science, he used some of the material from it in various shorter articles that he later published.

In one of these articles, published in 1814 as part of Flinders's *A Voyage to Terra Australis,* Brown estimated the number of Australian plant species known to him at 4,200. In other papers he introduced evi-

The Unlucky Collector

Between 1802 and 1818, a man named Thomas Horsfield collected nearly 2,200 specimens of plant species from the Asian island of Java. He turned them over to Brown to organize, name, and publish. Brown found the project slow and selected only "those subjects which appeared to possess the greatest interest, either on account of their novelty, or of their peculiarity of structure." The project dragged on for years, and Brown wrote on only 30 species. Some suspect that Brown may have lost interest in publishing on new species.

*genus category of biological classification; class, kind, or group of organisms that share common characteristics; *pl.* genera

dence for relationships among plants that helped clarify botanical taxonomy. Brown wrote no further major works but made important information available through casual references. In 1831, for example, he published a small pamphlet containing some observations about the pollen of orchids. Included in this paper was a discovery that was important for the development of cytology—a branch of biology that deals with the structure, function, and life history of cells. During his microscopic studies Brown had noticed a more solid area within the cells of plant tissues. He was the first scientist to show that this structure generally occurs in all plant cells and named it the nucleus.

While studying pollen grains, Brown made another discovery with applications outside botany. Noticing that fine pollen grains moved while suspended in a liquid, Brown studied other fine particles, including powdered coal, glass, rock, and metal. He found that particles small enough to hang suspended in fluids moved constantly. This movement, called Brownian motion, is known today to occur because of the collision of the particles with moving but invisible molecules. In 1905, one of Albert Einstein's famous papers provided the physical explanation of Brownian motion.

Over the years, Brown's mind became a rich repository of facts. The English naturalist Charles DARWIN, who knew Brown well, wrote, "He seemed to me to be chiefly remarkable for the minuteness of his observations and their perfect accuracy." Brown never put forth any grand biological theories but calmly pursued a series of absorbing studies. He turned down three offers of professorships but was a member of several learned societies, including the Royal Society of London. He was president of the Linnean Society, an organization of biologists, from 1849 to 1853. In later life Brown enjoyed trips to Germany and visits to his old hometown, Montrose. At the age of 80 he climbed a Scottish peak where he had first collected plants 60 years earlier. Unmarried and with no close relatives, Brown spent more than half his life in Banks's house in Soho Square. He died there in the room that had been Banks's library, 60 years after his first meeting with Banks that had opened the way to Australia and a scientific career.

Georges-Louis Leclerc
BUFFON

1707–1788

NATURAL HISTORY

*naturalist one who studies objects in their natural settings

*natural history systematic study of animals and plants, especially in their natural settings

The French naturalist* Georges-Louis Leclerc Buffon is probably best remembered for *Histoire naturelle* (Natural History), a multivolume work in which he brought together all existing knowledge in the fields of natural history*, geology, and anthropology*. Widely praised for its well-written descriptions and illustrations, *Histoire naturelle* was translated into several languages and published in many editions and became one of the most widely read scientific works of the 1700s.

Life and Career. Born in Montbard, France, Buffon came from a middle-class family. His father was an official in the state of Burgundy, and his mother was related to a wealthy banker. The eldest of five children, Buffon studied at the Collège des Jésuites in Dijon. Although only an average student, he showed an aptitude for mathematics, but because his father wanted him to have a legal career, Buffon studied law at Dijon. In 1728 he traveled to Angers in western France, where he may have studied medicine, botany, and mathematics. Two years later, forced to leave Angers because of a duel, Buffon began to travel through southern France and Italy with a young English nobleman and his tutor.

Buffon returned to France in 1732 and received an inheritance from his mother, who had died during his absence. Settling down on the family estate at Montbard, he began doing research in botany and forestry and continued his studies of mathematics. He later became interested in chemistry and biology as well, and he conducted some microscopic research on animal reproduction. Buffon also translated into French a number of works by other scientists, including Stephen HALES's *Vegetable Statiks*. In 1734 Buffon was elected to the Académie des Sciences, France's most prestigious scientific society.

Beginning in 1740, Buffon divided his time between Montbard and Paris. While in Paris he met with scientists, politicians, and other scholars and worked on his writings. He also worked as keeper and director of the Jardin du Roi (king's garden), which he developed into an important center for botanical and zoological research. Returning each spring to Montbard, Buffon administered his estates, continued his research, and edited his writings. He died in Paris at the age of 80.

Research and Writings. Buffon's work may be grouped into two main categories: the various reports, or *Mémoires,* that he presented to the academy; and *Histoire naturelle,* his masterpiece. The *Mémoires,* which appeared between 1737 and 1752, dealt with mathematics, astronomy, physics, forestry, and other subjects. Many of these subjects appeared again in the *Histoire naturelle.*

Of the proposed 50 volumes for the *Histoire naturelle,* Buffon published only 36 before his death. The rest were published later. The work covers a range of subjects related to biology, including birds, reptiles, fish, humans, and other animals; geology; astronomy; chemistry; and anthropology. It contains not only scientific observations and descriptions but also philosophical discussions about the nature and value of science. Breaking with the spirit of the times, Buffon attempted to separate science from metaphysics* and the religious ideas that had dominated science for centuries. His goal was to construct a science derived solely from nature.

One of the best-known sections of the work is the *époques de la nature* (Ages of Nature), which contains a new theory of the history of the earth. Buffon believed that long, long ago, the earth was a piece of the sun and that it had torn away, gradually solidified, and cooled into its present form. As the earth solidified, mineral deposits and mountains were formed, and as the planet cooled, water vapor condensed and covered the planet with great oceans, which were soon populated

*anthropology study of human beings, especially in relation to origins and physical and cultural characteristics

Buffon was the first scientist to create an autonomous (independent) science, free of any religious influence. His work was original, diverse, and influential, and established the intellectual framework within which naturalists worked for nearly a century.

*metaphysics branch of philosophy that deals with the fundamental principles or ultimate nature of existence

with marine creatures. Forces of erosion gradually shaped the planet, and finally, animal and human life appeared. The *époques* was the first book to present the earth's geologic history in stages. It also introduced the idea of lost species (represented by the fossils in rock), paving the way for the development of paleontology*.

*paleontology study of extinct or prehistoric life, usually through the examination of fossils

Buffon studied humans using the same methods he applied to animals. Although he believed that humans had the same history as animals, he proclaimed the absolute superiority of humans over animals because of their ability to reason. He maintained that because of their intelligence, humans have been able to adapt to different environments.

Buffon's work is of exceptional importance because of its diversity, richness, originality, and influence. Among the first to create a science free of religious influence, he also was one of the first to understand the important roles that other areas of science play in natural history.

Jean-Martin
CHARCOT

1825–1893

MEDICINE, NEUROLOGY

*pathology study of diseases and their effects on organisms

*lesion wound or injury

*atrophy wasting away of tissues or organs

The French physician Jean-Martin Charcot is considered one of the founders of the modern science of neurology, the study of the nervous system and its disorders. Born in Paris, France, Charcot studied at the Faculty of Medicine of Paris. In 1853 he received his M.D. and became a resident doctor at the Salpêtrière, a famous Parisian hospital, where he created the department of neurology. Charcot later became professor of anatomical pathology* at the Faculty of Medicine and served as chair of a study of nervous disorders at the Salpêtrière.

Early in his career Charcot published a series of papers that attracted the attention of fellow neurologists. He also developed a technique to trace symptoms of neurological disorders to lesions* in the brain. He described various types of neurological disorders including Charcot's disease, now known as multiple sclerosis. Charcot also discovered a progressive muscular atrophy* caused by neurological deterioration that was later named Charcot-Marie amyotrophy.

One of Charcot's most important contributions was his idea that control over certain abilities, such as speech or hearing, is centered in particular areas of the brain. This theory, called cerebral localization, has been supported by modern neurological studies. Another enduring achievement was his demonstration of the link between physical condition (physiology) and mental state (psychology). This finding stemmed from his work on hysteria, which stimulated the later investigations of Sigmund Freud.

Realdo
COLOMBO

ca. 1510–1559

ANATOMY, PHYSIOLOGY

During the 1500s many European scientists turned their attention to the structure and function of animal and human bodies. One such researcher was Realdo Colombo, an expert in anatomy and physiology*, who made the significant discovery that air enters the bloodstream in the lungs. His work contributed to an understanding of how the heart and the lungs work.

Little is known about Colombo's life. He was born in Cremona, Italy, the son of an apothecary*. Colombo received his early education at Milan and after a period of following his father's trade, he became an apprentice to Giovanni Antonio Lonigo, a surgeon in Venice. By 1538 Colombo had begun studies at the University of Padua, also in Italy. A few years later he became an instructor of surgery and anatomy at Padua, taking a position formerly held by Andreas VESALIUS, one of the foremost anatomists of the day. Vesalius and Colombo appear to have been friends and colleagues at that time, but later, after Colombo pointed out some errors in Vesalius's work and teaching, their relationship soured. Colombo, who settled in Rome in 1548, hoped to work with the artist Michelangelo on an illustrated book of anatomy that would replace that of Vesalius. The artist's advanced age made this impossible, however, and in 1559 Colombo published his text *De re anatomica* (On Anatomy) without illustrations.

The work reveals Colombo's attention to detail and the depth of his experience in surgery, anatomical dissection, vivisection*, and autopsy. Because it contains a good account of human anatomy in brief but clear terms, the text was popular in the later part of the 1500s.

Colombo's best-known achievement was his discovery of the pulmonary circuit, the process by which blood passes from the right ventricle* into the lungs, where it is exposed to air breathed in by the lungs, and then passes into the left ventricle. Before Colombo, some anatomists thought that blood moved between the two ventricles through tiny pores in the tissue wall that separates them. They also believed that air entered the heart through a large vein and then mixed with the bloodstream. By studying the breathing and blood flow of live animals, Colombo correctly determined that air enters the blood in the lungs, not the heart, although it was still uncertain how the heart distributed the enriched, life-giving blood to the body. He thought it was a process of ebb and flow.

Colombo was not the first to describe the pulmonary circuit, however. The Spanish physician Michael SERVETUS had done so a few years earlier in a work on theology*, but it is most likely that Colombo made his discovery independently, with no knowledge of Servetus's work. He also pursued the discovery in greater detail than Servetus did. Colombo also made significant progress in understanding the heartbeat. His observations led him to believe that the contraction phase of the heartbeat, in which the heart briefly becomes smaller and pushes blood out into the arteries, is more strenuous than the dilation phase, in which the heart expands and draws blood in from the veins. Colombo's observations on the heartbeat were used in the later studies of the English physiologist William HARVEY, who went on to discover the full circulation of the blood through the body.

*physiology science that deals with the functions of living organisms and their parts

*apothecary individual trained to make up the drugs necessary to fill prescriptions; also called pharmacist or druggist

*vivisection practice of dissecting or cutting into the body of a living animal for the purpose of scientific investigation

*ventricle muscular chamber of the heart

*theology study of religion

Georges
CUVIER
1769–1832

ZOOLOGY, PALEONTOLOGY,
HISTORY OF SCIENCE

*paleontology study of extinct or prehistoric life, usually through the examination of fossils

*naturalist one who studies objects in their natural settings

*invertebrate animal without a backbone

*mollusk marine animal with a shell of one or more pieces enclosing a soft body

*crustacean class of animals that typically have a body covered with a hard shell or crust, such as lobsters, shrimp, and crabs

Georges Cuvier rose from a humble background to achieve fame, honor, and wealth as one of France's leading scientists in the early 1800s. His primary areas of research were zoology and paleontology*, and he made several discoveries of lasting importance. Cuvier also wrote documents that are of interest to historians of science, such as reports on scientific progress, biographies of fellow scientists, and surveys of particular scientific fields.

Education and Career. Cuvier was born in Montbéliard, a part of France that had been under German control for several centuries. Unlike most of France, which was Catholic, its inhabitants had adopted the Protestant Lutheran religion. Weak and sickly as a child, Cuvier showed early signs of impressive intellectual ability. He enjoyed drawing and had an astonishing memory. He became very familiar with the works of Georges-Louis Leclerc BUFFON, a French naturalist* and paleontologist, and at age 12 he began his own natural science collection and founded a scientific society with some friends.

At age 15, Cuvier entered the Caroline University in Stuttgart, Germany, where he continued his investigations in natural science. He identified several new species of plants, formed close friendships with several teachers and fellow students, and again founded a scientific society. He completed his studies in 1788 and became a tutor to a prominent Protestant family in western France. Cuvier lived there for six years, remote from the events of the French Revolution in Paris, reading and pursuing his collections and undertaking the dissection of plants and animals.

In 1795 Cuvier went to Paris, seeking recognition from the scientific world. He presented a paper that marked a new stage in the study of invertebrate* animals and became the first to subdivide invertebrates into as many as six different categories, such as mollusks*, crustaceans*, insects, and worms, each with its own distinguishing features. He began working at the Muséum d'Histoire Naturelle (Museum of Natural History) in Paris and began teaching zoology at the university level. Because of his position at the museum, Cuvier was given a residence near the museum's zoo, and he lived there for the rest of his life.

After 1796, Cuvier held ever-higher posts in the world of education. In 1808 Napoleon Bonaparte, the emperor of France, appointed Cuvier a university counselor. Cuvier also helped reorganize higher education in Paris as well as in Italy, the Netherlands, and Germany. For these services, he received a salary as well as the titles of *chevalier,* or knight, and baron. In 1814 he became a member of France's council of state and four years later he was made a member of the Académie Française, an elite literary and learned organization. While Cuvier enjoyed these honors and his large income, he continued to produce a large amount of scientific and administrative work until his death in Paris in 1832. An examination of his brain conducted after his death found it to be unusually heavy and bulging, which some suggested was a sign of his impressive intelligence.

One of Georges Cuvier's contributions to the life sciences was the publication of three works of general zoology. A page from one of these books, showing different forms of insects, is illustrated here.

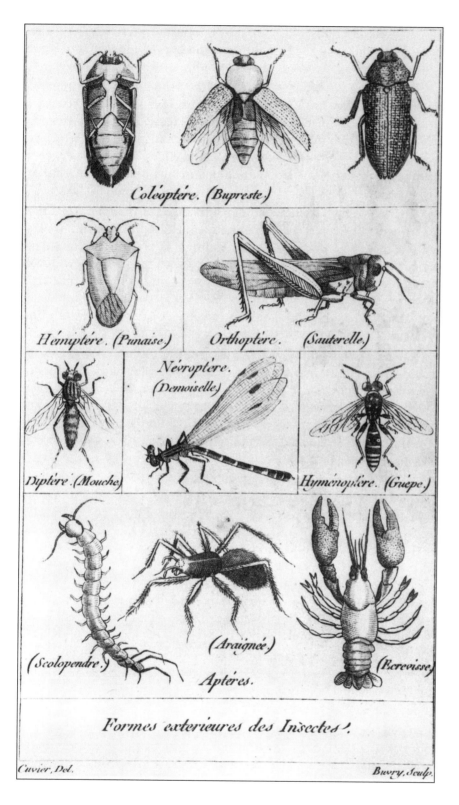

Coléoptère. (Bupreste.)

Hémiptère. (Punaise.)

Orthoptère. (Sauterelle.)

Névroptère. (Demoiselle.)

Diptère. (Mouche)

Hyménoptère. (Guêpe.)

(Scolopendre.)

(Araignée.)

Aptères.

(Ecrevisse)

Formes extérieures des Insectes.

Cuvier, Del.

Buvry, Sculp.

Abilities and Achievements. One of Cuvier's gifts was his extraordinary memory. By the end of his life his personal library, which he made available to all, held about 19,000 volumes on many subjects. He had memorized much of their contents and could recall information he

The Wizard of Science

The public regarded Cuvier as a bit of a wizard who brought to life animals long extinct. Cuvier said that from a well-preserved piece of bone he could determine much about the whole animal. He made mistakes, but his successes were spectacular. Once, in front of witnesses, he looked at a partly visible skeleton in a block of stone and predicted what the rest of the bones would look like. He then proceeded to remove the fossil skeleton of a small opossum from the stone, just as he had described it. By 1804 he had had the idea of using marks left by muscle on bone to reconstruct extinct animals, a technique that scientists use today.

needed within seconds. He made use of his memory as a teacher—after just a few minutes of preparation he could deliver a logical and confident lecture, illustrated with his own skillful blackboard drawings.

Despite the advantages it offered, Cuvier's remarkable memory might have contributed to one of his main weaknesses as a scientist. Believing in the primacy of facts, he was reluctant to develop theories that explained them. He opposed theorizing and declared, "We know how to limit ourselves to describing." This philosophy of science—a form of positivism—was popular among many of his contemporaries, such as the physiologists François MAGENDIE and Claude BERNARD.

Cuvier's contribution to zoology resulted chiefly from the fact that for many years he was the dominant scientist of the Museum of Natural History. When he arrived at the museum, its comparative anatomy collection consisted of a few hundred skeletons and a few dozen examples of animal anatomy. By the time of his death, the musuem's collection increased to more than 13,000 items in all. Collectors sent him fossils, skeletons, and other natural history materials from around the world.

Cuvier's own zoological research produced several books on animals and anatomy, but his masterpiece was a detailed natural history of fish titled *Histoire naturelle des poissons.* At his death he had completed editing nine volumes of this great work, which became the basis of the emerging science of ichthyology, the study of fish. Cuvier also was one of the first to describe the anatomy of mollusks, the invertebrates that inhabit shells.

Buffon, whose books Cuvier had devoured as a child, was among the earlier naturalists who had examined extinct animals and recognized their scientific importance. Cuvier, however, made great strides in studying these fossil remains with new accuracy. Unlike other scientists, he did not limit himself to assembling bones but focused instead on what the living creature had been like. His paleontological reconstructions, in which a few fossils served as the basis for his projection of the entire animal and its characteristics, became famous in an era when people were beginning to marvel at the notion that strange, unknown creatures had once roamed the earth.

One of Cuvier's ideas that was not fully developed until long after his time was the balance of nature. He saw living nature as an "immense network" in which species depended on each other, an understanding that is the basis of modern ecological studies.

From around 1802 until his death, Cuvier carried on a battle of words with many of his scientific colleagues, including Étienne Geoffroy Saint-Hilaire, who had given him his first job at the Museum of Natural History, and Jean Baptiste LAMARCK, the well-known zoologist and previously a director of the museum. These scientists believed that plant and animal species must be variable, or able to change, and that the species underwent change through time. Lamarck had developed a theory of transformation (evolution*) that was supported by Geoffroy. Cuvier, on the other hand, believed that these views contradicted bibli-

*evolution historical development of a biological group such as a species

cal teachings and that species were fixed, having been formed separately at the original creation.

Cuvier's long-standing disputes with Geoffroy and Lamarck reflected the tumult felt throughout the scientific world as revolutionary new knowledge and theories were beginning to upset the traditional view of nature. In fact, anything revolutionary disturbed Cuvier, who made no secret of his admiration for royalty and his respect for the established social order. Although he had considered more liberal or daring scientific ideas earlier in his career, by the end of his life Cuvier had become hostile to new theories.

B y demonstrating that species of plants and animals evolve, or change, over time, with new species created from ancestral ones, Charles Robert Darwin had made one of the most dramatic, important, and far-reaching contributions in the history of science. In addition to demonstrating evolution*, he outlined the chief method by which it occurs, a process called natural selection*. Darwin's work has had enormous influence not only on later scientific work but also on society and culture in general. He forever changed the human view of the natural world—and of humankind's place in the great web of interconnected life.

A man of wide interests, deep insight, and great patience, Darwin also did important research in geology and botany. His work in these fields, as well as in evolutionary biology, was influential in several modern branches of science.

Life

Darwin's early years were marked by uncertainty about what he was to do with his life. The uncertainty vanished during a remarkable voyage of discovery, after which Darwin was able to devote the rest of his life to his two great passions: biological research and his family.

Background and Education. Darwin was born in Shrewsbury, in the English county of Shropshire, into a prominent family. He was the grandson of Erasmus DARWIN and the son of Robert Waring Darwin, both successful physicians. His mother, Susannah Wedgwood, was the daughter of Josiah Wedgwood, founder of the large Wedgwood pottery-making firm. Charles was the fifth child of the family. Darwin received his early education at home, where he was taught by his three older sisters. He began to attend school at the age of eight but was declared a slow learner. In fact, Darwin—whose brilliant scientific work would one day bring him praise and many awards—failed to distinguish himself at school throughout his academic career.

Darwin later complained that at Shrewsbury School he was taught nothing but the classics (Greek and Roman language and literature, which were then considered central to a good education), ancient histo-

Charles Robert
DARWIN

1809–1882

NATURAL HISTORY, EVOLUTION, BOTANY, GEOLOGY

*evolution historical development of a biological group such as a species

*natural selection theory that within a given species, individuals with characteristics best adapted to the environment survive and successfully produce more offspring than other individuals, resulting in changes in the species over time

ry, and some geography. Even as a youth, he had developed an interest in collecting natural history specimens, performing chemical experiments, and hunting. Such pastimes, however, were not regarded as signs of future success. Darwin's schoolmaster publicly criticized him for wasting his time with chemistry, and his father declared in exasperation, "You care for nothing but shooting, dogs, and rat-catching, and you will be a disgrace to yourself and all your family."

When Darwin was 16, his father removed him from Shrewsbury School and sent him to Edinburgh, Scotland, to study medicine at the university there. Darwin, however, was not cut out for a medical career. He found the lectures unbearably dull, and he was horrified and sickened by the demonstrations of surgical operations, which were performed on conscious, screaming patients because anesthetic* drugs had not yet been discovered. Vowing that medicine was no career for him, Darwin left Edinburgh after two years, but his stay there had nourished his growing interest in natural history*. He had formed a friendship with a zoologist named Robert Grant, explored the countryside to study geology, and ventured to the seashore and neighboring waters to collect specimens of marine animals.

Darwin's father next decided to prepare his son for a career as a clergyman in the Church of England. He enrolled the young man in the University of Cambridge in 1827. Darwin's performance at Cambridge was lackluster, and he later said that his time there was "wasted as far as the academical studies were concerned, as completely as at Edinburgh and at school." His preferred activities once again revolved around hunting and riding with fellow sportsmen and around natural history pastimes. An older cousin, William Darwin Fox, introduced Darwin to the pleasures of collecting beetles, which remained one of Darwin's lifelong enthusiasms. Darwin also befriended two members of Cambridge's scientific community: geologist Adam Sedgwick and botanist John Stevens Henslow. Henslow, who became something of a second father to Darwin during this formative period of his life, fired the younger man's passion for natural history and inspired him with self-confidence. He also opened the door for the greatest adventure of Darwin's life.

anesthetic substance that causes loss of sensation with or without loss of consciousness

natural history systematic study of animals and plants, especially in their natural settings

The Evolution of Darwin's Family

Darwin had a reputation as a worrier. He worried not only about the health of his children, but about whether they would find interesting work and be successful in their own careers. As it turns out, however, he had no need for concern. George Darwin became a famous mathematician and astronomer; Francis Darwin a botanist; Leonard Darwin became a successful engineer; and Horace Darwin, also an engineer, founded a scientific instrument company. Several generations of Darwins were so successful in scientific careers that the family became the foundation for some theories about the inheritance of intelligence.

The Voyage. In 1831, after receiving his degree from Cambridge, Darwin received an invitation from the British government to accompany the ship *Beagle* on a surveying mission around the world. Henslow had suggested Darwin as a companion for the ship's captain, believing that the voyage would offer Darwin exceptional opportunities to study natural history. Darwin wished to accept the offer at once, but his father objected to the plan, fearing that it might be too risky for his son. On the urging of Charles's uncle from the Wedgwood side, Darwin's father changed his mind, and in December 1831, Charles left England on the *Beagle*. During the mission, which was expected to take two years but in actuality lasted for five, Darwin endured bouts of seasickness. The experience sharpened his skills as a scientific observer; as a collector of plant, animal, and rock specimens; and as a brilliant thinker.

The *Beagle* sailed southwest across the Atlantic Ocean, visiting several island groups before reaching South America. For several years the ship moved from place to place along South America's eastern and western coasts as its captain carried out his mapmaking duties. Darwin was often able to spend long periods of time ashore. He marveled at Brazil's tropical rain forests, galloped with cowboys across Argentina's plains, dug fossils out of riverbanks, crossed the towering Andes Mountains, and witnessed an earthquake that devastated the city of Concepción, Chile.

On the western side of South America, off the coast of Ecuador, the *Beagle* called at the dry, sparsely inhabited Galápagos Islands—a visit that would later play a key role in the development of Darwin's scientific thought. After leaving the waters off the South American coasts, the *Beagle* crossed the Pacific Ocean, stopping again in several island groups and in Australia. Eventually it crossed the Indian Ocean, rounded the southern tip of Africa, and entered the Atlantic, returning to England in 1836.

Darwin had set out on the voyage with an informal scientific training but no clear life goals. He returned a man of science, with a purpose in life. He had filled many notebooks and sent many geological and biological specimens home during the voyage. It would take years for Darwin and other experts to classify, study, and write about all the material gathered. All the while, Darwin was quietly mulling over an issue that he called "the species problem"—the question of how plant and animal species arise. Specimens and observations from the *Beagle* voyage not only raised the question in his mind but also helped him answer it, although he did not make his views on the species problem public until 1858, many years after he had formulated his new theory.

Scientist and Family Man. Darwin's journey around the world earned him a place in England's scientific community. He settled in London and within a few years was elected to three of the country's most distinguished learned societies: the Athenaeum, the Royal Society, and the Geological Society, of which he became secretary. In 1839 he published *Journal of Researches into the Geology and Natural History of the Various Countries Visited by H.M.S. Beagle,* a lively and popular summary of his experiences and observations on the voyage.

That same year, Darwin married his cousin Emma Wedgwood, and the couple had ten children, three of whom died in childhood. Soon after the marriage, Darwin began to suffer from ill health. In 1842 he moved his young family out of London to a small estate called Down House in the village of Downe in Kent. There he spent the rest of his life, living comfortably on money from his father and income from his investments. Although Darwin attended scientific meetings in London in the early years, poor health gradually limited his attendance and set a routine of four hours' work a day, walks in his garden, visits to his greenhouses, and strolls or pony rides in the neighborhood.

Darwin, Charles Robert

Darwin's lasting fame is rooted in the observations he made during his five-year voyage around the world. That trip was the single most important event in Darwin's intellectual life, and according to some historians, in the entire history of biological science.

Darwin's illness remains something of a mystery. The doctors of his day could never identify the cause of his exhaustion, weakness, and stomach troubles. Whatever its cause, illness turned the once-adventurous Darwin into an occasional invalid by middle age. But spells of poor health did not keep Darwin from being extraordinarily productive. He completed a set of three books on geological findings from the *Beagle* voyage, then spent eight years on a massive and detailed study of living and fossil barnacles, a class of small marine creatures. Later in his career he published six books on botany and one on earthworms. The central event of his scientific life, however, was the publication of his views on evolution and natural selection in a series of four books beginning with an essay in 1858 and his famous *Origin of Species* in 1859. Darwinism, as these views came to be called, instantly became one of the most hotly debated topics of the era as Darwin's supporters and critics sprang into action in scientific meetings, classrooms, learned journals, and church pulpits.

Despite the controversy, Darwin received recognition as one of the leading scientists of his age. Three foreign universities awarded him honorary doctoral degrees, and 57 foreign learned societies elected him a member. The British monarch and government, however, gave Darwin no official recognition—his demonstration of the fact of evolution and the natural mechanism that causes it was distasteful to Britain's religious authority, the Church of England. As Darwin himself remarked, "Considering how fiercely I have been attacked by the orthodox, it seems ludicrous that I once intended to be a clergyman." Nonetheless, when Darwin died in his home of a heart attack in 1882, his supporters, led by Thomas Henry HUXLEY, arranged for a full funeral service and burial in Westminster Abbey.

Darwin as Geologist

Geology was the first science in which Darwin published important contributions. In many ways, his geological studies were closely connected to his work in the life sciences, especially to his insights into evolution.

Catastrophism. At the time when Darwin sailed aboard the *Beagle,* the most commonly held theory in geology was catastrophism, which held that the forces that had shaped the earth in the past had operated on a much greater scale than any of the forces that were active today. The catastrophists believed that the earth had undergone a succession of creations of plant and animal life when massive floods and volcanic eruptions had wiped out each creation, accounting for fossil finds of animals no longer in existence. The most recent catastrophe was thought to have been Noah's flood, which is described in the Bible. Since that time the surface of the earth and the whole system of nature had been fixed and unchanging. This scheme of thought enabled people to believe in the literal truth of creation as described in the Bible.

The British geologist Charles Lyell challenged catastrophism in his three-volume *Principles of Geology,* of which the first volume appeared

46

in 1830. Darwin carried the book aboard ship and read it with great interest. Lyell argued that land could have risen from the seafloor by slow, gradual processes, such as a series of earthquakes over a long time. He also stated that ordinary processes such as rainfall and erosion could explain the wearing down of land and the deposition of thick layers of soil on ocean floors.

Darwin's observations during the *Beagle* voyage convinced him of the validity of Lyell's views. For example, Darwin witnessed the Concepción earthquake raise the land by several feet. Along the hillsides he saw fossil shells belonging to species still living and concluded that they had been raised from the sea bed only recently. In addition, he observed the effects of erosion.

The Age of the Earth. Like many other scientific thinkers of the time, Darwin began to believe that the earth must be far older than had traditionally been thought. He noticed that many homes in the Andes had been abandoned perhaps because of infertile soil and the lack of water, and speculated on the climate changes that regions must have undergone across geological time and within human experience. This emerging picture of the earth as immensely old, shaped throughout its long history by the same processes that continue today, became part of the foundation for Darwin's studies in the history of life. Finally, as Darwin crossed the Pacific he investigated many coral formations and developed insights into how such geological features as reefs and islands are formed by the slow activity of countless living creatures, the coral polyps. As one commentator put it, "Nature is generous in time and parsimonious [sparing] in violence." Between 1842 and 1846, after his return from the voyage, Darwin published three books on geological subjects: *Coral Reefs, Volcanic Islands,* and *Geological Observations on South America.*

A Revolution in Biology

Even before the first of his geological works appeared, Darwin had formulated his revolutionary views on the transformation or evolution of species. After a long period of carefully seeking confirmation, he published the theory, following it with three additional books about various aspects of evolution.

The Question of Species. Before the *Beagle* voyage, Darwin had no reason to question the accepted view that species of plants and animals had existed unchanged since the biblical creation. The concept of species evolution was not entirely unknown, however. A few earlier thinkers, such as Darwin's own grandfather Erasmus Darwin and French naturalist Jean Baptiste LAMARCK, had suggested it, but they had failed to develop a full theory or provide convincing evidence to explain how species could evolve. Most people, including scientists, opposed the idea of evolution. Some believed that such ideas threatened not just religious beliefs but also the social order of which religion was a part.

Darwin, however, began to doubt the accepted view of unchanging species. When he saw the similarities between the living species of South American armadillos and the extinct fossil species, he wondered why it was so, especially if the present species had been created afresh. He also observed that the Cape Verde Islands, located in the Atlantic near the coast of Africa, are very similar in their geological and physical features to the Galápagos Islands. Yet the animals in the Cape Verdes resembled African species, while those in the Galápagos resembled South American species. Somehow, the island species must be connected to the mainland ones, but how?

The Galápagos Islands held a key to the puzzle. Identical in climate and physical features and located very close to one another, the islands should have been inhabited by identical species. But Darwin noticed that the finches (songbirds) on different islands had different physical characteristics and food habits. Some of these birds ate insects, while others ate seeds, and their sizes and bill shapes varied depending on their diets and ways of life. At first Darwin thought they were only varieties of a single species, but later he learned that they were separate but closely related species. This knowledge led him to ask if a single type of bird could have been "modified for different ends."

Soon after his return to England, Darwin began to try to explain how species might change into other species or diverge from each other, with one species giving rise to two or more new ones. In mid-1837, Darwin opened a notebook in which he recorded his ideas on the subject. Evolution, he soon saw, explained many biological mysteries, such as why each region of the earth has its own types of plants and animals, why organisms fall into groups that can be classified by shared features, and why older fossils differ more from living species than recent fossils do. He hypothesized that species are related because they descended from common or shared ancestors.

Darwin kept his ideas largely to himself, sharing bits only with one or two close associates, because he saw the great obstacles that lay ahead and because his insight would cause an uproar in the scientific world and among the public. Moreover, he could not yet explain *how* evolution might have occurred. He viewed evolution as the change that species undergo to adapt to their environment and way of life. The woodpecker, for example, has toes that grip tree trunks, stiff tail feathers that prop it against the trees, a stout bill for poking holes through bark, and a long tongue for reaching grubs through the holes. But how had the woodpecker evolved to have these features?

For thousands of years people had been cultivating plants and breeding domesticated animals, producing many new varieties of each. Because there are differences among members of the same species, growers and herders use a process of selection, choosing the plants and animals with qualities they favor to become the parents of the next generation. Darwin wondered whether some sort of selection process had been operating in nature since the beginning of life on earth.

In 1838 Darwin acquired the final piece of the puzzle. He read *Essay on the Principles of Population* by Thomas Robert Malthus, an

Evolution in Action

Shortly before Darwin died, his son Leonard asked how soon he thought scientists would find conclusive evidence of natural selection. The reply, 50 years, proved to be an accurate forecast. In the 1930s the British scientist Ronald Fisher showed that the way genes shape organisms' physical forms is a result of natural selection. Soon researchers were seeing evolution in action, such as moths in industrial areas growing darker over generations to blend into their increasingly sooty environment. *The Beak of the Finch,* an award-winning 1994 book by science writer Jonathan Weiner, describes current evolution among the Galápagos species that inspired Darwin.

English clergyman and economist, who argued that human populations could increase at a far faster rate than the food supply increases. Human populations expand until they outgrow the necessary resources, resulting in famine, starvation, war, or some other limit to population growth.

Darwin quickly concluded that he could apply Malthus's argument to plants and animals. Survival is a constant struggle or competition in nature because the number of plant and animal offspring produced is far greater than what the available resources can support. If an organism's individual variations improve its chances to survive and breed, it will pass on those useful characteristics to the next generation, which will also benefit from them and pass them on. As these well-adapted creatures interbreed, the adaptive characteristics will become more pronounced. Under the pressure of competition for survival, the distant descendants of a bird with an unusually stiff tail and long tongue will one day form a distinct species, the woodpecker. Darwin called this process natural selection, in contrast to the artificial selection practiced by growers and breeders. "At last," he said, "I have a theory to work by," the mechanism through which evolution operates.

Darwin's Greatest Work. In mid-1842 and 1844 Darwin wrote two essays about his theory of the origin of species through natural selection. He did not publish them then, but by the mid-1850s he had begun to share his ideas with a few of his scientist friends. One of them, the geologist Lyell, urged Darwin to write a book on the subject, and he began to do so.

Other scientists had also begun to investigate "the species problem," and in 1858 Darwin received a manuscript from one of them, Alfred Russel WALLACE. To Darwin's dismay, Wallace had perfectly summarized the very same argument that Darwin had secretly developed and for which he had been collecting evidence for 20 years. Lyell and several of Darwin's other scientific supporters, who knew something of the history of Darwin's thought, arranged for Wallace's paper and Darwin's essay to be read at a meeting of the Linnean Society and published together later that year. Wallace is considered Darwin's codiscoverer of the principles of evolution and natural selection, but Darwin came to be chiefly associated with those principles, mainly because the book he published in 1859 outlived the basic theory of evolutionary biology.

That book, *On the Origin of Species by Means of Natural Selection,* was shorter than the volume Darwin originally intended to write on the subject but its several hundred pages were substantial enough to stir up a storm of protest. Two aspects of the *Origin* were especially disturbing to religious leaders. First, the notion that humans and apes had descended from a common ancestor took humans out of their privileged position as beings created in God's image to rule the earth. Second, although Darwinism did not deny the existence of God, it claimed that the design of nature could be explained by natural instead of divine means.

*genetics branch of biology that deals with heredity

The turmoil caused by the wide publication and discussion of Darwin's views lasted for some time—indeed, some religious groups still claim on the authority of the Bible that evolution does not occur. The fact of evolution, however, has been well established and scientific debate centers on its mechanisms rather than its existence. One of the most important advances in evolutionary biology since Darwin's time has been the growth of genetics*, which has revealed how individual variations occur among organisms and how characteristics pass from parents to offspring—questions Darwin himself never answered satisfactorily.

Later Works on Evolution. Some of Darwin's scientist friends, notably the biologist Thomas Henry Huxley, became stalwart public defenders of Darwin's ideas. In fact, Huxley was often called "Darwin's Bulldog." For the most part, Darwin himself remained busy with research and writing at Down House. In 1868 he published *The Variation of Animals and Plants Under Domestication,* in which he attempted to explain how animals pass on their characteristics.

Three years later Darwin published a more important work titled *The Descent of Man, and Selection in Relation to Sex.* In this work he tackled the subject that he had ignored in the *Origin.* As early as the late 1830s, when he became more certain that species had evolved over time, Darwin had realized that his insight involved humans as well as animals and plants. He had written, "Animals . . . they may partake of our origin in one common ancestor—we may be all netted together."

Darwin did not claim in the *Descent* that humans are descended from apes, but he argued, on the basis of the many physical, behavioral, and psychological similarities between humans and apes, that both are descended from some common ancient ancestor.

*paleontologist one who studies extinct or prehistoric life, usually through the examination of fossils

Paleontologists* now believe this claim to be correct. In the *Descent,* Darwin also discussed how mental and moral qualities might have evolved in humans. The book includes a section on the role played in evolution by sexual selection, which refers to the improved chances of mating that members of one sex (usually male) have because of special features or behaviors they use in courtship.

The fourth and last of Darwin's books on broad evolutionary issues was *The Expression of the Emotions in Man and Animals,* published in 1872. Again treating humans as part of the animal world, Darwin examined facial and vocal expressions in people and other mammals, attempting to show how such expressions are related to particular emotions. With this book Darwin provided the bases for the science of ethology, the study of animal behavior.

Contributions to Botany

Plants as well as animals contributed to Darwin's insights into evolution and natural selection. In the later stages of his career, Darwin grew increasingly interested in botany, and after publishing the *Origin* he wrote several books on botanical subjects. These included the results of many observations and experiments conducted in his gardens.

In an 1862 book on how orchids are fertilized by insects, he showed that the adaptations of plants are as varied and complex as those of animals. By the mid-1870s Darwin had published several more books on the methods by which plants become fertilized.

Darwin also studied climbing plants, hoping to determine the adaptive value of climbing. He measured the growth of climbing plants and found that some climb by twining their stems around other objects. Climbing enables young, weak plants to raise themselves from the ground and receive more sunlight and air without having to build strong woody stems. Darwin discovered that plants will not twine around objects larger than six inches in diameter—this prevents them from climbing up large trees whose leaves would deprive them of air and light. Darwin also investigated the mechanical cause of bending and twining in plants and found that growth was related to a substance in the plant that was sensitive to light. His researches and experiments, reported in *Climbing Plants* and *The Power of Movement in Plants,* were an early insight into what became the science of growth hormones in plants.

Through a series of studies and experiments on insect-eating plants, Darwin showed how such plants trap and digest insects. He was particularly impressed by the fact that the living cells of these plants have certain qualities in common with the nerve cells of animals. He published these findings in *Insectivorous Plants* in 1875. Darwin's last book, *The Formation of Vegetable Mould Through the Action of Worms, with Observations on Their Habits,* was a pioneering study in ecology that showed that on a single acre of land, 18 tons of soil are brought to the surface each year by the tunneling activities of worms.

At the end of his life, the man who had revolutionized biology with his bold, sweeping concepts remained fascinated with nature's small but vital details.

Erasmus DARWIN

1731–1802

MEDICINE, BOTANY, TECHNOLOGY

Erasmus Darwin, the grandfather of the great English naturalist* Charles DARWIN, was the author of several important works on medicine and natural sciences. He was also an accomplished physician and a diverse scientific thinker who drew up plans for an impressive array of practical inventions.

Born near Nottingham, England, Darwin studied the classics, mathematics, and medicine at Cambridge, where he earned a master's degree. He spent several years at the Edinburgh Medical School before beginning his private practice in 1756 in Nottingham. Because he attracted few patients, he moved to Lichfield, where he established his reputation by healing a patient who had been declared incurable by another physician. An innovative doctor, Darwin tried new treatments, supported the practice of inoculation* to prevent disease, recognized the role of heredity in some diseases, and held progressive views on treatment of the mentally ill and matters pertaining to public health.

Darwin was also deeply interested in the natural world and an active student of botany and zoology. In 1779, he began working on

*naturalist one who studies objects in their natural settings

*inoculation introduction of a disease agent into an animal or plant to produce a mild form of the disease and render the organism immune

*natural philosophy set of theories or ideas about the natural world; theoretical basis for research in the natural sciences

*evolution historical development of a biological group such as a species

*natural selection theory that within a given species, individuals with characteristics best adapted to the environment survive and successfully produce more offspring than other individuals, resulting in changes in the species over time

The Botanic Garden, a scientific treatise on natural philosophy* written in the form of an extended poem. The work covers the important studies, inventions, and discoveries of contemporary scientists such as the Scottish engineer James Watt and the Swedish botanist Carl LINNAEUS. It also contains an early statement of a theory of biological evolution*. Between 1794 and 1796, Darwin released his second major work, *Zoonomia.* In this two-volume treatise on medicine and natural science, he defined and explored the physical and psychological bases of disease as he understood them. He also further developed his theory of evolution, which had hints of the mechanism of natural selection* that became the cornerstone of his grandson Charles's theory of evolution. In *Zoonomia,* Darwin expressed his belief that the earth was millions of years old, and he advanced the notion that all forms of life may have arisen from a common ancestor. It was among several early theories of evolution that took into consideration all life on earth and that raised several issues that became central to his grandson's work.

Darwin's two other major works were *Phytologia* and *The Temple of Nature.* The former deals with matters of scientific agriculture, such as draining and watering land and identifying and treating plant diseases. It also outlines chemical means of pest control as well as ecological methods such as breeding predatory birds to eat the larvae of destructive insects. *The Temple of Nature* is a nature poem in which Darwin argues that ancient myths embody basic truths about the natural world that can be incorporated into the body of scientific knowledge.

In addition to his publications, Darwin kept a journal in which he noted his ideas for various inventions. These included canal locks, a speaking machine, a rocket motor powered by hydrogen and oxygen, and a copying machine. He also joined in founding organizations to discuss science and its application to technology. At age 70, Darwin suffered what appears to have been a heart attack. He never fully recovered from its effects and died two years later.

Paul
EHRLICH
1854–1915
MEDICINE, IMMUNOLOGY

*immunology science that deals with the immune system, which protects the body from foreign substances, cells, and tissue by causing the body to produce substances to counteract the infectious materials

*physiology science that deals with the functions of living organisms and their parts

One of the most original, industrious, and successful medical scientists of his generation, Paul Ehrlich is perhaps best known for his pioneering work in immunology* and for his discovery of a successful treatment for the sexually transmitted disease syphilis. Ehrlich shared the 1908 Nobel Prize for physiology* or medicine with Élie METCHNIKOFF in recognition of their work on immunity.

Early Life and Education. Ehrlich was born in Strehlen, Germany (present-day Strzelin, Poland), a small country town. The only son of a respected Jewish innkeeper, he entered the local primary school at age six. Four years later he was sent to the Gymnasium, a college preparatory school, in the city of Breslau (present-day Wroclaw, Poland), where he lived in a professor's home. Although not an outstanding student, Ehrlich was often near the top of his class.

In 1872 Ehrlich graduated from the Gymnasium and took a course in the natural sciences at Breslau University. He later studied at the University of Strasbourg, where he devoted many long hours to developing staining techniques (making tissue preparations with dyes) for use in studying organic tissues. In 1874 Ehrlich returned to Breslau, where he resumed studies for his medical degree. He also studied at Freiburg and Leipzig.

Early Work and Career. After graduation from university, Ehrlich was appointed head physician at the Charité Hospital in Berlin, a renowned medical clinic. While there he did histological* and biochemical* research and gained important insights into problems of medical diagnosis and therapy. Ehrlich's studies on blood cells advanced the field of hematology* into a new era by establishing methods of detecting and differentiating types of leukemia and anemia. He also applied new tissue staining techniques to the study of bacteria and protozoa*. Ehrlich's application of these techniques to the tuberculosis bacteria discovered by German scientist Robert KOCH proved to be of crucial importance for the diagnosis of tuberculosis.

Continuing his work with dyes, Ehrlich investigated the distribution of oxygen in animal tissues and organs. He demonstrated that bodily organs could be classified into three categories based on their oxygen content. He also developed a technique using dyes to kill nerve pain, or neuralgias. Another outcome of Ehrlich's ingenuity with dyes was the development of a test that became useful in diagnosing severe infections, such as typhoid fever.

After a change in administration at the Charité Hospital in 1885, unfortunately, Ehrlich found his researches increasingly impeded. Three years later, when he was diagnosed with tuberculosis, Ehrlich left the clinic and traveled to Egypt, where he stayed for more than a year. He returned to Berlin in 1889, apparently cured. Nevertheless, he received Koch's newly discovered tuberculosis treatment and never had a recurrence of the disease.

Later Career. Back in Berlin, Ehrlich set up a small private laboratory and launched a series of fundamental studies in immunity. Using certain toxic (poisonous) plant proteins as antigens*, he demonstrated that young mice could be protected against these toxins if fed or injected with them in tiny but increasing dosages. He observed that such actively immunized mice developed high levels of specific antibodies* in their blood. He also showed that the offspring of an immunized mother inherited a certain amount of immunity.

In 1891 Ehrlich joined the Institute for Infectious Diseases in Berlin, then headed by Koch. There he dedicated himself to the institute's goal of solving problems related to infections. He worked with Emil von BEHRING to create a serum* against diphtheria (infectious disease characterized by inflammation of the heart and nervous system), and he developed a method to measure the effectiveness of the serum that was soon adopted throughout the world.

*histological relating to histology, the branch of anatomy that deals with the minute structure of animal and plant tissues, observable only through a microscope

*biochemical referring to biochemistry, the science that deals with chemical compounds and processes occurring in living organisms

*hematology study of the formation, structure, and diseases of the blood

*protozoa group of one-celled microorganisms

*antigen substance that stimulates the production of antibodies, substances in the blood that help fight or counteract a specific disease toxin

*antibody protein produced by the immune system to neutralize the presence of a foreign protein in the body

*serum fluid in the blood that carries substances that provide immunity against disease

In 1899 Ehrlich became director of the Royal Prussian Institute for Experimental Therapy, a new research institution established in Frankfurt. Later renamed the Paul Ehrlich Institute, the organization was responsible for the routine control of immune agents used in therapy as well as for research and training in experimental therapy. Ehrlich remained there until his death in 1915.

Important Research. Between 1899 and 1906 Ehrlich developed the side-chain theory, which states that each cell has a center of protein substance and a series of receptors*, or side chains, that absorb nutrients as well as certain toxic substances. Ehrlich believed that if an organism is exposed to a toxin, the cells will produce great quantities of side chains, each one "matched" to the disease-causing agent. These "immune" side chains prevent a renewed infection, thereby giving the organism active immunity. This theory, and Ehrlich's later work on immunity, had a profound influence on later scientists and the understanding of immunity.

During the course of his work, Ehrlich realized that many infectious disorders did not respond well to treatment with serums. He then began to experiment with the identification and production of synthetic chemicals that could kill toxins or slow their growth. He created and tested several hundred synthetic compounds, marking the beginnings of the field of chemotherapy*.

Another avenue of research Ehrlich devoted attention to was to find a substance that could treat syphilis. In 1909 Ehrlich began intensive trials with a compound that appeared to provide an effective treatment for syphilis in rabbits. Soon, physicians around the world were clamoring for the new remedy. Ehrlich hoped to conduct further tests before the drug could be released for general use, but the demand was overwhelming, and a German chemical company soon began to manufacture the drug, called Salvarsan.

The invention of Salvarsan brought Ehrlich four years of both tragedy and triumph. He battled problems stemming from the drug's imperfections and the harmful side effects that sometimes resulted from its use. He struggled against human carelessness, greed, and the ill will of critics. He closely scrutinized the tricky manufacturing process for each batch of Salvarsan. During this four-year period, Ehrlich continued to test the drug and worked to make it safer by combining it with other compounds.

Last Years and Honors. These burdens caused Ehrlich's frail health to worsen, and his peace of mind was disturbed by vicious attacks against him by critics, who accused him of fraud, profiting from the misery of others, and ruthless experimentation. Finally, the outbreak of World War I drew public attention elsewhere, and Ehrlich suffered no further indignities.

However, Ehrlich was distressed by World War I and Germany's role in it. He also brooded over his isolation from scientific friends abroad and the effect the war had on slowing or halting work at the

*receptor specialized organ or cell that is sensitive to and responds to certain stimulating agents

*chemotherapy treatment of disease by means of chemicals that have a specific effect on certain disease-producing organisms

In the early 1900s, Ehrlich discovered Salvarsan, a compound used to treat syphilis. Salvarsan is also known as "606" because it was the 606th compound that Ehrlich tested in his quest to find a drug to cure the disease.

institute. He suffered a slight stroke in 1914, and the following year he entered a clinic for treatment and rest. Shortly after his arrival at the clinic he suffered a second, fatal stroke. He died at age 61.

Ehrlich received many honors. In addition to winning the Nobel Prize in 1908, he was awarded several honorary degrees and he held memberships in many scientific and medical societies. The Paul Ehrlich Prize for outstanding achievement in one of his fields of research is still given every other year as a living memorial to him.

Jean Henri
FABRE
1823–1915
ENTOMOLOGY

A keen observer of nature and a talented writer, Jean Henri Fabre is a perfect example of the self-taught scientist of the nineteenth century. As a pioneer in entomology, the study of insects, Fabre made many important discoveries and interested others in the subject.

Fabre was born in Saint-Léons, France, and was educated at Rodez and at the École Normale Primaire in Avignon. He worked as a schoolteacher from 1842 until 1854, when he received his doctoral degree in natural science. He spent the rest of his life studying insect biology and behavior, first in Avignon and then in Sérignan, where he lived after 1879. To earn a living, Fabre wrote textbooks and about 40 volumes of popular science for young people, on topics ranging from mathematics and physics to biology. He also wrote poetry.

In 1855 Fabre began to publish papers on such topics as wasps that paralyze beetles and the metamorphosis, or change in form, of beetles. In 1859, when the English biologist Charles DARWIN mentioned Fabre in his book *On the Origin of Species,* it was a valuable encouragement for the poorly paid young researcher. Although Darwin admired Fabre's work, Fabre remained opposed all his life to the idea of evolution*.

*evolution historical development of a biological group such as a species

Fabre's major scientific work was the ten-volume *Souvenirs entomologiques* (Entomological Notes), published between 1879 and 1907. This popular work on the lives and habits of insects inspired many to pursue entomology. Much of Fabre's work attempted to grapple with the problem of instinct in insects and how each species acquired the habits and responses that its members exhibited. Although sometimes criticized by other scientists, these researches showed that insects are governed largely by inborn instinct, not by reasoning powers like those of higher animals or humans, as some earlier investigators had thought.

Girolamo
FABRICI
ca. 1537–1619
ANATOMY, PHYSIOLOGY,
EMBRYOLOGY, SURGERY

The Italian physician and anatomist Girolamo Fabrici, also known as Geronimo Fabrizio or Fabricius ab Aquapendente, dominated the study of anatomy at the University of Padua in Italy, one of Europe's foremost universities for many decades in the late 1500s and early 1600s. Fabrici was a pioneer in embryology*, and his studies of the structure of blood vessels helped prepare one of his students, the English physiologist* William HARVEY, to explain the workings of the body's circulatory system.

*embryology branch of biology that deals with embryos, organisms from the first division of the fertilized egg through the early stages of development before birth or hatching

*physiologist one who specializes in physiology, the science that deals with the functions of living organisms and their parts

A Room with a View

Medical students have long learned anatomy by observing skilled anatomists at work as they operate on the living or dissect the bodies of the dead. In Fabrici's time the University of Padua recognized the need for a chamber designed so that students could clearly see and hear the anatomist. Thanks largely to Fabrici's efforts, the university built a new, oval-shaped anatomical theater, which Fabrici inaugurated in 1595. It became famous as a seat of advanced anatomical study. The theater still stands in Padua and bears Fabrici's name.

Life and Career. Fabrici was born in Aquapendente, near Orvieto, Italy. The exact year of his birth is unknown, but is probably 1537. He was the oldest son of a noble family that had once been wealthy. As a young man Fabrici had a classical education; he studied Greek, Latin, logic, and philosophy at the University of Padua. He also studied medicine, and around 1559 he received a degree in both medicine and philosophy.

Fabrici studied anatomy with the famous Italian physician Gabriele Falloppio, and when Falloppio died in 1562, Fabrici took his place as teacher of anatomy. Several years later the university appointed Fabrici as a lecturer in anatomy and surgery and he held that position until 1609, when anatomy and surgery began to be taught as separate subjects. He continued as the head of anatomical study until his retirement in 1613, after nearly 50 years of service to the university.

Those years did not pass without strife for Fabrici. In addition to quarrels with some of his colleagues, he had troubled relations with his students. In 1588 his students publicly accused him of neglecting his teaching. There was probably some truth to this charge—Fabrici was frequently ill, and he devoted much time to scientific research. Trouble arose again when he ridiculed the manner in which his German students spoke, and they resented the insult. German students in Italy seem to have been a lively lot, for in later years, Fabrici defended one student from a charge of murder and helped others who had gotten into trouble for carrying weapons. Despite his sometimes difficult character, his excellent reputation as a surgeon and physician brought him many famous and wealthy patients, including several dukes and the astronomer Galileo Galilei.

Contributions to Medical Science. As a scientist Fabrici was a careful and exact observer, but he most often interpreted his observations in ways that fit traditional ideas or principles. Only on some occasions did he offer new theories or interpretations.

Fabrici intended to publish a monumental work that would encompass all of his researches, discoveries, and ideas. Although he never completed this masterwork, he did publish a series of shorter volumes, beginning in 1600. They dealt with such topics as vision, voice, and hearing; the valves of the veins; and the eggs and embryos of birds, animals, and humans. Among other notable discoveries, he was the first to describe how the larynx produces speech and to show that the pupil of the eye can grow larger and smaller to admit more or less light. In 1600 Fabrici also completed an important set of 300 color plates illustrating human anatomical features.

One of the best known and most thoroughly studied of Fabrici's works is *De venarum ostiolis* (On the Valves of the Veins), published in 1603. It gives the first clear anatomical description of structures that were later seen as necessary to regulate the flow of blood within the veins. However, he did not understand their function at the time. An important feature of his work on the veins is that his student William Harvey later drew on it when he described the system by which blood circulates within the body. Harvey, who not only studied with Fabrici but also lived for a time in his house, first became interested in the motion of the heart (heartbeat) and circulation while observing Fabrici's anatomical dissections at Padua.

Fabrici's other contribution to medical science concerned the structure of the fetus before birth. In 1604 he published *De formato foetu* (On the Formation of the Fetus), which dealt with fetal development in birds, sharks, mice, rabbits, cats, dogs, horses, pigs, and humans. Fabrici described the umbilical cord and provided the first clear description of the placenta*. He explained many of his findings using the traditional medical theories of his time. His skillful dissections and reports were important to the foundation of the study of embryology.

*placenta flattened organ in pregnant mammals that connects the fetus to the maternal uterus and facilitates the exchange of nutrients

Girolamo
FRACASTORO
1478–1553
MEDICINE, PHILOSOPHY

The Italian physician and poet Girolamo Fracastoro was learned in many areas of both the arts and natural history*, and he produced works on topics ranging from astronomy to syphilis, a sexually transmitted disease. His chief contribution to the life sciences was his theory of infections, which was an early attempt to explain how diseases pass from one person to another. His major scientific work was a landmark study of contagious diseases.

*natural history systematic study of animals and plants, especially in their natural settings

Life and Career. Fracastoro was born in Verona, Italy. His mother died when he was very young and his father began his education in literature and philosophy. As a young man, Fracastoro was sent to the University of Padua to complete his education. Under the guidance of a family friend from Verona who taught and practiced medicine in Padua, Fracastoro studied literature, mathematics, astronomy, philosophy, and medicine.

Immediately after receiving his degree in 1502, Fracastoro became an instructor of logic at the University of Padua. He was also involved in the study of anatomy, and in addition became acquainted with the great Polish astronomer Nicolas Copernicus. In the early 1500s, when war between Venice and Emperor Maximilian I loomed over the region, the university closed and Fracastoro left Padua. After a brief period of military service, apparently as a doctor, Fracastoro returned to Verona around 1509. He dedicated himself to his studies and to reorganizing the estate he had inherited on his father's death. For some years he also maintained a medical practice, treating patients from all over Italy, and was one of the administrators of the local medical college.

Beginning in 1511 Fracastoro began spending long periods at a country house in Incaffi (the present-day hamlet of Affi), outside Verona. His learned friends gathered there for philosophical and scientific meetings. Fracastoro's own cultural interests continued to widen, and he became knowledgeable in each area that claimed his interest, including botany and geology. He died suddenly of a stroke in 1553, probably at his country residence, and was buried in Verona, where a statue was erected in his honor in 1555.

Contributions to Science. Fracastoro's scientific personality took shape at Padua and reflected a key intellectual trend of his time: an increased interest in the study of nature. His philosophy of science was that nature operates by its own laws, which are a mixture of good and bad from the human point of view. To live profitable and happy lives, humans should not hope for supernatural aid but should rely on their capacity for reason to gain a better understanding of the principles that govern the natural world. These ideas emerge in a long poem that brought Fracastoro far-reaching fame after it was published in 1530. Titled *Syphilis sive morbis Gallicus,* it deals with the symptoms and treatment of syphilis. Through this work, the name of the sickness (derived from Sifilo, the name of the poem's hero) was definitively established. Fracastoro's mythological tale contains an exhaustive description of the various symptoms of the disease, demonstrating his lucid knowledge of the clinical events and the related course of the illness.

Fracastoro's greatest achievement in science, published in 1546, was *De contagione et contagiosis morbis et curatione.* This work earned him a lasting place in the history of epidemiology, the study of how diseases spread. Fracastoro in clear fashion describes a number of contagious diseases. In the most significant part of the work, he illustrates three ways contagions can spread: by direct contact, or touching; through carriers such as sheets or clothing; and at a distance, without direct contact or carriers.

Fracastoro believed that the seeds of contagious disease were tiny, invisible particles that had certain properties, such as being able to multiply and to endure for long periods, even when alienated from the sick person in whom they had originated. Fracastoro seems to have visualized something very much like microbes, tiny infectious organisms whose existence would not be established for hundreds of years. Later scientists found Fracastoro to be accurate in many of his ideas about the causes and pathways of infection.

Leonhart
FUCHS

1501–1566

MEDICINE, BOTANY

L eonhart Fuchs was an important professor of medicine in the German universities of the 1500s. He was born in Wemding, Germany, and educated in Erfurt and Ingolstadt. As a youth, he took long walks in the countryside with his grandfather Fuchs, learning the names of different species of flowers. This interest guided him through his academic career. He received a doctorate in medicine at the age of 23. He practiced and taught medicine in Munich and Tübingen and then served as physician to a German noble in Ansbach, where he gained respect for his treatment of an epidemic of English sweating sickness.

In 1535 Fuchs became professor of medicine at Tübingen, where he remained for the rest of his life. He had a strong influence on those around him, and he was an influential force for the study of ancient Greek and Roman medical texts by such men as GALEN and HIPPOCRATES. His main talent was the organization and presentation of knowledge, and he produced major medical textbooks and a valuable book in which he described 400 native and 100 foreign plants.

Because human dissection was forbidden in Galen's time, most of his contributions to medicine were based on animal anatomy. In this woodcut, a group of men observe Galen while he performs a surgical procedure on a pig.

For nearly 1,500 years, Western and Arabic thought were dominated by Galen's views on medicine, anatomy, and physiology*. He was one of the most important physicians of ancient times. His extensive writings formed the basis of medical theory and practice during the Middle Ages* and the Renaissance*, and much of modern medical knowledge developed from commentaries and critiques of his theories.

GALEN

ca. 129–ca. 200

MEDICINE

*physiology science that deals with the functions of living organisms and their parts

*Middle Ages period between ancient and modern times in western Europe, generally considered to be from the A.D. 500s to the 1500s

*Renaissance period that marked the beginnings of modern science and the rebirth of interest in classical art and literature that occurred in Europe from the late 1300s through the 1500s

Life and Work

Galen was born in Pergamum, Asia Minor (present-day Turkey), then an important city of the Roman Empire. His father was an architect who was trained in geometry, a discipline that would exert a powerful influence on Galen's own ideas about medicine and physiology. Many sources cite his first name as "Claudius," but the name is not documented in the ancient texts and appears to have been added during the Renaissance.

Education and Early Career. Galen's education focused on mathematics and various fields of philosophy, but he claimed that a dream he had at age 16 set him on the course of his life's work—medicine. Although scholars are not certain if this story is true, it appears that Galen's exposure to so many different philosophical ideas led him on a search for certainty. He found that only the systematic logic of geometry satisfied this need, and he hoped that by studying medicine he would find a similar certainty of knowledge about the workings of the body. Galen studied under the physician Satyrus, who introduced him to some of the leading personalities of Pergamum. From this circle of scholars, he became exposed to philosophical ideas that shaped his thinking. During this time Galen wrote several medical works, including a work on the anatomy of the uterus and one on the importance of medical experience. These topics remained important in his later writings.

When Galen was about 20, his father died and shortly thereafter Galen left Pergamum to study with a physician named Pelops in the city of Smyrna. He later went to Corinth in Greece and finally to Alexandria in Egypt, which was the most renowned center of learning in the ancient world. There he had access to the collected knowledge of his day, as well as an opportunity to study human skeletons. At age 28 he returned to Pergamum to become physician to the gladiators* of the city. By that time, he had been studying medicine for nearly 12 years, a

*gladiator in ancient Rome, a person engaged in a fight to the death for the sake of public entertainment

Galen

Medical Forgeries

Galen was such a prominent authority that forgeries and works published by others under his name sprang up even during his own lifetime. In some cases, authors used Galen's name to try to legitimize their point of view. Others "borrowed" Galen's name to increase the sales of material written on a popular subject, such as the use in the Middle Ages of urine for medical prognosis. Some medical works that appeared in the late ancient period and the Middle Ages were distorted summaries and simplifications of Galen's writings. Forgeries of Galen's works continued to be produced as late as the Renaissance.

*cadaver dead body, especially one intended for anatomical dissection

very long time by the standards of the day. His work with the gladiators gave him valuable experience in nutrition, the treatment of wounds, and the study of nerves and muscles.

Galen and Rome. Three years after his return to Pergamum, Galen went to Rome and established his own practice there. His patients included many influential Romans, one of whom convinced him to write his first major works on medicine and anatomy. The same official, Flavius Boethus, also inspired Galen to give public lectures and demonstrations in anatomy, which attracted many important politicians and philosophers. Galen made a name for himself, but he also made enemies because of his high opinion of himself and his contempt for those who disagreed with his ideas. He left Rome at age 34 to return to Pergamum and then traveled for a brief time for scientific study. He returned to Rome at the order of Emperor Marcus Aurelius and served as the personal physician for the emperor's son Commodus. He remained with the imperial household when Commodus became emperor in 180 and later served under the Septimus Severus, who succeeded Commodus in 193. During this second stay in Rome, he traveled throughout Italy and became a leading figure in Roman society. Galen died around the year 200, but it is not clear whether he spent his final years in Rome or in Pergamum.

Scientific Philosophy and Accomplishments

Galen's medical ideas were based on the teachings of HIPPOCRATES, and his philosophical ideals were derived from the teachings of ARISTOTLE. Although his abilities as an anatomist and physiologist were unquestioned in his time, he often had to use questionable arguments to make his ideas on medicine fit his philosophical beliefs.

Philosophy and Achievements. Hippocrates' medical ideas were based on the interaction of many factors. These included the bodily humors (fluids), the elements (earth, air, fire, and water), the seasons, and age. This system provided a structure that satisfied Galen's need for certainty, but it also led him to make errors. For example, he argued strongly for anatomy as the foundation of medicine and made many advances in this field. However, cultural taboos prevented him from working with human cadavers*. With no practical knowledge available to him from dissection, he often substituted guesswork based on his philosophical convictions. Nevertheless, his achievements in many areas of medicine cannot be doubted. He was an outstanding physiologist who stressed the importance of experimentation and direct observation. He developed a thorough knowledge of the nervous system, was gifted at diagnosing illnesses based on their symptoms, and was a first-rate dietitian.

Galen's Hippocratic views led him to place importance on predicting illness based on such factors as "critical days," which had a basis in arithmetic and numerology. While he made accurate diagnoses, he also

60

used medical evidence in unsystematic ways to predict the course of a disease or the possibility of future illness. He believed that medicines should be tested to ensure their effectiveness, even though neither he nor his contemporaries understood how they worked. At times he defended the use of magic charms or the value of unproven "medicines." Despite his wide knowledge of anatomy and physiology, Galen strongly opposed surgery, except for the treatment of wounds. Without anesthetics (painkillers) or the ability to prevent or control infection, surgery was difficult to practice and often ineffective.

Physiology and Anatomy. Although Galen's ideas on physiology and anatomy were derived from the work of earlier physicians, he provided systematic accounts and made several important improvements on their work. At the time many scholars believed that blood was produced in the liver and traveled through the veins to the right side of the heart. The heart then pumped blood to the lungs to nourish the tissues there. The arteries and the left side of the heart were thought to contain breath, air, or *pneuma,* which was pushed through the body by the same action of the heart that pushed blood to the lungs. Galen showed by experiment that the arteries and the left side of the heart actually contain blood, not air. Based on this discovery he argued that the function of breathing was to cool the excess heat of the heart. He thought that air passed from the lungs through the veins along with blood, and that it nourished and cooled the heart before returning to the lungs. The arteries drew blood from the veins as well as *pneuma* from the surrounding air and pushed both through the body to maintain the body's "vital heat." Galen described a mechanism by which he believed that blood distributes *pneuma* or air throughout the body. Although he was working at a time when there was little knowledge of the motion of the heart and blood, he did describe a "system" of the heart and blood that linked many of the body's important functions.

These and other ideas of Galen's formed the core of medical knowledge for many hundreds of years and served as the basis for medical practice and a starting point for subsequent medical research.

Francis
GALTON

1822–1911

PSYCHOLOGY,
HEREDITY, EUGENICS

Francis Galton of Great Britain was a self-trained scientist. He never completed his formal education or held any academic or professional position, but he was endlessly curious about the natural world, especially human beings. Able to immerse himself in whatever subject interested him, Galton contributed to several fields, studying statistics, genius, and human intelligence. He is best remembered as the founder of the science of eugenics*.

Galton was born in Birmingham, England, into a family with scientific connections. His maternal grandfather was the physician, poet, and zoologist Erasmus DARWIN, and he was a first cousin of Charles DARWIN, who became one of the best-known naturalists*. Despite the great intelligence noted by many who knew him, Galton's only achieve-

*eugenics study of improving human heredity by means of genetic control

*naturalist one who studies objects in their natural settings

61

ments as a student were a few mathematics courses at the University of Cambridge and some unfinished medical studies in London. At the age of 22, when he came into a large inheritance, Galton abandoned medicine and began to travel. A journey through previously unknown parts of southwestern Africa in the early 1850s gained him a reputation as a bold explorer. He spent the rest of his life in London, however, except for occasional vacations on the European continent.

The driving force in Galton's scientific work was his belief that everything could be quantified, or measured and expressed using numbers. He devised methods for measuring and comparing all sorts of phenomena, including feminine beauty, body weights of three generations of British aristocrats, the effectiveness of prayer. Galton also originated several concepts in the science of statistics and set the foundation for elements of psychology, including mental testing and measuring sensory acuteness.

In 1880, the British science journal *Nature* published papers Galton wrote describing human fingerprints as unique and permanent. Galton investigated fingerprints and established that they are an easy and almost error-free way to uniquely identify people. He also developed the first system for classifying fingerprints, naming their various kinds of patterns as arches, loops, and whorls. Galton's work established the basis for categorizing fingerprints still used in forensic* identification.

*forensic referring to the use of science in criminal and legal investigations

Galton's well-known and controversial work concerned the inheritance of scholarly, artistic, and athletic talent. Using the records of prominent families, he found strong evidence that such qualities were inherited, even though there were differences in the individuals' environments and upbringing. One outcome of this investigation was Galton's deep belief, which many others shared, that a society that wanted to maintain and improve its quality and status should promote a program of eugenics to increase talent and healthiness in its population, and to minimize stupidity and sickliness. In 1883 Galton coined the term *eugenics* to refer to the program. He was knighted in 1909 and died two years later in Surrey, England. Galton left money in his will to fund a professorship in eugenics at University College, London.

Luigi GALVANI

1737–1798

ANATOMY, PHYSIOLOGY, PHYSICS

*obstetrics branch of medicine dealing with pregnancy and childbirth

Trained as a physician, Luigi Galvani's noteworthy contributions came from his research on nerves and nerve impulses. Born in Bologna, Italy, he studied at the University of Bologna and later became professor of anatomy there. He served as curator of the city's anatomical museum and professor of obstetrics* at its Istituto delle Scienze (Institute of Science). Galvani was fired from these posts in 1790, however, when he refused to swear loyalty to the government set up by Napoleon Bonaparte after he had conquered the city. Galvani died in Bologna at age 61.

Early in his career Galvani studied standard topics in anatomy, but during the 1770s he became interested in the electrical stimulation of the nerves and muscles of frogs. He prepared the frogs for his experiments by dissecting as a unit the animal's spinal cord, nerves, and lower legs. When he touched the spinal cord or nerves with an electrical conductor, the muscles in the legs contracted, indicating an irritable response to the stimulation.

Galvani noticed that he could produce the same effect merely by placing the frog on an iron plate and pushing a brass hook against it. He also observed that the muscles contracted when he touched one end of the metal hook to the spinal cord and the other end to the legs. The strength of the contractions depended on the metal used, but there were no contractions if he used a nonconductor. He had uncovered the phenomenon of galvanism—the production of electric current from contact of two different metals in a moist environment. But he misinterpreted the results as evidence of the presence of "animal electricity" produced in the brain and stored in the nerves and muscles.

Galvani's conclusions were the subject of much debate. The famous Italian electrician Alessandro Volta at first agreed with Galvani, but later correctly concluded that the contact of different metals produced the electricity. Although Galvani's concept of animal magnetism was later disproved, his findings were important in helping later researchers uncover the nature of the transmission of nerve impulses.

Konrad Gesner, an observer of the natural world, wrote influential early works in botany and zoology. Surprisingly, most of his formal academic preparation was in theology*, and it was not until late in his studies that he turned to medicine, which prepared him for a career in the sciences.

Born in Zurich, Switzerland, Gesner was the godson of Ulrich Zwingli, a prominent Protestant reformer. He studied theology from an early age and attended theological seminaries. Zwingli died when Gesner was 15, and the following year young Konrad left Zurich for France.

Gesner soon lost interest in theology and turned to the field of medicine. He attended the Universities of Bourges, Paris, and Basel and received his doctorate in 1541. Following the advice of his close friend Christophe Clauser, Gesner decided to pursue work in botany, which had fascinated him as a boy. He returned to Zurich and was named chief physician of the city, a position he inherited from Clauser. In addition to his duties as chief physician, Gesner devoted a great deal of time to preparing his manuscripts on botany and zoology. He traveled widely and collected a wealth of information that he incorporated into his two important scientific treatises, *Opera botanica* (Botanical Works) and *Historia animalium* (History of Animals).

Opera botanica, a large format two-volume work published posthumously*, contained nearly 1,500 detailed illustrations drawn by Gesner. He collected more than 500 plant species that were not described in ancient texts. He was one of the few botanists of his day to realize that plants could be classified according to the structure of their flowers as compared to earlier systems that often used medicinal quali-

Konrad
GESNER

1516–1565

NATURAL SCIENCES, MEDICINE

theology study of religion

posthumous occurring after the death of an individual

ties. He was also able to establish the relationships among plants by studying and comparing their seeds. The great Swedish botanist Carl LINNAEUS, who later created the basis of the modern system of classification, frequently noted that his work owed much to Gesner's efforts.

Historia animalium, which was published during Gesner's lifetime, ran more than 4,500 pages in length and remained popular hundreds of years after his death. He proposed a classification system for animals based on body parts and functions. Gesner's interest in animal life included studies of animal physiology* and pathology*. He studied fossils and wrote memoirs on extinct forms of vegetable life. An epidemic that struck Zurich in 1565 claimed Gesner's life. He was not yet 49 years old.

*physiology science that deals with the functions of living organisms and their parts

*pathology study of diseases and their effects on organisms

Johann Wolfgang von GOETHE

1749–1832

ZOOLOGY, BOTANY, GEOLOGY, OPTICS

Goethe was celebrated for scientific findings as well as for his literary achievements. Many consider his play *Faust* his masterpiece. Goethe began writing *Faust* around 1770, but he did not publish the first part until 1808. He completed the second part in 1832.

*evolution historical development of a biological group such as a species

Best known as one of Germany's finest poets, Johann Wolfgang von Goethe also had a strong interest in the sciences, and he published several papers on a variety of topics including zoology, botany, and geology.

Life and Career. Goethe was born in Frankfurt and educated at the University of Strasbourg, where he obtained a law degree in 1771. Four years later, because of his literary fame from his early writings, Goethe was summoned to the court of Emperor Charles Augustus II in Weimar. There he took on a number of duties, including the supervision of irrigation and mining activities in the region. His observations in the mines stimulated many of his theories about the origin of rocks and rock formations.

Beginning in 1786, Goethe spent two years traveling in Italy. The trip convinced him that he was destined to be a writer, and it was after his return to Germany that he composed his most important literary works. By this time Goethe had turned decisively toward literature as a career, devoting much less time to scientific inquiry. He spent the rest of his life in Weimar, where he died in 1832.

Scientific Philosophy. Goethe held that all of nature had an underlying unity that could be discovered by close observation. He believed that every plant, animal, and rock was a variation of an original ideal form, or archetype. All plants were based on an "ideal plant," and individual varieties of plants were simply variations of this archetype. He called his search for the unity among all natural forms "morphology," and it would become one of the most widely used approaches in investigating the natural sciences for many years.

Goethe's goal was to create a theory that would explain all living things and identify their original forms. He was not interested in determining how the many variations of a particular plant or animal came about. Goethe never proposed that similar organisms evolved from the same general form, but he agreed that differences in climate or food could cause one species to develop into another. Notwithstanding his disinterest in the subject, Goethe supported ideas of development that were used by some scientists to propose theories of evolution*.

Explorations of Morphology. In his first scientific paper, based on the idea of morphology, Goethe attempted to prove that humans possess a bone in the upper jaw called the intermaxillary. He noted that the bone appeared in some mammals even though the upper incisors, which it normally supports, are absent. Goethe believed that a bone so important to these mammals must be part of the archetype of the vertebrate* skull and would thus be present in all vertebrates. Moreover, because humans have well-developed upper incisors, he felt that the intermaxillary bone must be present in them. When Goethe found evidence of the three sutures* that define the intermaxillary bone in humans, he believed he had proved his claim. However, other scientists later showed that the sutures were either indistinct or absent in humans.

In his idea of morphology, Goethe also suggested that just as organisms are variations of a single archetype, the type itself consists of parts, each of which are identical to the others. He argued, for example, that all parts of the plant are variations of the ideal form of the leaf. However, he did not mean that the parts develop or evolve from the leaf, but that the ideal leaf is the essential unity that underlies all the parts. He also proposed that the bones of the skull are actually variations of the vertebrae that make up the spinal column. This theory achieved popularity but was later challenged by Thomas HUXLEY, who performed extensive studies of the skulls of embryos*.

Geological Investigations. When Goethe was supervisor of mines, he studied rock formations. At the time, most scientists believed that the sea once covered the entire planet, that the granite core of mountains was the original form of rock, and that all other rocks were created by chemical deposits left by the receding seas. To Goethe, granite was the archetypal rock, deposited as crystals piled atop one another. Because he could not believe that nature was formed by violent disturbances, he rejected the now-accepted notion that many geological formations are the result of the rocks uplifted by collision or volcanic forces.

Goethe's rejection of violent force as a mechanism for shaping nature led him to develop an explanation for the presence of large boulders throughout northern Europe far from their places of origin. Earlier geologists claimed that the rocks had been displaced by violent catastrophes. Goethe argued that the glaciers confined in his time to the Alps had once covered the entire continent and that they carried the boulders as they moved. The German geologist Johann de Charpentier later credited Goethe as one of the pioneers of this theory.

Seeing Red; Then Green

Goethe's longest-lasting scientific work was an attack on Isaac Newton's theory that white light is a mixture of all colors. Although Goethe's premise was incorrect, he helped explain some visual phenomena. He was the first to suggest that the eye works in a polar fashion. That is, when presented with one color, it automatically projects the opposing, or complementary color. For example, if you stare at a red square and then turn to look at a white surface, you will see an image of a green square. He also said that purple was psychologically the purest form of red. Both ideas were supported by later research.

*vertebrate animal with a backbone

*suture division between the bony plates of the skull

*embryo organism from the first division of the fertilized egg through the early stages of development until birth or hatching

The Italian researcher Camillo Golgi is known primarily for his investigations of the anatomy and functioning of the nervous system, for which he shared the 1906 Nobel Prize for medicine or physiology*. Golgi was born in Cortena in the province of Brescia in northern Italy. He received his M.D. from the University of Pavia in 1865 and worked for a short while in a psychiatric clinic. During this time, he

Camillo
GOLGI
1843–1926
HISTOLOGY, PATHOLOGY

*physiology science that deals with the functions of living organisms and their parts

*histology branch of anatomy that deals with the minute structure of animal and plant tissues, observable only through a microscope

*pathology study of diseases and their effects on organisms

*cytoplasm organic and inorganic substances outside the cell's nuclear membrane

*metabolism set of chemical reactions in organisms that convert food into energy and tissue

also pursued his main interests—research in histology* and pathology*. However, financial problems forced him to cease research for a time and take a position at a local hospital.

In 1875 he became a lecturer in histology at the University of Pavia. Four years later he obtained the chair of anatomy at the University of Siena, but he returned to Pavia the following year and remained there until his retirement in 1918, teaching histology and pathology. In 1900 Golgi became a senator in Pavia where he tackled problems of public health and took part in the administration of the university.

Golgi is best known for inventing a completely original method to study the features of nerve elements—he developed a technique to stain certain nerve cells and fibers while leaving others unstained. Based on his work, he concluded that the axons, or the long fibers that join nerve cells, are used solely for transmitting nerve impulses. He also differentiated between sensory nerves and motor nerves based on the length and structure of the axon. Golgi also identified unique networks of fibers in the cytoplasm* of nerve cells. Known as Golgi's internal reticular apparatus, these networks are considered basic to cell metabolism*. Although some of his conclusions were later challenged by the Spanish physiologist Santiago Ramón y Cajal, with whom he shared the Nobel Prize, Golgi's investigations remain important to modern neuroanatomy and neurophysiology. He died in Pavia in 1926 after a lifetime of remarkable achievements and distinctions in the life sciences.

Asa
GRAY

1810–1888

BOTANY

*evolution historical development of a biological group such as a species

*mineralogy study of the properties of minerals

Asa Gray was the foremost botanist in the United States at a time when explorers of North America and the world were introducing thousands of previously undiscovered plants to science. His most noteworthy contribution to botany was his work in taxonomy, the task of identifying plant species and organizing them into larger groupings on the basis of their structure and their relationships with other plants. Gray also wrote important textbooks and was one of the earliest supporters of the English biologist Charles DARWIN's theory on the origin and evolution* of species.

Life and Career. Gray was born in Sauquoit, New York, to a family that had moved from England to upstate New York after the American Revolution. At the age of 15, Gray entered Fairfield Academy in New York and a year later he began to study medicine at Fairfield's College of Physicians and Surgeons. There he was instructed by a talented group of teachers who introduced him to chemistry, mineralogy*, and botany. Gray was especially interested in botany and began collecting plants.

After receiving his medical degree in 1831, Gray practiced medicine for a short time in Bridgewater, New York, but his growing interest in botany led to him seek a career in that field. He had already been in contact with the leading botanist in the United States, John Torrey. After less than a year practicing as a physician, he abandoned medicine to assist Torrey, relying on a series of part-time teaching and library jobs to support himself.

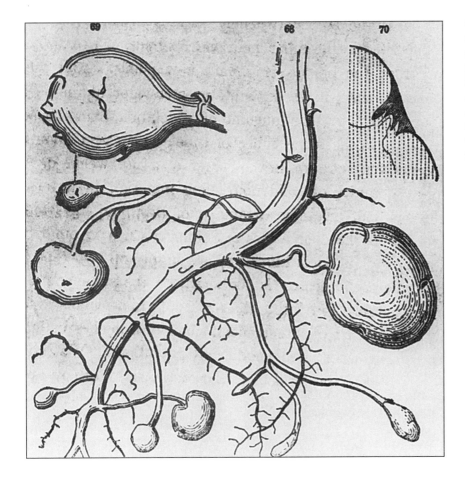

Gray had the exciting opportunity to identify and classify scores of previously undiscovered plants throughout North America. His findings were published in *Flora of North America, Manual of Botany of the Northern United States,* and *Synoptical Flora of North America.* Gray published other books on botany as well, including the one from which this illustration of the root system of a plant is taken.

In 1836 Gray became one of the scientific experts of the U.S. Exploring Expedition, a planned voyage around the world. However, when the expedition's departure was postponed by many delays, he tired of waiting and accepted a job as professor at the University of Michigan in 1838. The university sent him to Europe for a year to buy library books and study plant specimens in European collections. He returned in 1839 but discovered that Michigan was nearly bankrupt and unable to employ him. He then began collaborating with Torrey on a multivolume work called *Flora of North America,* which was published between 1838 and 1843. Three years after his return from Europe, Gray was offered a professorship in natural history* at Harvard University.

At Harvard, Gray's activities were focused on botany and on developing the school's botanical garden, making him the only full-time botanist in the country who also had adequate financial support. He taught an elementary course in botany and worked with some advanced students until his retirement from teaching in 1873. He also took frequent trips to Europe, the American West, and Mexico to collect specimens. He lived and worked in his home in the botanical garden until his death at age 78.

natural history systematic study of animals and plants, especially in their natural settings

Research, Publications, and Influence. Gray's contributions to the development of botany in the United States were significant. When he

The Gray Herbarium

During his years at Harvard, Gray spent his spare time and money on his library of botanical books and pamphlets and on his herbarium (collection of preserved plant specimens). Both collections eventually occupied much of his house. In 1864 he offered them to Harvard if the university would house them in an appropriate building. Harvard agreed, and Gray's 200,000 plant specimens and 2,200-item library were moved into a specially constructed building. The Library of the Gray Herbarium, now with more than 63,000 volumes, remains a valuable source of botanical research material and features an on-line index of American plants.

*natural selection theory that within a given species, individuals with characteristics best adapted to the environment survive and successfully produce more offspring than other individuals, resulting in changes in the species over time

entered the field, its greatest need was a program of classification for North America. Torrey and Gray's *Flora of North America* helped meet that need, but they never completed the work because Gray was swamped with his duties at Harvard and with cataloging the flood of plant specimens from expeditions in the United States and overseas.

Between 1843 and 1873 Gray and Torrey spent much of their time studying plants collected by returning expeditions. Gray also sponsored individual collectors who accompanied boundary survey and military expeditions. In addition, he produced a manual that covered all of the flowering plants and some nonflowering ones of the northeastern United States. This *Manual of the Botany of the Northern United States* was a useful and successful volume that was widely used for many years. In 1878 he published the *Synoptical Flora of North America*, an expanded version of his earlier work with Torrey.

In taxonomy and the naming of plants, Gray dominated American botany more than any other scientist ever did. He launched the study of botany at Harvard, and by starting a garden, a specimen collection, and a library dedicated to botany, he created a permanent center of botanical research there. His textbooks shaped botanical education in the United States from the 1840s into the 1900s. He also trained and assisted a generation of collectors and part-time specialists who comprised the U.S. botanical profession until the 1870s.

Gray and Darwin. The high point of Gray's career was his relationship with Charles Darwin, whom he met in England in 1851. Gray had already entered into a correspondence with Joseph Hooker, an English botanist and one of Darwin's closest associates, about the geographical distribution of plants. Gray's letters to Hooker impressed Darwin, who by 1855 had begun corresponding directly with Gray.

At the time, Darwin was developing his revolutionary theory about the origin of species through the process of natural selection*. In an 1857 letter to Gray, he described the theory, which he had shared with almost no one else. The following year, the theory made its first public appearance in a session at London's Linnean Society and in joint publications with the Welsh natural historian Alfred Russel WALLACE. The letter that Darwin had sent to Gray was included in the publication and became a major document in one of the most important scientific discoveries of the era. It served as proof that Darwin had developed the idea independently, before learning of Wallace's work.

Gray agreed with Darwin on species formation and used Darwin's ideas as the basis for an explanation of how related plants could appear in both eastern Asia and eastern North America; both had evolved from the same ancestors, plants that had once grown all around the northern polar region. When Darwin published *On the Origin of Species* in 1859, Gray was one of the prominent reviewers of the book, insisting on a fair hearing for Darwin in America. In 1876 he published *Darwiniana*, a collection of essays in which he sought to find points of agreement between Darwinism and Christianity. Gray and his work appear prominently in Darwin's later books on botanical subjects, one of which Darwin dedicated to Gray.

Nehemiah Grew is known for his study of plant anatomy. His most important work, *The Anatomy of Plants,* represented a great advance in the understanding of plant structure and function. The son of a clergyman and schoolmaster, Grew was born in Manchester, England. He began his education at Cambridge, but had to complete his studies abroad because Cambridge would not grant an advanced degree to those who were not members of the Church of England. He received an M.D. from the University of Leiden in Holland and made his living through the practice of medicine.

Grew first earned a reputation for his studies of animal anatomy and was invited to become a member of London's Royal Society. There he had access to the society's compound microscope, which he used to conduct in-depth studies of plant anatomy. He began by using naked-eye observations and later went on to detailed microscopic studies. He sketched stem and root structures using many cutaway views that were influential in later botanical studies.

He also confirmed the existence of plant cells first seen by the English natural scientist Robert Hooke, and noted the existence of vessels in wood through which sap flowed, the stomata (pores) in leaves, and the vessels in bark. He discovered that roots have an outer skin, bark, and a core that also contains vessels. His studies also enabled him to recognize structural differences in plants within the same family or species. Since Grew was never formally a teacher, he left behind no students to carry on his work after his death.

Nehemiah
GREW
1641–1712
PLANT ANATOMY

Ernst Haeckel's zoological research led to discoveries and technical publications on marine life-forms, such as sponges and starfish. He is remembered for his enthusiastic acceptance of Darwinism—the ideas of English biologist Charles DARWIN, especially his concept of evolution* by natural selection*. Haeckel's support for Darwinism in his popular scientific writings helped make evolution a central element in the formation of new biological theories.

Background and Career. Haeckel was born in Potsdam, Germany. From a very early age he enjoyed drawing and painting, and during his school years he was greatly interested in botany. After reading a book about scientific expeditions, including the South American adventures of Darwin and of the German scientist Alexander von HUMBOLDT, the young Haeckel wanted to study botany and undertake expeditions of his own. In 1852, however, he gave up those plans to follow his parents' wish that he study medicine. He resisted the idea until he realized that medical school would offer a solid foundation for future scientific study, but he did not intend to become a practicing physician.

Ernst Heinrich Philipp August
HAECKEL
1834–1919
ZOOLOGY

*evolution historical development of a biological group such as a species

*natural selection theory that within a given species, individuals with characteristics best adapted to the environment survive and successfully produce more offspring than other individuals, resulting in changes in the species over time

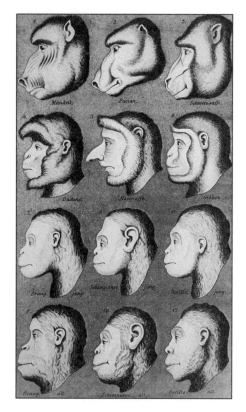

Haeckel was a passionate supporter of Darwin's theory of evolution, producing several writings advocating and expanding the English naturalist's ideas. This lithograph from one of Haeckel's works illustrates the process of evolution in the development of facial features.

---

*embryology branch of biology that deals with embryos, organisms from the first division of the fertilized egg through the early stages of development before birth or hatching

Haeckel studied medicine in Berlin and Würzburg, Germany, and in Vienna, Austria. In 1857 he received his medical degree in Berlin. Four years later he qualified as a lecturer in anatomy in the medical school of the University of Jena, Germany. He was later appointed associate professor of zoology there, and in 1865, he was made full professor and director of the Zoological Institute.

Throughout his career, Haeckel worked quickly and intensely over long periods and relaxed by taking long hikes and traveling. His work brought him many honors over the years, and he belonged to more than 90 scientific associations and learned societies, including the Imperial Academy of Sciences at Vienna, the Royal Swedish Academy of Sciences, the American Philosophical Society, and the Royal Society at Edinburgh, Scotland. Haeckel remained at the University of Jena until his retirement in 1909. He died in Jena ten years later.

Influence of Darwinism. In the mid-1850s Haeckel undertook a zoological expedition to the Mediterranean, where he discovered 144 new species of radiolarians (tiny forms of marine life). In 1859 he read Darwin's newly published *On the Origin of Species,* and immediately became a supporter of Darwinism and of evolution.

Darwin's book provided the foundation and direction for Haeckel's future work. Haeckel produced many technical writings, some of them lengthy, about the form and embryology* of such creatures as sponges and sea urchins. Over the course of his career, he described nearly 4,000 new species of lower marine animals. At the same time, however, he was concerned with the larger issue of the nature of life.

At first Haeckel simply interpreted the results of his studies in light of Darwin's theory, arguing that the biological systems of the organisms he described were products of their evolutionary history. Soon Haeckel was no longer content with interpreting Darwin's theory of evolution. Instead, he became interested in further developing Darwinism—a development that he hoped would not only reform all of biology but also provide the foundation for a science-based world view that applied evolutionary thinking to areas such as politics, religion, and social organization. Such topics were hotly debated at the time, as people began to question whether human societies also followed the "laws" of evolution. Although Darwin himself did not participate directly in such discussions, Haeckel refused to limit himself to biology. The concept called "social Darwinism," the idea that evolution operates on human groups and societies in the same way that it operates on species, is often associated with Haeckel.

Haeckel's major scientific works were less successful in scientific circles than he had hoped. However, the evolutionary views he expressed in lectures, essays, and books for a broader public had far greater influence. In 1899 Haeckel published an all-inclusive statement of his beliefs, *Die Welträthsel* (Riddles of the Universe). With sections on humans, the soul, the universe, and God, this work was very successful and was translated into many languages. However, among churchmen, philosophers, and some scientists, the work was controversial because it attempted to conform belief with scientific advances. Some of Haeckel's statements were so extreme that opponents of Darwinism used them to cast doubt on the theory of evolution.

Major Zoological Concepts. In his search for a unified vision of life, Haeckel introduced many influential concepts. He wanted not only to describe life-forms but also to account for their evolution. For him, the study of life-forms had two aspects. Anatomy was the study of developed forms as they exist in the world. The study of emerging or developing forms included ontogeny, the development of an individual organism; and phylogeny, the evolution through time of the species to which it belongs. Haeckel was the first to formulate the relationship between the important concepts of ontogeny and phylogeny. He coined the phrase *ontogeny recapitulates phylogeny*—a single organism goes through the stages that the species underwent in evolution.

Haeckel was also the first to formulate the idea of ecology (he named the concept), which he defined as "the comprehensive science of the relationships of the organism to the environment." He invented the term *chorology* to refer to the study of the geographical distribution of organisms and species. Both concepts—now integral parts of biology— reveal Haeckel's desire to go beyond the scientific description of organisms. He wanted biology to rest on an understanding of the natural world as a complex, interrelated system shaped by evolution.

Although heredity is central to Darwinism, the mechanism through which it operates was not yet understood. In 1876 Haeckel put forth his own ideas about the mechanism of heredity. Like many other scientists of the time, he believed that organisms that acquired characteristics during their lifetimes could pass those features to their descendants. He defended this idea until the end of his career, even though it became increasingly clear that it was not true.

Haeckel inspired many to take up zoology, especially the study of marine animals. Yet his real importance lies mainly in the ideas he put forth that stimulated further work by other scientists.

Many English scientists of the 1700s were clergymen who made time to study and experiment in the sciences. One such scientific clergyman was Stephen Hales, whose experiments with plants made him an important figure in the establishment of the science of plant physiology*. Hales also investigated the nature and chemistry of air, the circulation of blood in animals, and various medical problems. He also developed ventilators, which helped improve the quality of air in confined spaces, such as prisons and holds of ships.

Education and Career. Hales was born in Bekesbourne, England. Little is known about his childhood, but it is known that in 1696 he entered Benet College (now Corpus Christi College) at Cambridge University. He received an M.A. in 1703 and six years later, when he was made a deacon in the Church of England, left Cambridge for

Stephen
HALES

1677–1761

PHYSIOLOGY, PUBLIC HEALTH

*physiology science that deals with the functions of living organisms and their parts

In a dramatic experiment, illustrated here, Hales tied a live mare on her back and attached one of her arteries to a glass tube nine feet high. The mare's blood pressure drove the blood eight feet up the tube, enabling him to calculate the pressure of the blood. When he detached the tube at intervals and allowed a measured quantity of blood to flow out, he noted that the horse's blood pressure changed at these times.

Teddington, Middlesex County, where he served as a minister. Hales spent the rest of his life in Teddington and carried out most of his scientific work there.

Hales became interested in science while at Cambridge, where he joined another student, William Stukeley, for work in botany and anatomy. Together they collected plant specimens, dissected frogs and other small animals, and attended lectures.

Plant Physiology. Almost ten years after Hales settled in Teddington, he was elected to England's Royal Society, an organization of scientists and people interested in science. Stukeley, by then a doctor in London, had recommended him for membership. Several years passed before Hales displayed his work to the society.

After leaving Cambridge, Hales continued his animal experiments, studying the flow of blood and taking measurements of the pressure of blood in different animals. During this time he wrote, "I wished I could have made the like Experiments, to discover the force of the Sap in Vegetables." In early 1719, he adapted techniques used on blood to develop a method of measuring the volume and pressure of the flow of sap; he attached a glass tube to a cut in the stem of a plant and observed the height to which the sap rose. He proceeded to carry out a systematic program of plant experiments, using his own garden as well as plants and trees from a nearby royal garden at Hampton Court.

Hales was guided by the belief that the life processes of plants—such as breathing and circulation—are similar to those of animals. His principal method of studying living things was called "staticks," the weighing or measuring of substances that flow through organisms, including blood, sap, air, and water. Hales believed that by determining when, where, and how organisms use these substances, he could arrive at insights into how they function. Consequently, he devised experiments that focused on precise measurements.

To measure the sap pressure, Hales employed a "mercurial gage," a bent tube filled with mercury, which he fixed to the cut stem. While observing rising sap through glass tubes, he noted how the sap flow varied with the weather and the time of day. He also devised a system of glass tubes to measure how much water the root of a plant absorbed. To show "the great force" with which plants absorb moisture, Hales filled an iron pot nearly to the top with peas and water and then weighted the lid with 180 pounds. As the peas absorbed water, they swelled, lifting off the heavy lid.

In perhaps his most brilliant series of experiments, Hales measured how much water a sunflower transpired, or "breathed" out. He carefully measured each of its leaves and was able to calculate how much water was lost in relation to the surface area of the leaves. In other experiments Hales sliced off sections of tree bark to observe the direction of the sap flow, which was always upward and never downward. Plants, he determined, unlike animals, did not have true circulation—the flow was always in one direction. Hales presented the results of his plant experiments to the Royal Society and in 1727 published his findings in *Vegetable Staticks,* making contributions critical to the establishment of the science of plant physiology.

The Analysis of Air. His studies of plants had convinced Hales that plants release air—that they perform a kind of breathing. Although scientists of Hales's time did not yet understand that "air" is comprised of many gases, they were aware that various materials either absorb or release "airs" under certain circumstances. In *Vegetable Staticks* Hales included a chapter, titled "The Analysis of Air," in which he dealt with the experiments that he had performed to discover the amount of air or gas given off or absorbed by such substances as hog's blood, powdered oyster shell, amber, honey, and various plant materials, when he heated them in a glass or iron vessel.

An ingenious and persistent experimenter, Hales devised several instruments to help him study air. One of them, a bladder equipped with valves and a breathing tube, let him breathe his own exhaled air. He could do so for only about a minute, but he discovered that if he passed his exhaled air through a chemical solution, he could re-breathe it for more than eight minutes. Scientists now know that the chemical Hales used, salt of tartar, absorbs carbon dioxide from exhaled air.

Animal Circulation. After publishing *Vegetable Staticks,* Hales turned his attention to completing and publishing his earlier experiments on blood circulation in animals. This work appeared in 1733 under the title *Haemastaticks;* the two volumes were later combined and published as *Statical Essays.*

Hales's study of animal physiology was influenced by the ideas of the iatrophysicists, physicians who believed that the best way to understand living organisms was by applying the principles of mechanics*. At Cambridge, Hales had read a book by James Keill, a Scottish iatrophysicist, who gave quantitative estimates of the amount of blood in the human body, the velocity of the blood as it left the heart, the amounts of various animal secretions, and similar functions. Hales wanted to use what he called "the statical way of inquiry" to arrive at accurate information about such aspects of animal bodies.

Focusing on blood pressure and circulation, Hales conducted dissections and vivisections* to study the amount and force of blood in the systems of horses, dogs, and other animals. He studied their pulse and heartbeat, noting that the pulse was faster in small animals than in larger ones. He injected the animals with various chemical substances—brandy, saline solutions, and extract of Peruvian bark—and noted that these chemicals changed the rate at which blood flows through an organ. He correctly concluded that the chemicals caused blood vessels to shrink or expand, although he did not observe these phenomena directly.

Practical Uses of Scientific Knowledge. For Hales science was more than a hobby—it was a natural outgrowth of religious faith. Although he believed that living organisms and nature were complex machines, he considered them evidence of the wisdom, power, and goodness of

Disagreeable Dissections

Perhaps one reason Hales liked studying plants is that he disliked dissecting animals to study their anatomy. Around 1713 he abandoned animal experiments because of "the disagreeableness of anatomical Dissections." However, because such experiments were vital to biological research, Hales resumed the practice of dissection in the late 1720s.

*mechanics science that studies how energy and force affect objects

*vivisection practice of dissecting or cutting into the body of a living animal for the purpose of scientific investigation

their creator. Hales also believed that science should be useful, and he was always alert to the practical possibilities of his discoveries. After studying the effects of alcohol on animal blood circulation, he warned people of the medical consequences of heavy drinking and joined the campaign to reduce alcohol consumption in Britain.

One of Hales's medical concerns was the formation of stones in the bladder and kidneys. He hoped to find a solvent that would dissolve the stones without surgery. Although he failed to find such a solvent, he did invent a surgical tool that surgeons used successfully to remove stones from the human urinary tract.

His experiments on air and breathing led to the invention that made him famous in his own time—ventilators that removed stale air from enclosed spaces. Although the ventilators did not eliminate diseases caused by airborne bacteria and viruses, they reduced the incidence of some illnesses. His studies made Hales an important contributor to public health.

Albrecht von
HALLER

1708–1777

BIOLOGY, BOTANY

*embryo organism from the first division of the fertilized egg through the early stages of development until birth or hatching

Albrecht von Haller's principal fame as a scientist rests on his researches into anatomy and physiology—investigations into the form and function of organic bodies. Haller conducted research on the heart, respiration, the nervous system, and the development of embryos*, contributing many insights that became the basis of future research. A notable botanist and a bibliographer, Haller also compiled lists of books on various medical and scientific subjects.

Life and Career. Haller was born in Bern, Switzerland, into a family with little wealth or political influence. Many members of the family were said to be nervous, secretive, and eccentric. During his own career, Haller earned a reputation for being high-tempered and irritable, and although he could be pleasant, he was intolerant of opinions that did not match his own. He was often embroiled in controversy stemming from his criticisms of others.

As a child Haller suffered from poor health, and later in life he was plagued by headaches, dizziness, stomach pains, sleeplessness, and other ailments. As a young man, however, he was an active mountaineer who enjoyed hikes in the Alps. While still a teenager, Haller had decided to become a physician. He studied in universities in Tübingen, Germany, and Leiden, Netherlands, and received his medical degree in 1727. He then traveled to London and Oxford in England and to Paris and Strasbourg in France, studying a variety of subjects—including advanced mathematics—with learned instructors. He also explored the Alps, collecting plants. By 1729 he had established a medical practice in Bern and he had begun independent anatomical research.

In 1736 Haller was appointed professor of anatomy, surgery, and medicine at the University of Göttingen in Germany, but he returned to Bern in 1753 in the hope of pursuing a political career there. He held administrative and political offices and continued his scientific work, publishing an eight-volume handbook on physiology titled *Elementa Physiologiae Corporis Humani* (Physiological Elements of the Human Body). He was a member of many scientific societies and received several honors. Early in his career, Haller had written poetry, and later he turned to fiction, writing three novels in which he set forth his ideas about government. Haller died in Bern at the age of 69.

As a scientist, Haller was unable to bear another's error in silence, becoming embroiled in many debates and controversies throughout his career. He was also intolerant in politics and religion, considering every opinion that opposed his own a personal insult.

naturalist one who studies objects in their natural settings

Contributions to Anatomy and Physiology. Haller contributed to medicine by showing the problems and inaccuracies of many long-accepted ideas. For example, many scientists and philosophers of his day believed that the human soul or personality was located in a particular physical part of the organism, such as the blood. While studying deformities, Haller examined a pair of premature, joined twins who shared a heart and blood but had separate nervous systems, which meant that in theory each could express an individual will. From this, Haller concluded that the soul (anima) does not reside in the blood.

In his research on the heart, Haller showed how its blood vessels are distributed and accurately described the alternate contraction of the atria and ventricles, the heart's chambers. He also investigated blood cells and blood vessels, describing blood vessels so small that only one blood cell could pass through them at a time, later named capillaries. His observations also helped reinforce the idea put forth by the Dutch naturalist* Antoni van LEEUWENHOEK and others that the blood circulates through a closed pathway. He also observed how breathing affects the motion of blood. His interest in respiration led him to study the diaphragm, a large muscle involved in the expansion and contraction of the lungs.

Haller also conducted important studies of the nervous system, including how muscle fibers contract in response to such sensations as touch, cold, heat, or electricity—a response that he called irritability. Although some of his conclusions were challenged, such as his belief that electricity played no part in the stimulation of muscle fibers, his experiments laid the basis for neurophysiology, the study of the functions of the nervous system.

In his studies on the development of embryos, Haller took on one of the major questions of the day—the origin of new organisms. At the time, some believed that the male parent was more important in creating the embryo, and some others believed it was the female. In a related controversy, some researchers felt that entirely new parts formed as the embryo developed, while others believed that the embryo simply grew from complete but tiny, preformed organisms in the egg or sperm. Haller adopted the second view, and his authoritative support of this theory made him part of a sharp controversy that he ultimately lost. However, he created a valuable mathematical method to demonstrate the rate of growth in a fetal body and its parts. He showed that a fetus grows faster in the early stages of development than in the later ones.

Botanist and Bibliographer. Haller also pursued research in botany, a subject that had interested him since the late 1720s. At the time, he

An Experimental Example

One of Haller's most significant contributions to anatomy and physiology was the fact that he based his conclusions on his experiments instead of on ideas of how things *might* work. Even when his conclusions were wrong, they illustrated the scientific method. For example, in studying the normal structure of the human body and its parts, Haller pioneered the use of quantification and statistics. He used the decimal system to number his observations and then analyzed them, concluding that the measurements that recurred most often were the norm or standard.

William
HARVEY
1578–1657
PHYSIOLOGY, ANATOMY

started an extensive plant collection, and the collection grew over the years as correspondents sent him specimens. Preserved in Paris and Göttingen, the collection is still useful to scholars.

Haller's goal was to create a complete study of Swiss botany. He addressed one of the most pressing botanical problems of the time—how to name plant species and identify members of each species. Haller was meticulous in his work, describing a species only after examining many examples of it, both wild and cultivated. His major work on Swiss plants—*Historia stirpium indigenarum Helvetiae inchoate*—published in 1768, was for a long time considered a model study of the subject. The work contains a geographical description of Switzerland, a survey of how climate influences vegetation, and beautiful botanical illustrations, and it brought Haller much fame and recognition.

Throughout his career, Haller had made it a practice to read everything that had been published on any subject that interested him. As a result he was familiar with books published on many subjects, and he began publishing bibliographies, first in medicine and physiology, then of sciences in general, and finally of botany. He planned a final, all-inclusive bibliography of the medical sciences, and although he never completed it, the existing parts list more than 50,000 titles. Haller marked with a star those volumes that he possessed, enabling scholars to determine the contents of his personal library.

Best known for discovering the circulation of blood, the English physician William Harvey also made major advances in the understanding of generation, sensation, and locomotion. His experimental methods inspired a fundamental change in the study of anatomy and the functioning of the body, sharply undermining the system of medicine established by the ancient Greek physician GALEN. Harvey's accomplishments helped fuel the popular enthusiasm for science that was a hallmark of the late 1600s. His work played a major role in the scientific revolution that marked the beginning of modern science.

Life, Career, and Philosophy

Born in Folkestone, Kent County, Harvey was the oldest of seven sons and the only one who did not pursue a career in business. His father took up commerce after many years as a farmer and landowner, and his brothers achieved success in the same field. William, however, studied arts and medicine at Cambridge. He finished his education at the University of Padua in Italy, the leading medical school in Europe, where he studied under some of the most prominent medical scholars of his day. He graduated at the age of 24 and returned to England to practice medicine. In 1607 he was elected to the Royal College of Physicians, and he rapidly rose to a position of great importance in that organization. He performed a series of anatomical demonstrations at the college and the notes from these lectures contain the earliest suggestions of his later the-

King Charles I took an interest in Harvey's work, providing him with deer from the royal parks to dissect as part of his anatomical investigations. Here, Harvey stands before Charles as he explains the circulation of blood to the king and several members of the king's court.

ories on the motion of the heart and circulation of the blood. In 1618 Harvey was named a physician to King James I. He retained that position when Charles I succeeded James seven years later.

Publications and Later Life. Harvey published *Exercitatio anatomica de motu cordis et sanguinis in animalibus* (On the Motion of the Heart and Blood in Animals) in 1628 to announce his discovery of the circulation of the blood. Three years later he became a physician at the royal court, and in 1639 he was named the king's senior physician. He developed a close relationship with Charles and traveled with him on military expeditions to Scotland. He also took part in a special embassy that Charles sent to the Holy Roman Emperor Ferdinand II. He stayed with the king and moved with him to Oxford during the English Civil War (1642–1646). However, after the Parliament defeated the royal forces and beheaded Charles, Harvey returned to his private practice in London.

In 1651 Harvey published his other major work, *De generatione* (On Generation). He continued to lecture at the Royal College until a year before his death, and late in life he donated money to the college for the establishment of a library. In old age Harvey was plagued by gout* and kidney stones, and he often relieved his pain with large doses of a powerful drug called laudanum. He survived one overdose in 1652, but another one five years later led to a stroke that took his life.

Philosophical Roots of Harvey's Work. As with many scientists of the time, Harvey's discoveries stemmed from his close observation of animals of all types. What set Harvey apart, however, was his ability to

*gout disease marked by painful inflammation of the joints

grasp the importance of what he saw, formulate theories based on his observations, and test his theories through experimentation. He was also not afraid to challenge accepted theories that did not adequately account for the phenomena he observed.

When Harvey began his scientific career, knowledge of anatomy and physiology* was based largely on the works of the ancient Greek philosopher ARISTOTLE and the physician Galen. He studied under teachers who supported the theories proposed by both men, but his own views were more influenced by those of Aristotle.

One of the basic ideas that Harvey shared with Aristotle was the belief that the soul and the body are inseparable. By contrast, most scholars of the day believed that the body was merely a passive object that was animated by the soul and that separate forces directed the activities of different parts of the body. These forces supposedly flowed to the various parts from a central source. Like Aristotle, Harvey contended that the life force resided simultaneously in all parts of the body. However, Harvey was not single-mindedly devoted to Aristotle's ideas; although they served as a starting point for his studies, he was more than willing to criticize and modify Aristotle's theories when his own observations led him to different conclusions.

Harvey drew on the writings of other authors as well, but he was independent in his judgments and did not uncritically accept traditional views of medicine, anatomy, or physiology. At the same time, he never completely rejected the philosophical foundations on which Renaissance* medicine was based. He used some of Aristotle's ideas to criticize Galen's teachings at a time when Galenic beliefs were paramount.

Studies in Circulation

Harvey's research on circulation was stimulated by his belief that blood was the most important substance in the body, that the soul resided in the blood, and that the blood was the only part of the body that was truly alive. He maintained that an embryo* began as a single drop of blood, which then formed the basis of the organs and other bodily structures and supplied them with the heat and nutrition they needed to live and function properly. He also claimed that the body existed to serve the blood and that the heart was the "center" of the body.

Prevailing Thoughts on Circulation. To understand the significance of Harvey's discovery, it is necessary to discuss the beliefs of his day concerning the heart and blood vessels (veins and arteries). The prevailing medical view was that the veins and arteries comprised two separate systems that performed different tasks. The venous system was concerned with nutrition. Nutrients from the intestines were soaked up by blood and carried by veins to the liver. This nutrient-rich blood then flowed into a large vein near the heart, called the vena cava, that distributed it to the other veins in the body. The right ventricle* of the heart pumped some of this blood to the pulmonary artery that supplied blood to the lungs.

*physiology science that deals with the functions of living organisms and their parts

*Renaissance period that marked the beginnings of modern science and the rebirth of interest in classical art and literature that occurred in Europe from the late 1300s through the 1500s

*embryo organism from the first division of the fertilized egg through the early stages of development until birth or hatching

*ventricle muscular chamber of the heart

The arteries, along with the lungs, left ventricle, and pulmonary vein, formed a separate system that provided the body with heat and *pneuma* (air). The left ventricle and arteries supplied *pneuma* to the heart during inhalation and exhalation, causing the heart and arteries to contract and dilate (expand) and produce pulse. At no point did the arteries and veins connect with or interact with each other.

Harvey's Views. In 1559 the Italian anatomist Realdo COLOMBO challenged the existing view of the role of the heart and arteries. Colombo's investigation of circulation showed that the primary function of the heart and the arteries is to supply the body with blood. However, Colombo still believed that arterial and venous systems served different purposes. Harvey adopted Colombo's ideas and set out to investigate whether the arteries pulsated on their own or because the heart pumped blood. Colombo had identified both a passive phase of the heartbeat (dilation), when the heart relaxes and receives blood, and an active stage (contraction), in which it squeezes out the blood it contains. The previously accepted view was that both phases were active and that dilation was the stronger of the two.

Through experimentation Harvey demonstrated that the active phase of the heartbeat occurred during the contraction phase of the ventricles, not during their dilation. He proved this by showing that a punctured heart expels blood powerfully during contraction. He also noted that the walls of the heart become thicker during contraction, which meant that the cavities in the heart that receive the blood must become smaller at the same time. Turning to the arteries, Harvey demonstrated that their pulse was the result of blood being forced into the arteries by the contraction of the heart. To support this theory he showed that a cut artery expels blood much more forcefully when the heart contracts.

This new view of the heartbeat suggested that the amount of blood that flowed into the arteries had to be quite large. It was so large that unless the blood somehow returned to the heart, all of it would be emptied into the arteries in just a few beats. How then did the heart and veins replenish themselves with blood? Harvey concluded that blood pumped from the heart into the arteries must pass into the veins at some point before returning to the heart. To prove this, he tied a cord tightly around a subject's arm, cutting off the arterial pulse. The arteries above the cord swelled with blood. When he loosened the cord, the swelling in the arteries went down, and the veins in the arm below the cord swelled with blood. In this manner he showed that the blood from the arteries clearly flowed into the veins.

Harvey's theory of the circulation of the blood was well received, but his critics noted that it failed to specify a precise connection between the arterial and venous systems. Harvey insisted, without empirical evidence, that the arteries and veins were connected, but with only a magnifying glass at his disposal, he made no progress on this problem. Later, in 1661, the Italian physician Marcello

New Buildings, Old Foundations

Harvey's work on circulation illustrates his sympathy for some of the basic philosophical concepts of his day. Traditional philosophy considered circular motion to have a special preservative character that set it apart from regular motion. Harvey's familiarity with and support of this idea might have provided a spark of insight that helped him recognize the circular nature of the blood's movement and shaped his theory. In fact, his essay on circulation compares the movement of blood to other circular processes—he likens the heart to the sun—noted by earlier natural philosophers.

MALPIGHI observed that the two systems were connected by very small blood vessels (capillaries), which he observed through a microscope. The area of connection was called anastomoses.

Although Harvey had discovered circulation, he failed to grasp its full purpose—to replenish the supply of "airs" in the blood by cycling it through the lungs—because the presence of "airs" was not yet known. He instead believed that supplying the body with heat obtained from the heart was a prime purpose of blood circulation. He continued to explore this topic to find a fuller explanation for circulation, but he never arrived at the correct answer. Still, his discovery revolutionized physiology not only by showing the new functions of the heart and blood vessels, but also by introducing new methods of experimentation.

Generation

In another series of studies, Harvey's investigations led him to challenge the accepted views of the formation of new life, or generation. The old view was that semen combined with menstrual blood in the uterus to form the heart of a fetus. (Observations had shown the heart to be the first visible organ.) The heart then used additional menstrual blood to create the rest of the fetus. All of the organs and structures of the fetus were assumed to be present at the moment of conception. During pregnancy they grew until they assumed their final form. The same process supposedly occurred in animals that laid eggs, except that the fetus grew inside an egg rather than in the uterus.

Harvey carefully observed developing chick embryos and found no evidence that semen ever enters or even touches eggs while they are forming within a hen. He also dissected the uteruses of female deer at various stages of mating and pregnancy and observed no menstrual blood before mating. He noted that the fetus does not appear until quite some time after the male's semen has disappeared from the female's body.

Based on these observations, Harvey concluded that the purpose of semen was simply to make the female fertile. In egg-laying animals, the fertile female produces an egg that has the ability to nourish itself and to generate a fetus from material contained within itself. This material begins as a homogenous substance, but eventually differentiates (specializes) itself into different organs and structures that become a new individual. Harvey called this gradual emergence of the fetus epigenesis.

He based his conclusions about generation of live-bearing animals on his ideas about egg-bearing ones. The semen fertilizes the female, enabling her uterus to produce a fertilized conceptus, which is similar to the egg. The conceptus then grows within, and is nourished by, the uterus. Although Harvey's thinking on this topic has been displaced, he was the first to realize that it was a new entity, the fertilized egg, which develops into an embryo and then into a new organism.

Sensation and Locomotion

In an unfinished and unpublished paper, *De motu animalium* (On the Motion of Animals), Harvey outlined his ideas about sensation and locomotion, again challenging existing theories. Earlier physicians believed that the brain created both sensation and movement. Consequently, cutting a nerve to one part of the body destroyed that part's mobility and sensibility. This belief also implied that the muscles involved in voluntary movement were fundamentally different from organs of involuntary movement, such as the heart.

Harvey argued that the brain does not actually create sensation or movement, but that the organs and muscles contain these powers as long as they receive blood, heat, and spirits. The nerves transmit sensations from the organs to the brain, which then analyzes and makes sense of them. Similarly, he argued, the brain does not supply the power to move muscles, it simply coordinates the movements they make. The nerves supply the external sensations to which the brain reacts. He stated that cutting a nerve does not destroy a muscle's mobility but its ability to take part in coordinated activity.

Other Works. From comments in his writings it appears that Harvey planned to conduct a comprehensive program of research. Unfortunately, little of this additional work was ever printed. He lost many notes and manuscripts when his room was looted in 1642. The rest were probably consumed in the great fire that destroyed much of London 14 years later. All that survives of his work are his lecture notes, drafts of his papers on muscles and movement in animals, and a few letters. However, his published essays represent discoveries and explanations that established Harvey as one of the most brilliant minds of his time.

The foremost German scientist of the late 1800s, Hermann von Helmholtz helped reform that nation's universities into leading research institutions. He had great influence on nineteenth-century science and made important contributions to the fields of physiology*, particularly to the study of how the senses of hearing and sight work, and physics, which was the primary basis of his career. He also invented the ophthalmoscope, an instrument that enabled doctors to examine the retinas of patients' eyes.

Background and Career. Helmholtz was born in Potsdam, Germany, where he began his education. His father, a teacher, was passionately fond of the arts and shared that passion with his son. Much of Helmholtz's later research into the workings of the senses was shaped by his deep interest in music and painting.

Helmholtz wanted to study physics, but his father could not afford to send him to the university and instead encouraged him to take up medical studies, for which the state would provide financial aid for

Hermann von
HELMHOLTZ
1821–1894
PHYSIOLOGY, PHYSICS

*physiology science that deals with the functions of living organisms and their parts

education and training. In return for that aid, Helmholtz agreed to serve for eight years as a surgeon in the army. He received his medical degree in Berlin in 1842. While studying in Berlin, he became part of a group of young scientists who vowed to reform physiology. Rejecting the formerly popular idea that life processes depended on nonphysical (or vital) forces, the group sought to explain the workings of living organisms using the principles of physics and chemistry. This approach, called mechanism, was characteristic of Helmholtz's work.

In 1849 Helmholtz was released from his army duty and he was appointed associate professor of physiology at the University of Königsberg. Later he taught at universities in Bonn, Heidelberg, and Berlin. In 1851 Helmholtz began to tour German universities on behalf of the government, inspecting their physiological institutes. Thereafter he influenced and witnessed the transition of German universities from purely teaching academies to institutions devoted as well to organized research. In the late 1880s, he was appointed president of a new state institute for research, and by that time he had gained recognition as a dominant figure in German science and the state's top adviser on scientific matters. Although his productivity did not wane, his health began to fail in the mid-1880s and he turned to music and mountaineering in the Alps for relief. He died in 1894 in Berlin after suffering what appears to have been a paralytic stroke.

Physiological Researches. Helmholtz's first area of physiological research concerned the sources of energy and heat in the body. Late in his career he would return to the study of energy, focusing on the physics of electricity and the production of heat in chemical reactions. His most famous work was done in physics and came early in his 1847 paper "On the Conservation of Force," which enunciated the principle of the conservation of energy through the transformation of one sort of energy (such as electricity) into another (such as heat). The work in physiology for which he became best known began in 1850 and concerned the physiology of the senses.

Because Helmholtz had mastered both physics and mathematics, he was able to subject physiological problems to a mathematical and physical analysis. He applied such an analysis to the question of the source of animal heat and concluded that it was the product of mechanical forces within the animal.

Helmholtz next turned his attention to physiological acoustics, or the science of hearing. Building on the work of earlier researchers, he investigated the ear's ability to hear certain complex tones. His principal achievement in acoustics was the resonance theory of hearing, which states that sound waves cause the structures of the inner ear to resonate (vibrate) at frequencies that activate nearby nerve endings, sending to the brain the nerve impulses that convey sounds. In 1863 he wrote *Die Lehre von den Tonempfindungen als physiologische Grundlage für die Theorie der Musik* (On the Sensation of Tone as a Physiological Basis for the Theory of Music), in which he applied his research on the mechanism of hearing to explain how the ear interprets music.

Helmholtz also explored physiological optics, the science of how light produces vision in the eye. A colleague had recently shown how the human eye could be made to glow with reflected light, like the eyes of cats, deer, and other animals. Helmholtz was preparing a lecture demonstration of this phenomenon when he realized that with a simple device he could project the reflected light to obtain a clear, enlarged image of the retina. This discovery led Helmholtz to invent the ophthalmoscope, bringing him recognition throughout Europe.

Next, when attempting to solve the problem of color vision, Helmholtz came to support the theory, put forward half a century earlier by the British scientist Thomas Young, that each nerve ending in the retina possesses three distinct receptors, one each for green, red, or violet wavelengths of light. Helmholtz's massive two-volume work on optics, *Handbuch der physiologischen Optik* (Handbook of Physiological Optics), published in 1856 and 1867, contains all previous research in the field and sets forth his own experimental results and theories.

In 1871 Helmholtz abandoned physiology for physics, claiming that physiology had become too complex for any individual to comprehend the whole field. By the time of his death, that was true of all fields of scientific inquiry, and scientists were beginning to specialize in narrower areas of research. Helmholtz was one of the last scientists whose work embraced the sciences, philosophy, and the fine arts.

Friedrich Gustav Jacob
HENLE
1809–1885
ANATOMY, PATHOLOGY

F riedrich Gustav Jacob Henle was a pioneer in cytology, the study of cells, and histology, the study of animal tissues. Henle was also interested in pathology, the study of disease. By recognizing that diseases are carried by tiny living organisms such as bacteria, his studies helped pave the way for the science of microbiology*.

Henle was born into a Jewish family near Nuremberg, Germany. His early education focused on classical and modern languages. Henle was a talented artist and musician, and later in life he enjoyed hosting musical gatherings and concerts in his home. In 1821, when his family converted to Christianity, Henle considered becoming a minister, but after meeting the famous German physiologist Johannes MÜLLER, his thoughts turned to medicine, which he studied in Bonn and Heidelberg. He received his M.D. at Bonn in 1832 and became Müller's assistant. Henle later taught anatomy and physiology* at universities in Berlin and in Zurich, Switzerland. His spent the final 33 years of his career at the university in Göttingen, where he died at the age of 75.

Henle was introduced to scientific work when he helped Müller edit a journal on natural science. He became interested in microscopic research and investigated the smallest structural elements of animal tissues. One of the first authors to call these units cells, he described the cellular structure of the tissues forming the epithelium, a membrane that lines the inner cavities and canals of the body.

*microbiology study of tiny organisms that can only be observed through a microscope

*physiology science that deals with the functions of living organisms and their parts

The causes of diseases was another topic of interest to Henle. Many scientists of the time distinguished between a cause of disease that acted from outside the body, called "miasma," and a cause that acted from within the body, called "contagia." Henle argued against this distinction because diseases originating from miasma could become contagious. His most important contribution was his emphasis that diseases are carried by living microorganisms* that colonize the host body. Although this idea was not new, it would not be accepted widely for another 30 years.

microorganism tiny living thing that generally can be seen clearly only through a microscope

Henle wrote influential textbooks on anatomy and pathology and used new advances in microscope technology to study the fundamental units of organisms: cells and tissues. He conducted research on renal* anatomy, and although that work contained errors, it led scientists to complete an accurate investigation of the kidneys in the 1860s.

renal of or relating to the kidneys

HIPPOCRATES

460 B.C.–ca. 370 B.C.

MEDICINE

Hippocrates of Cos was the most famous physician of the Greek world until GALEN in the A.D. 100s. He was the leading representative of an important school of ancient medicine and he contributed to a group of influential medical writings, including a statement of professional ethics that is called the Hippocratic oath in his honor. The key feature of the type of medicine that Hippocrates practiced was the importance he placed on observation and rationality, or reasoning.

Life and Legends. Little is known about Hippocrates' life. Some scholars have concluded that no provable facts about him exist and that he is a figure of rumor and guesswork. Others are confident that some truths must lie in the facts that were recorded in ancient times.

Hippocrates studied, practiced, and taught medicine on Cos, a Greek island off the southwest coast of present-day Turkey, and is thought to have been born there. He studied with his father, Heraclides, and with Herodicus, a physician who was probably from Cnidus, an ancient Greek city in southwestern Turkey. The cities of Cos and Cnidus were the seats of the two influential schools of medicine.

During his career, Hippocrates traveled widely within Greece and achieved considerable fame as both a physician and a teacher. He was well known in Athens, the principal Greek city. In fact, the Athenian philosopher Plato mentions Hippocrates in one of his early works, *Protagoras,* in a passage that reveals that Hippocrates took paying students who expected him to teach them how to practice medicine. As a prominent professional man, Hippocrates would have been welcomed anywhere. He is believed to have died around 370 B.C. in Larissa, the chief town of Thessaly, a region in northern Greece.

One difficulty in uncovering the facts of Hippocrates' life is that legends began to develop around him. In some, he is a heroic sage, while other accounts claim that he was a Greek patriot who rejected an offer from Artaxerxes I, a Persian king who wanted to conquer Greece. Still other accounts state that he saved Athens from the plague*. These

plague contagious, widespread, and often fatal disease

stories probably have no basis in historical fact, but they cloud the picture of what little is known about Hippocrates' life.

The Coan School and Writings. Hippocrates was not only a physician and a teacher but also a writer. Plato and others recorded that Hippocrates had written medical books, and his name became attached to a number of famous ancient works on medical subjects. Many of these works from the school of Cos have survived, and it is likely that Hippocrates himself wrote some of the most outstanding among them. But many were probably produced by other members of the school of Cos. At that time, individual authorship of a text was not given the same importance that it is today—some books later said to have been written by Hippocrates were probably written by other authors or even by groups of authors. All of the writings from Cos, however, probably reflect Hippocrates' thought and his teaching.

The writings associated with Hippocrates consist of about 60 medical works. At some point in the centuries after Hippocrates, these texts were brought together into a body called the *Hippocratic Corpus* or *Collection*. Most of these texts date from the late 400s and early 300s B.C.; a few were added centuries later. The authorship of most of the works in the *Collection* is not known for certain. The philosopher Aristotle recorded that one of the most important texts, *Nature of Man*, was written by Polybius, who was both Hippocrates' student and his son-in-law. Hippocrates wrote at least two of the texts, *Joints* and *Prognostic*, and may have written several others. He may also have written books that have since disappeared, because works in the *Collection* frequently mention other books that have not survived. Not all the works in the *Collection* belong to Hippocrates' Coan school—some appear to come from the school of Cnidus, such as *Epidemics* I and III; *Airs, Waters, Places*; *Wounds of the Head*; *Humors*; and *The Sacred Disease*, which is about epilepsy.

Some key ideas of the Coan school appear in a text that dates from the A.D. 100s and is about 1,900 lines long. Errors and other features of the writing suggest that it was a set of notes made by a medical student for his own use, not a finished document. This text reproduces the work of Meno, a disciple of Aristotle, who lived around the time of Hippocrates. Meno outlines the ideas and beliefs of 20 physicians, including Hippocrates and Polybius.

According to Meno, Hippocrates believed that bad air and bad diet caused disease, that air was essential for health and must circulate freely in the body, that poor air or blocked circulation of air would result in epidemics, that proper nourishment was essential, and that defective nourishment could cause a variety of diseases. He also stated that too much food, or food of poor quality, would upset the stomach and generate waste products in the body; and that winds arising from these waste products spread into the body, causing illnesses. *Nature of Man* and other works from Cos confirm that the Hippocratic physicians believed that food and environmental factors directly affected health.

The Hippocratic Oath

Physicians today still abide by the Hippocratic oath, which sets forth their responsibilities: to help, or at least do no harm, and to respect the privacy, or confidentiality, of what they learn about people. The oath says:

In whatever houses I enter, I will enter to help the sick, and I will abstain from all intentional wrongdoing and harm, especially from abusing the bodies of man or woman, bond or free. And whatsoever I shall see or hear in the course of my profession in my intercourse with men, if it be what should not be published abroad, I will never divulge, holding such things to be holy secrets.

Hippocratic Medicine and Science. Several themes practiced by Hippocrates' school are basic to medicine. The concept of humors—four fluids in the body—is found in both the Coan and Cnidian schools and undoubtedly existed before Hippocrates. As Hippocrates and the Coans interpreted it, the four humors were phlegm, blood, black bile, and yellow bile; but the Cnidians believed the humors were water, blood, phlegm, and bile.

According to the Coan writings, imbalances in the humors caused internal diseases. These imbalances were called fluxes, and when they occurred, the body experienced coction, or a kind of slow cooking or heating, which restored the balance of the humors and returned the body to normalcy. The disease then reached a crisis, a point at which the outcome becomes favorable. The crisis was marked by critical signs and symptoms and occurred on particular days in the course of the illness. Another idea that appears less frequently than humors is that of the deposit, a complaint in a specific part of the body that might be the beginning or the aftermath of a disease. The deposit could travel from one part of the body to another, changing one disease into another.

Environmental factors and diet were basic to Hippocratic medical teachings. *Airs, Waters, Places* is devoted to the role of air, climate, season, and other factors in causing, curing, and preventing disease. Many of the Coan texts stress the importance of diet. These topics were not unique to the school of Cos, however—they appear in many of the Cnidian texts as well.

In terms of medical practice, Coan physicians began by examining the symptoms, without questioning the patient. They then stated the past and present conditions of the disease and predicted its future course. However, Coan medicine recognized the importance of the patient's psychological state and its influence on the body. Coan physicians viewed each living being as an interdependent whole, not a collection of parts. These approaches, too, appear in Cnidian writings.

The original contributions of Hippocrates are hard to identify. He did not bring about a revolution in medical practice, and his ideas and beliefs do not seem to have been greatly different from those of other physicians of his day. His importance lies partly in his status as a teacher, partly in his skill and success at practicing medicine, and partly in the writings that he or his school produced, which have more style and interest than the monotonous writings of the Cnidians. Hippocrates was not a lone genius or scientific visionary, but he was in the front rank of medicine in his age.

Modern historians of science regard the emphasis on science and reason as an important feature of Hippocratic medicine. Medicine had long been intertwined with religion and magic in ancient Egypt, Greece, and Mesopotamia, where people believed that magic could cause and cure illnesses and that the gods took a direct role in a person's medical state, whether for good or for harm. The medicine that the Hippocratics promoted was strictly rational, a great step forward from the magic- and religion-based medicine of earlier eras. Many sound Coan principles came from this desire for rationality. For example, physicians were

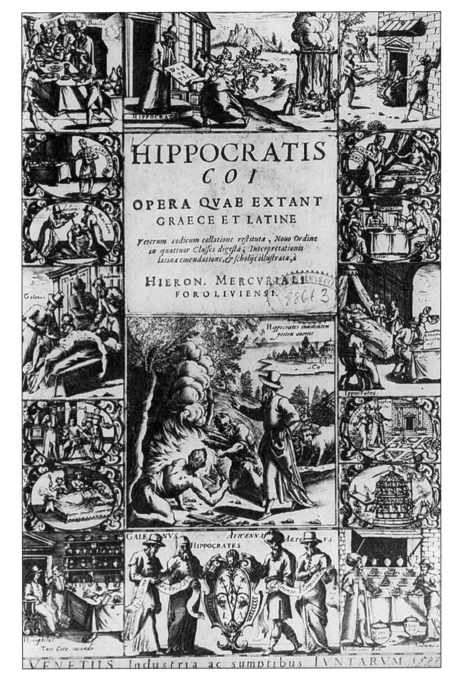

According to Hippocrates, physicians had many responsibilities, from instructing patients on proper diets to prescribing medicines, from advocating the use of herbs to performing surgery. This title page from a Hippocratic work shows physicians performing these duties.

advised that "Examining the body requires sight, hearing, sound, smell, and taste," and were told to consider all the evidence before making their diagnosis. This resulted in a program of careful observation of a patient's symptoms. Physicians could then compare and contrast symptoms to determine the unique qualities of each case.

The rational approach enabled physicians to recognize their errors and to see the usefulness of admitting and studying them. After describing an unsuccessful treatment, for example, the author of *Joints* adds, "I relate this on purpose, for it is also valuable to know what attempts have failed and why they have failed." The rational approach also permitted the Hippocratic physicians to view the unity of the animal kingdom, with man as one species among many, and to design experiments to test their theories.

Another important element of Hippocratic medicine was its concern with ethics. The author of *Precepts*, a component of the *Collection*, wrote to other physicians, "I urge you not to be too unkind, but to consider your patient's wealth and resources," and urged giving "full assistance" to all, including foreigners and the poor, regardless of their ability to pay. And Hippocratic medicine—perhaps even Hippocrates himself—produced the best-known statement of medical ethics, which is still used today and commemorates the great teacher of Cos with its title, the Hippocratic oath.

Friedrich Wilhelm Heinrich Alexander von
HUMBOLDT
1769–1859
NATURAL SCIENCE

*geomagnetism of or relating to the earth's magnetic field

*orography study of the physical geography of mountains and mountain ranges

*meteorology science that deals with the atmosphere, especially the weather and weather predictions; also known as atmospheric science

*mineralogy study of the properties of minerals

*asphyxiation death caused by lack of oxygen

*geophysical of or relating to geophysics, the scientific study of the physics of the earth, including weather, magnetism, volcanoes, earthquakes, and ocean structure

Alexander von Humboldt made many contributions to a range of scientific fields. He was a pioneer in the study and measurement of geomagnetism*, developed climatology and geography as separate sciences, and established the fields of plant geography and orography*. During his extensive travels, he made discoveries in geography, meteorology*, mineralogy*, and astronomy. As a mining supervisor in Prussia (former kingdom and state of Germany), he tackled many practical problems in that field. In addition to his scientific work, Humboldt was a champion of humanitarian causes such as the abolition of slavery.

Life and Career. Humboldt, the son of a Prussian officer, was born in Berlin, Germany, and educated by private tutors until he entered the University of Frankfurt at age 18. He also studied at the University of Göttingen, the academy of commerce in Hamburg, and the academy of mining in Freiberg, where he obtained a background in economics, mining, geology, botany, and chemistry. He visited Paris a year after the start of the French Revolution, an experience that both moved him and reinforced his liberal political views. After graduation Humboldt entered the Prussian mining service, where he invented safety lamps and a rescue device for miners facing asphyxiation*. He tested these devices on himself in often dangerous experiments.

During the next several years, Humboldt traveled throughout Europe on mining expeditions and continued his scientific research on geomagnetism, which included taking geophysical* and astronomical measurements. On a journey to Spain he collected data that he later used to prepare the first detailed relief map of a large area. He followed this with his most extensive and productive trip, a five-year voyage (from 1799 to 1804) to South America that has been called "the scientific discovery of America." After returning to Europe he spent the next several years publishing the results of his journeys. He later took a 9,000-mile scientific trip through Siberia.

Humboldt spent the last years of his life compiling his scientific writings into a multivolume work called *Kosmos*. The work presents

research in natural science and geography in a popular form, and the first two volumes were very successful with readers. He also devoted time to humanitarian causes and offered encouragement and financial support to many promising young scientists. Humboldt was honored with awards and honorary degrees from six universities and membership in all the major scientific societies. While still working on a volume of *Kosmos,* Humboldt died in Berlin at the age of 89.

Scientific Philosophy. Humboldt believed that all of nature demonstrates harmony and unity. One example of this belief was his early enthusiasm for the idea of *vis vitalis,* a common life force shared by all living things. He set up experiments to investigate these "chemical processes of life," attempting to find similarities between the life processes of plants and animals. However, while he pursued this romantic notion, Humboldt never abandoned his conviction that nature could only be understood through precise measurement and the reduction of scientific phenomena to numbers. He later abandoned his belief in the *vis vitalis* but always retained his insistence on accurate measurement and mathematical analysis.

Expedition to South America. Humboldt's trip to South America is perhaps the best example of the wide range of his interests and his scientific originality and curiosity. Traveling with the botanist Aimé Bonpland, Humboldt explored the region occupied by present-day Venezuela, Cuba, Colombia, Peru, Ecuador, and Mexico. The two men journeyed by foot, horseback, canoe, and ship, recording and describing virtually every natural object they encountered.

They collected some 60,000 specimens, more than 6,000 of which were previously unknown in Europe. In addition to drawing many maps, Humboldt gathered data on magnetism, meteorology, climate, geology, mineralogy, oceanography, and zoology. He proved that the Orinoco River flows directly into the Amazon and set a new mountaineering altitude record by climbing Mount Chimborazo (20,561 feet) in Ecuador.

In addition to his scientific work, Humboldt studied the history, languages, social conditions, population figures, and economic development of South American Indian societies. He studied connections between climate and vegetation, between altitude and fertility, and between human productivity and property ownership. He was the first to treat geography in terms of science, politics, and economics. He also proposed that the Isthmus of Panama be leveled and a canal constructed to join the Atlantic and Pacific Oceans nearly 100 years before the building of the Panama Canal. His work provided a major stimulus to the study of the Americas.

Geomagnetism and Geophysics. Many of Humboldt's noteworthy contributions stem from his study of geomagnetism and geophysics. During a trip through the Alps in 1795, he recognized the importance of geomagnetic and astronomical measurements as the only true basis for precise geography. On his landmark trip to South America, he cre-

Humboldt's extensive travels enabled him to conduct research on both sides of the Atlantic Ocean. His voluminous, never-finished travel journal was published in 34 volumes over a 25-year period. These and other works based on his travels helped establish geography as a science.

For the Love of France

Humboldt's humanitarianism and love of liberty drew him to the ideals of the French Revolution and to France in general. When the European forces finally defeated Napoleon in 1814, Humboldt used his influence to preserve French scientific institutions such as the Muséum d'Histoire Naturelle (Museum of Natural History). He also fought to save the property of French citizens from seizure by occupying troops. However, he was not an uncritical admirer of the French. For instance, he wrote against the fraud, extortion, and violence of French administrators in Algeria, which was controlled by France from the early 1800s to 1962.

ated maps and collected extensive geomagnetic data. When back in Europe, he refined his astronomical calculations and used the results to prepare more accurate maps of the places he had visited. Humboldt often stressed the importance of setting up geomagnetic observatories to take precise measurements of large areas. During his trip to Siberia, he measured and compared relative temperatures and magnetic values at different locations. He also collected geological and mineralogical data that enabled him to predict the existence of diamonds in the Ural Mountains; the power of his methods was proven when diamonds were discovered there.

Other Contributions. Humboldt's interest in astronomy was not limited to taking bearings to aid in geography and mapmaking. He prompted astronomers to become more interested in shooting stars, which we now know to be meteors entering the earth's atmosphere, and he developed a method for determining the light intensity of stars in the Southern Hemisphere. He was also the first to notice that the earth's magnetic intensity decreases during the appearance of the aurora borealis, or "northern lights." In the field of audiology* he mathematically explained the amplification (increase) of sound at night, which is now known as the "Humboldt effect." Humboldt also conducted experiments on the chemical composition of air and studied the properties of the newly discovered gases nitrogen and oxygen.

*audiology scientific study of hearing

Humboldt was also a supporter of liberal and humanitarian causes. He introduced Prussian laws abolishing slavery, which he considered the greatest evil affecting humankind. He spoke out against racism and anti-Semitism (discrimination against Jews). Humboldt was an enthusiastic supporter of the ideal of individual freedom and corresponded regularly with Simón Bolivar, who led the revolution that freed much of South America from Spanish rule. He not only advised Bolivar on scientific matters, but also urged him to pursue a moderate political course in leading his newly independent land. Bolivar once said, "Humboldt has done more for South America than all her conquerors." Although Humboldt admired the freedom of thought and action in the United States, he regretted that nation's indifference to slavery. Humboldt's dedication to science and humanitarianism marks him as one of the remarkable figures of his time.

Thomas Henry
HUXLEY
1825–1895
ZOOLOGY, EVOLUTION, PALEONTOLOGY

Thomas Henry Huxley is widely known as one of the earliest and most ardent supporters of the English naturalist* Charles DARWIN's theory of evolution*. Huxley, who earned the nickname "Darwin's Bulldog," was an outstanding scientist in his own right. His groundbreaking studies in anatomy and paleontology* not only established his reputation as one of the leading scientific figures of his day, but they also provided evidence of evolutionary processes at work. Huxley was equally recognized as a vigorous reformer of university education and as a popularizer of the new sciences.

At the Government School of Mines, Huxley gained the reputation of being an outstanding teacher. He engaged his students in their work by making them conduct dissections, believing that the practical experience would help them to better understand the material in their textbooks.

Life and Career

Huxley's early life gave few clues that he was destined for a brilliant scientific career. The youngest child of a schoolteacher in Ealing, England, Huxley was largely self-taught, receiving only about two years of formal education at his father's hands. He showed no particular gift for academics, but he was an excellent artist. The young Huxley hoped to be a mechanical engineer, but instead became an apprentice to his brother-in-law, John Godwin Scott, a physician in London.

Education and Naval Service. At age 17 Huxley won a scholarship from Charing Cross Hospital to study medicine. During this time he wrote his first scientific paper about his discovery of a layer of cells at the root sheath of the hair (today known as Huxley's layer). He earned his M.D. in 1845 and became a member of the Royal College of Surgeons. The following year he joined the Royal Navy and was assigned as ship's surgeon aboard the H.M.S. *Rattlesnake*, which was to conduct a survey of the coast of Australia. His equipment consisted of a microscope and a net for collecting specimens, and he put both to good use.

During the four-year voyage, Huxley closely studied tiny marine creatures known as plankton, which at the time were lumped into a single scientific category. By closely studying their anatomy, Huxley showed that these creatures should be divided into several separate groups. The importance of his findings was immediately apparent to zoologists. Huxley's work also involved observations that would prove critical in the later debate over evolution.

Huxley sent several papers about his findings on plankton to the Linnean Society, an organization of biologists, but he heard nothing

*naturalist one who studies objects in their natural settings

*evolution historical development of a biological group such as a species

*paleontology study of extinct or prehistoric life, usually through the examination of fossils

in response. Papers he submitted to London's Royal Society, however, earned him both election as a fellow in that prestigious scientific organization and ultimately the society's Royal Medal. After returning from his voyage in 1850, Huxley took a leave of absence from the navy to pursue his scientific interests. During this time he became involved in a dispute with the Royal Navy regarding payment for publishing the results of his work done aboard the *Rattlesnake*. The navy ordered him back to active duty, but he refused. For the next four years, Huxley earned a meager living by publishing the findings of his research.

Later Research and Teaching. In 1854 Huxley took up positions as a naturalist with the Geological Survey and as a lecturer in natural history at the Government School of Mines. These posts provided him with enough income to marry and the means to continue his research. At the Geological Survey he worked on fossils, and he also began to study the development of embryos* in vertebrate species (organisms with a backbone). Both lines of research would be important in his later defense of Darwin's ideas. They would also lead him to divide birds into three main groups and to reclassify all vertebrate species into three distinct divisions. Modern scientific classification of these animals is based on Huxley's work.

At the Government School of Mines, Huxley became an outstanding teacher who lectured to both academic and lay audiences. He also held professorial appointments at the Royal Institution and the Royal College of Surgeons, where he made laboratory work a key component of his natural history course; students dissected and observed specimens to verify what they had read and heard in lectures. An innovation at the time, this incorporation of laboratory work has since become standard educational practice. Huxley was perhaps most interested in his popular series of "workingmen's lectures," in which he spoke to average men and women on scientific topics. Refusing to speak down to his audiences, he was convinced that most people could understand even the most complex ideas if they were presented in a clear and logical manner. Huxley's interest in teaching extended to service on the London School Board, where he helped shape primary education in the city. He wrote many textbooks on physiology* and anatomy.

Huxley was also appointed to ten royal commissions to investigate problems of education, fisheries, and the use of live animals for research (vivisection). He was a member of several scientific societies and received many scientific and civic honors. By the time of his death in 1895, he was regarded as a leading public figure in Great Britain and as one of the world's finest scientific researchers and educators.

Scientific Accomplishments

Huxley was not only a dedicated educator but also a fine researcher, a well-respected member of the scientific community, and an advocate of

*embryo organism from the first division of the fertilized egg through the early stages of development until birth or hatching

*physiology science that deals with the functions of living organisms and their parts

Darwin's evolutionary theory. His research interests spanned the fields of zoology and paleontology, and his work in these disciplines provided the evidence that he needed to support Darwinian theory.

Invertebrate and Vertebrate Anatomy. Huxley's work on the *Rattlesnake* focused on three groups of marine invertebrates: medusae, tunicates, and cephalous mollusca. He noted that all medusae are comprised of two foundation membranes that develop into the inner and outer parts of the organism, and that they lack blood, blood vessels, and a nervous system. He concluded that the membranes were comparable to layers found in a typical embryo, but he did not comment further on the topic. His findings suggested that the earliest developmental forms of all animals were similar, whether they were marine invertebrates or higher primates, such as apes and humans. This observation was later developed further by the German naturalist Ernst HAECKEL.

Huxley wrote and presented two major papers on tunicates, confirming that this organism's life cycle alternates between solitude and the generation of colonies of offspring. Having observed a great abundance of specimens at various growth stages, he concluded that the solitary stage is the product of sexual generation and that the colony results from asexual reproduction or budding. Thus there were two separate processes that accounted for the forms seen in colonial species. Huxley's work with cephalous mollusca led him to the notion of the archetype (typical structure). He stated that each group of animals has an archetype and that all members of that group represent a "more or less complete evolution" of that archetype. He used the term *evolution* to mean the development of the embryo to its final form, without suggesting progress from a lower to a higher type within the group.

Huxley's work with vertebrates reinforced the evolutionary ideas that he noticed in his invertebrate studies. A major contribution in this work was his insistence that a researcher could show homologies* only by studying and comparing anatomical structures of organisms from their earliest stages of development. At the time, scientists typically drew such conclusions by comparing the features of adult animals only. In an 1858 lecture, Huxley proved his point by showing that, despite their differences, all vertebrate skulls are modifications of the same basic type. He showed that the skulls of higher vertebrates develop in three stages: they begin as a membrane, then become cartilage, and finally harden into bone. Huxley then compared vertebra development to the steps that can be observed in the skulls of amphioxus (membranous animals), sharks (cartilaginous animals), and higher vertebrates (which have bones). This comparison suggested to him that parts of the developmental processes that occur in humans and higher vertebrates can be observed in lower animals.

Paleontology. While Huxley was studying vertebrate anatomy, he was also engaged in extensive fossil study. He was one of the first to notice that, on the one hand, some dinosaur skeletons were remarkably simi-

Huxley versus "Soapy Sam"

Huxley's most notable confrontation on the topic of evolution occurred in 1860 during a debate with Bishop Samuel Wilberforce, known as "Soapy Sam." In the course of their debate, Wilberforce made several questionable scientific assertions; toward the end of his talk he turned to Huxley and asked whether Huxley was related to an ape on his grandfather's or his grandmother's side of the family. After correcting Wilberforce's errors, Huxley replied that he would rather be related to an ape than to a man of learning and importance who used his intellect to distort the truth. The incident not only established Huxley as Darwin's main defender, but it also showed that evolutionists would not back down in the face of religious opposition.

*homology relationship characterized by similarity in structure and evolutionary origin

lar to bird skeletons and that, on the other hand, many of their skeletal features differed from the features of most reptiles that had originally appeared more similar. Based on his findings he classified birds and dinosaurs as members of the same order of animals, a classification widely accepted today.

Huxley also studied fossil horses and noted that later forms of the horse were increasingly specialized. He was convinced that evidence of an ancient five-toed horse would eventually be discovered. As he predicted, paleontologists later discovered remains of an ancestral horse that proved to be more generalized than all later forms of horses. This provided further evidence that evolutionary modification occurred over time and that, as evolutionary theory suggested, earlier forms were less specialized and more generalized than later ones.

The Evolution Controversy. In the late 1850s, when Charles Darwin completed his famous book *On the Origin of Species,* he sent a copy to Huxley, who at the time had little regard for theories of species change. However, Darwin's arguments convinced Huxley to believe in the theory of evolution, and a few months after he had read the book, he had a chance to write a favorable review in the London *Times.* Shortly thereafter he wrote a supportive article in the *Westminster Review* and gave a lecture in which he argued that humans differ less from apes than apes differ from other primates. To prove his point to the public and to his critics, he dissected the brains of various primates and showed that human brains were not anatomically different from those of apes. His work also showed greater differences between apes and the lowest primates than between apes and humans. Huxley did not accept all of Darwin's ideas at once or uncritically. He felt that evolution was a fact, but that natural selection* had not been fully proven as the mechanism by which evolution operated. He argued that while it was the most probable mechanism, it still awaited experimental proof.

For years Huxley remained an advocate of Darwin's views despite a great deal of criticism. In addition to using his own research findings to defend evolution, he compared human and animal anatomy and physiology to show their similarities and differences. Instead of discussing humans as distinct from other animals, he hoped that by taking a reasoned and dispassionate approach to humankind's place in the animal kingdom he could convince people to see evolution as a fact and natural selection as its most likely mechanism. The prominent support from such a respected figure as Huxley won Darwin many converts and gave his ideas credibility in the eyes of a wider audience. Huxley became the most vocal public advocate of Darwinian evolution.

*natural selection theory that within a given species, individuals with characteristics best adapted to the environment survive and successfully produce more offspring than other individuals, resulting in changes in the species over time

IBN RUSHD

1126–1198

MEDICINE

Ibn Rushd, known in the west as Averroës, was one of the greatest Islamic philosophers of the Middle Ages* and among the leading physicians of his time. His major medical work, *Generalities,* was well known in the Arab world and was later translated and brought to Europe, where it gained wide popularity.

Life and Training. Ibn Rushd was born in Cordoba, Spain, the son and grandson of Islamic judges. He received thorough training in Islamic law and theology* and studied medicine under the Arab scholar Abu Ja'far Harun al-Tajali, who was well acquainted with the ideas of the Greek philosopher ARISTOTLE and of many ancient physicians. While a young man, Ibn Rushd traveled to Marrakech, Morocco, where he met the philosopher Abu Bakr ibn Tufayl, who would have a major influence on his later career.

Ibn Tufayl introduced Ibn Rushd to the prince Abu Ya'qub Yusuf, who would become his patron. According to one source, the three men had a meeting during which the prince asked if heaven was a substance that had a beginning, or if it had always existed and would always continue to exist. Ibn Rushd was at first not confident enough to participate in the discussion, but as the conversation progressed he participated increasingly until the brilliance of his arguments won over Abu Ya'qub Yusuf.

Prince Abu Ya'qub Yusuf reigned for more than 20 years, during which time Ibn Rushd served him in many capacities. In 1169 the prince named Ibn Rushd the judge of Seville. When the prince asked Ibn Tufayl to make commentaries on the works of Aristotle, Ibn Tufayl passed the job on to Ibn Rushd. In addition to his scholarly and legal duties, Ibn Rushd traveled extensively throughout the prince's empire. At age 56 he returned to Marrakech and replaced Ibn Tufayl as the prince's chief physician.

In 1184, when Abu Ya'qub Yusuf died, he was succeeded by his son al-Mansur Ya'qub ibn Yusuf, and Ibn Rushd served the new prince for the next ten years. Shortly thereafter Ibn Rushd angered conservative religious authorities because he had made public his criticisms of Islamic theological reasoning. In 1195 Ibn Rushd's philosophical teachings were banned, his philosophy books were burned, and he was exiled to the city of Lucena. Al-Mansur later overturned these decisions and recalled Ibn Rushd from exile. Unfortunately, Ibn Rushd did not survive long after his recall; he died in 1198.

Medical Works. The *Generalities*, written between 1153 and 1169, is derived mostly from the works of the ancient Greek physician GALEN. It is divided into seven books on the anatomy of organs, health, sickness, symptoms, drugs and foods, hygiene, and therapy. Ibn Rushd asked his friend and colleague Ibn Zuhr to write a companion book to the *Generalities*. This work, on the treatment of head-to-toe diseases, was meant to extend the coverage of material in the *Generalities*. The combined works may have been conceived as a replacement for IBN SĪNĀ's *Canon,* the most famous medical work of the time.

Ibn Rushd was an outstanding physician. He was familiar with all the branches and principles of the medical science of his day, and his cures were often successful. The measure of his stature as a physician is evident in the fact that, while his philosophical works were burned, his medical works were spared.

The Arab physician and philosopher Ibn Rushd, known in the West as Averroës, is most famous for his Arabic commentaries on the teachings of the Greek philosopher Aristotle.

*Middle Ages period between ancient and modern times in western Europe, generally considered to be from the A.D. 500s to the 1500s

*theology study of religion

IBN SĪNĀ

980–1037

MEDICINE

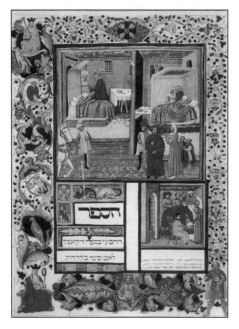

Ibn Sīnā's greatest contribution to the field of medicine is his comprehensive *Canon of Medicine.* In this illustration, taken from the *Canon,* the three basic stages during a physician's visit with a patient are represented: the examination of the patient, the consultation with the patient's caregivers, and finally, a written prescription or treatment procedure.

---

*Middle Ages period between ancient and modern times in western Europe, generally considered to be from the A.D. 500s to the 1500s

*theology study of religion

*cosmology study of the origin, history, and structure of the universe

Ibn Sīnā, known in the West as Avicenna, was one of the most important Muslim philosophers and scientists of the Middle Ages*. His book *Canon of Medicine* was one of the most influential medical texts of all time, and it was used in European universities into the 1600s.

Life and Travels. Ibn Sīnā was born near the central Asian city of Bukhara, one of the most important trading centers of the time. He received his early education from his father, whose house was a gathering place for many outstanding scholars. By the time he was ten, Ibn Sīnā had memorized the Qur'an, the Muslim holy book, as well as a great deal of Arabic poetry. He also studied law, philosophy, and medicine, and by the time he was 16 he was a practicing physician. His successful treatment of prince Nuh ibn Mansur earned him the gratitude of the Samanid rulers of Persia, who granted Ibn Sīnā access to their royal library. This rich store of knowledge provided a great boost to his learning. By age 21 Ibn Sīnā had not only established himself as an outstanding physician, but also served in several government posts under the Samanids.

Ibn Sīnā's life changed dramatically, however, when the Turkish leader Mahmud of Ghazna overthrew the Samanids. Ibn Sīnā was forced to flee, and he spent most of the rest of his life wandering the region occupied by present-day Iran and Iraq. This was a period of turmoil and disruption in central Asia, with various factions struggling for political control. It is a testimony to Ibn Sīnā's great intelligence and focus that he was able to continue to study and write during this upheaval. For a time he made a living as a physician in several towns of central Iran, but he had too little financial and political support to concentrate on his work. He finally settled in the western Iranian city of Hamadan, where he found favor with the ruling prince Shams ad-Dawleh. During his stay in Hamadan he twice served in important political offices, but he also made enemies and was imprisoned for a time.

When Shams ad-Dawleh died in 1022, Ibn Sīnā fled to the city of Esfahan, where he lived for the remainder of his life. He became a favorite of the ruler of that city, Ala ad-Dawlah, who brought Ibn Sīnā along on his military campaigns. In Esfahan, Ibn Sīnā completed his most important works, including the *Canon.* He also spent several years researching the roots of the Arabic language, which was the subject of a book that remained unfinished at the time of his death. In 1037, while accompanying Ala ad-Dawlah on a military campaign, Ibn Sīnā became ill and died of colic, although some sources suggest that he may have been poisoned.

Ibn Sīnā's Writings. Ibn Sīnā composed more than 250 books during his lifetime, many of them devoted to topics such as philosophy, theology*, cosmology*, mathematics, physics, music, and astronomy. However, he is best known in medicine and science for his work *Canon of Medicine.*

The *Canon* is a compilation of the most outstanding works of the ancient Greek physicians, along with Arabic writings and Ibn Sīnā's own notes. In the first of five books, the *Canon* covers a variety of subjects, including the four ancient elements (earth, air, fire, and water), which form the four humors (blood, bile, black bile, and phlegm). According to ideas of the time, the humors mix in different proportions to form the simple organs, whose anatomy is also discussed in book one. This is followed by a discussion of the basic forces of the body. The psychic force, dealing with thinking and reasoning, was centered in the brain. The natural force, which is responsible for preserving the human being, was centered in the liver and testicles. The heart was the seat of the animal force, which controls movement and the senses. Book one also treats the etiology (cause and origin) and symptoms of diseases, hygiene, the causes of health and sickness, and the inevitability of death. Types of therapy, diets, the use of drugs, and procedures such as bloodletting and various types of surgery are also featured in that book.

Book two of the *Canon* presents an alphabetical list of drugs and discusses their physical properties, their benefits, and how to preserve them. Book three covers diseases from head to toe, beginning with diseases of the brain and ending with those of the nails. This book also includes details of anatomy not covered in book one, such as the anatomy of the compound organs. Book four examines diseases that are not specific to certain organs. This includes the classification and symptoms of fevers, as well as the knowledge necessary for predicting illness, such as "critical days." He also deals with the most important principles of diagnosis and therapy here. In addition, book four looks at sores, wounds, poisons, diseases of the hair, obesity, and emaciation (extremely low body weight). Book five covers various pills and ointments and their use.

Many Arab scholars considered the *Canon* to be complete and perfect, and claimed that it could not be improved by adding material from other sources. Unfortunately, this attitude only served to arrest any progress in Arabic medicine. Other Arab physicians, such as Rhazes and IBN RUSHD, argued strongly for the importance of experimentation and observation. They criticized the practice of relying on logic and the untested authority of books as a guide to medical practice. However, the beauty of the *Canon*'s writing and presentation overwhelmed these arguments and the book became the world's foremost source of medical knowledge. Along with the Greek physicians HIPPOCRATES and GALEN, Ibn Sīnā was one the most revered medical scholars of the Middle Ages, and his ideas influenced both Western and Arabic medicine for hundreds of years.

Sciences and Pseudosciences

In addition to medicine, Ibn Sīnā wrote treatises on all of the sciences known during his day, including what would today be called pseudosciences, or false sciences. Ibn Sīnā believed in the effectiveness of some of these sciences, such as the practice of predicting the future based on dreams (oneiromancy) and the use of talismans. However, unlike most scientists and thinkers of his time, he did not believe that either alchemy (medieval chemical science with the goals of turning base metals into gold and finding the means for prolonging life) or astrology were valid sciences.

English physician Edward Jenner was interested in many aspects of natural history*, but he was a pioneer in the study of communicable diseases. By promoting the practice of inoculation* to immunize people against the deadly disease smallpox, Jenner launched a practice that was very important in preventive health care.

Born in Berkeley, Gloucestershire, England, Jenner was raised by an older brother after both his parents died when he was five. The

Edward
JENNER

1749–1823

NATURAL HISTORY, IMMUNOLOGY, MEDICINE

natural history systematic study of animals and plants, especially in their natural settings

inoculation introduction of a disease agent into an animal or plant to produce a mild form of the disease and render the organism immune

young Jenner showed his interest in science by collecting fossils. After a nine-year apprenticeship with a surgeon, Jenner went to London in 1770 to study anatomy and surgery. Three years later he returned to Berkeley and began to practice medicine. In his leisure time he wrote poetry and observed birds. Jenner married in 1788 and fathered four children.

As a physician Jenner was often asked to inoculate people against smallpox, which was responsible for 10 percent of all deaths in London in the 1600s. Inoculation, which began in England in the early 1700s, involved infecting a healthy person with material taken from a smallpox sore. This usually gave the inoculated person a mild case of smallpox that would prevent future, more severe, infections. Sometimes, however, the inoculations were fatal. Unless the inoculated people were isolated, they would infect others, starting an epidemic. As he performed inoculations, Jenner discovered that some people were completely resistant, or immune, to smallpox.

Many had previously been infected with cowpox, a nonfatal disease that affected milk cows and could be transferred to people who handled them. Jenner believed that cowpox inoculations could protect people from smallpox. In 1796 he inoculated an eight-year-old boy with matter taken from a milkmaid's cowpox sore. When Jenner later inoculated the boy with smallpox, no infection resulted. Jenner had found a safer, more effective way to protect people from smallpox.

After he published the results of his researches in 1798, the practice of preventive inoculation, or vaccination, spread with astonishing speed. Jenner discovered that material taken from sores could be dried, stored, and shipped around the world. He sent this vaccine to India and to President Thomas Jefferson of the United States, who vaccinated his family and neighbors.

For the rest of his life Jenner was occupied with writing about vaccination, providing vaccines, and supervising what became England's national vaccination program. Among the honors that he received were cash grants from the British government and a gold medal from Napoleon Bonaparte of France. He is recognized as a founder of what was later called immunology, the science of preventing illness by strengthening the body's own defense systems.

Heinrich Hermann Robert KOCH

1843–1910

BACTERIOLOGY, HYGIENE, TROPICAL MEDICINE

Considered the founder of modern bacteriology*, Heinrich Hermann Robert Koch was also the first to identify and isolate the organisms responsible for many infectious diseases, including tuberculosis, cholera, and anthrax. Koch's efforts led to the widespread adoption of public health measures to fight infections caused by microbes*. They also stimulated an awareness of the importance of controlling disease through immunization and improved hygiene. In 1905 Koch received the Nobel Prize in physiology* or medicine for his investigations and discoveries in relation to tuberculosis.

Life and Career

Koch had a restless and inquisitive nature that he exercised during his extensive travels to study the origins and development of various diseases. He also possessed great self-confidence that bordered on stubbornness, leading to personal conflicts with several colleagues.

Early Life and Career. Koch, one of 11 surviving children of a mining official, was born in Clausthal, Germany. He grew up in an environment that fostered an appreciation for nature. He often accompanied his uncle on natural history* trips in the countryside that helped develop his interest in the sciences as well as the new art of photography. Koch became an avid collector of plant and animal specimens, dissecting and mounting larger animals and preparing their skeletons. He taught himself to read and write before entering elementary school, where he excelled in his studies. However, his teenage years were marked by emotional difficulties that hurt his academic performance and required him to repeat his final year of high school. In 1862 Koch entered the University of Göttingen to study natural science but later pursued medical studies. An outstanding student, he graduated four years later with highest honors.

During the six years that followed, Koch struggled to find a location to practice his profession. He wanted to be a military physician or ship's doctor, but those opportunities were scarce and he was forced to take a job in an institution for retarded children. Unfortunately, financial cutbacks threatened Koch's salary and he moved to the town of Rakwitz, where he finally established a successful practice in 1869. A year later, however, the Franco-Prussian War began. Koch volunteered for service at a field hospital, but after a year he returned to Rakwitz in response to a petition by the citizens. In 1872, he moved to the town of Wollstein (present-day Wolsztyn, Poland), where he lived for the next eight years.

Research and Travel. At Wollstein, Koch had the time and money to pursue research into infectious diseases. During the next several years, he isolated *Bacillus anthracis*, the bacterium that causes anthrax, and developed rigorous methods for isolating, cultivating, and analyzing other disease-causing bacteria. He also studied the effectiveness of various disinfectants and how they acted against disease organisms. At that time Koch also began his investigations into the causes and treatment of tuberculosis. These studies brought him worldwide acclaim but caused professional rivalries with several fellow researchers, including the German physician Rudolf VIRCHOW and the French scientist Louis PASTEUR.

At the age of 40, Koch was finally able to satisfy his taste for travel when he went to Egypt and India to investigate local cholera epidemics there. On this trip he identified the bacteria responsible for the disease and proposed better sanitation methods to reduce the risk of future outbreaks. After his return to Germany he continued his research on tuberculosis, developing a highly controversial antitubercular drug. In the early 1890s, Koch dealt with a cholera epidemic in Germany and

*bacteriology science that deals with bacteria, microscopic organisms that can cause infection and disease

*microbe microscopic organism

*physiology science that deals with the functions of living organisms and their parts

*natural history systematic study of animals and plants, especially in their natural settings

Koch, Heinrich Hermann Robert

The Experimenter as Subject

In Koch's day, it was not unusual for scientific researchers to act as subjects in their own experiments. For instance, to study the body's production and excretion of succinic acid, which aids metabolism, Koch consumed food that included half a pound of butter each day. During the later cholera controversy, some of his rivals swallowed cultures containing bacteria that Koch claimed was the cause of the disease. Although a few developed cholera-like symptoms, none developed the disease. Because none of the researchers died, some scientists claimed that Koch was wrong about the cause of cholera.

---

*culture to grow microorganisms, such as bacteria or tissue, in a specially prepared nutrient substance for scientific study

*bacillus rod-shaped bacterium

*spore single-celled, environmentally resistant body produced by plants and some microorganisms and capable of development into a new individual directly or after mixing with another spore

*flagella whiplike structure used by certain organisms to move through a fluid medium, such as water or blood

*parasitic relating to a parasite, an organism that lives on or within another organism from whose body it obtains nutrients

then left to spend several years abroad studying and combating various infectious diseases. His travels again took him to India and to parts of Africa as well as New Guinea.

Final Years. Between 1896 and 1907, Koch spent more than seven years in the tropics. He spent his final years in Germany developing methods to control tuberculosis. During this time he received tributes and honors from many nations and scientific academies. In 1910, three days after delivering a lecture on tuberculosis to the Berlin Academy of Sciences, Koch died of heart failure. He was 66.

Scientific Accomplishments

In addition to his work on anthrax, tuberculosis, and cholera, Koch also studied other infectious diseases, such as typhoid and sleeping sickness. He pioneered techniques for bacteriological study that remained standard practice for many years.

Anthrax and General Bacteriology. Koch had begun to investigate anthrax during his time in Wollstein. He confirmed earlier studies that showed anthrax was caused by rodlike microorganisms seen in the blood of infected sheep. He invented techniques to culture* these organisms and in this manner, traced their growth and development. He discovered that, while the bacillus* itself was short lived, it produced spores* that could live for many years even when dried out. This finding helped explain the recurrence of the disease in long unused pastures. Koch also proved that mice infected with the bacillus only developed anthrax if active spores were present. He announced his findings in 1876, and scientists were so impressed that one remarked: "I regard it as the greatest discovery ever made with bacteria and I believe that this is not the last time that this young Robert Koch will surprise and shame us by the brilliance of his investigations."

Based on his work with the anthrax bacterium, Koch developed new techniques for the modern field of bacteriology, including how to fix bacterial cultures on glass slides, stain them with dyes, and use microphotography to record their structures. His photos showed details such as the flagella* on mobile bacteria, which enabled him to distinguish between harmless and harmful organisms. Koch also formulated rules, known today as "Koch's postulates," with which he determined whether an infectious disease was caused by a parasitic* microorganism. He concluded that most human infections were caused by parasites and that different bacteria were responsible for diseases.

He stressed the use of sterile techniques for culturing bacteria colonies for research and championed the use of gelatin as a medium for growing pure cultures. He urged researchers to study how easily newly discovered disease organisms could be transmitted to animals, where they were found in the host, and what their natural habitats and their susceptibility to harmful agents were. He investigated disinfectants to determine their ability to kill or inhibit the growth of certain bacilli. Koch's work was later compiled into an instruction manual that became a standard reference work for bacteriological laboratories.

Koch's early studies led to disputes with fellow researchers. He took issue with the anthrax research conducted by the German bacteriologist Hans Buchner and the French microbiologist* Louis Pasteur. Koch called Pasteur's work inaccurate, claimed his cultures were impure, and accused him of copying many of his results. He also disagreed with Pasteur's notions of how animals contracted anthrax and his assertion that earthworms brought anthrax spores to the surface. The dispute flared up on repeated occasions over a period of years.

microbiologist scientist who studies microscopic life-forms, such as bacteria and viruses

Tuberculosis Studies. Perhaps Koch's most important, yet controversial, work was his investigation into tuberculosis. He began his research in secret, determining that the disease was infectious and isolating the bacillus responsible for it. The latter task was quite difficult because the tubercle bacillus is very small, resists staining, grows very slowly in a test tube, and has very precise nutritional requirements. Through painstaking efforts Koch was able to reproduce the conditions that are conducive to the bacillus's growth, and he eventually discovered an effective staining technique. In 1882 he surprised the scientific world by revealing his findings in a paper that he read to the Berlin Physiological Society. Most scientists applauded his findings, but Virchow remained unconvinced. Although Koch's final report contained several errors, his main findings were verified by researchers across the world.

In 1890, eight years after his landmark report, Koch again amazed his colleagues by announcing that he had produced a substance that prevented the growth of tubercle bacilli. When injected into healthy guinea pigs, the substance made them resistant to the bacilli, and in infected animals it stopped the course of the disease. The German government planned to monopolize manufacture of the substance, called tuberculin, but when reports surfaced that the drug was highly toxic, the demand for revelation of the drug's formula intensified.

For a long time Koch refused to reveal the formula, and when he did the description was lacking in essential details and was misleading. After some hospitals and medical centers banned its use, however, Koch provided the complete formula. When researchers working with the drug were unsuccessful in immunizing animals, Koch returned to the laboratory to prepare new forms of the drug. Around the same time, Emil von BEHRING also began work on a treatment for tuberculosis. Koch resented what he saw as an invasion of his territory by Behring, whose fame was growing. The two finally fell out completely when, despite Koch's objections, Behring and a pharmaceutical company obtained patents for two different preparations of tubercle bacilli.

Koch continued his work on tuberculosis and discovered that human saliva was the main source of human infection. He also declared that, contrary to his previous beliefs, the human tubercle bacillus could not infect cattle, or vice versa. This finding placed him at odds with the famed British physician Joseph LISTER and in opposition to the findings of British scientific commissions that had banned the

Robert Koch was the first scientist to demonstrate that certain diseases are caused by specific bacteria. Here, Koch is shown diligently searching for the cause of rinderpest, a viral disease that affects animals, mainly cattle.

consumption of milk from cows with tuberculous udders. Although a professional meeting was called to resolve these differences, it came to nothing because of Koch's inability to compromise with his opponents.

Cholera and Other Diseases. On a trip to Egypt and India in the mid-1880s, Koch and his coworkers identified a comma-shaped bacillus in more than 70 cholera victims. Although the bacillus failed to produce infection when introduced into animals, Koch nevertheless identified it as the source of the disease. He suggested procedures to control the disease, including disinfecting areas contaminated with the feces of infected individuals and maintaining sanitary water supplies. Several colleagues disputed the role of the bacillus that Koch had isolated, but their objections were soon overruled, and Koch's prescriptions for controlling cholera were widely adopted.

Among the other diseases that Koch investigated were malaria, typhoid fever, sleeping sickness, and several cattle diseases. He identified mosquitoes as the carriers of malaria and recommended the destruction of mosquito breeding grounds as a control method. Where this was impossible, he developed a treatment regimen using the drug quinine. When epidemics of typhoid fever arose in Germany, Koch recommended many of the same precautions he had suggested for cholera, including increased attention to sewage disposal and sanitation, and quick identification and isolation of infected individuals. These efforts ended the epidemic and led to a decrease in the incidence of typhoid. His work with animal diseases such as rinderpest resulted in the development of an immunization using the blood of infected animals together with the blood of those who had recovered from the disease.

Koch's lifelong passion to explore and eradicate infectious diseases made a major contribution to the modern field of bacteriology and many breakthroughs in disease treatment and prevention. Although he was often at odds with colleagues, his work won worldwide recognition. A fitting tribute was the establishment in 1908 of the Robert Koch Medal, which is presented to the world's greatest living physicians. Fittingly, Koch was the first recipient of the award.

Jean Baptiste Pierre Antoine de Monet de
LAMARCK

1744–1829

BOTANY, ZOOLOGY, PALEONTOLOGY, EVOLUTION

The French scientist Jean Baptiste Pierre Antoine de Monet de Lamarck earned a place in the history of the life sciences with his significant contributions to botany and to the study of living and fossil invertebrates*. He is most remembered, however, for developing one of the first theories of how plant and animal species evolve, or change into new forms, over long periods of time.

An element of Lamarck's theory of evolution* was a concept called the inheritance of acquired characteristics. He believed that organisms could pass to their offspring qualities they had not been born with but had acquired during their lives. Of equal importance were his beliefs that organisms had an inborn tendency to develop complexity and that through use or disuse, organs would be enhanced or reduced in succeeding generations. Lamarck's theory of evolution was replaced in 1859 by the more comprehensive theory developed by the English naturalist* Charles DARWIN in his famous book *On the Origin of Species*.

Life and Career

Lamarck was born in Bazentin-le-Petit in the Picardy region of northern France. His family belonged to the minor nobility but had fallen on hard times. Lamarck's father, following family tradition, had served as a military officer. With little money to educate or equip his younger son for a similar career, the elder Lamarck decided that the boy should become a priest. At the age of 11, young Lamarck was sent to a religious school, but he found that he was not interested in pursuing that line of study.

Life in the Army. In 1759, when Lamarck's father died, he left school and joined the French army. After fighting in the Seven Years' War (1756–1763), he spent five years serving in a series of forts along the French borders. It was during this time that he began collecting and studying plants. Because of an illness, however, he left the army in 1768 and found a job in a Paris bank. Later he studied medicine for four years.

Interest in Science. During the 1780s, Lamarck's scientific interests broadened to include meteorology*, chemistry, and shell collecting. In 1779 the French naturalist Georges BUFFON arranged for Lamarck to be elected to the Académie des Sciences, France's leading scientific organization. Four years later, Lamarck became assistant botanist to the academy, and for the rest of his life he remained associated with the organization, from which he received an income.

Lamarck was also involved with a newly formed natural history group called the Société d'Histoire Naturelle, to which many prominent French naturalists belonged. He helped edit several of the society's publications and also contributed original articles on botany and invertebrates. His most significant association was as a botanist in the Jardin du Roi (king's garden) and its affiliated natural history museum, which Buffon had made into a major scientific center. In the early 1790s, in response to changes brought by the French Revolution, the Jardin du Roi was converted into the Muséum National d'Histoire Naturelle (National Museum of Natural History) and Lamarck was elected a professor of zoology there.

Personal Life and Reputation. Misfortune and poverty shadowed Lamarck's private life. He was married several times and had six children, of whom one was deaf and another insane. Lamarck's own health began to fail in 1809, when he developed eye problems. By 1818 he had become completely blind, although he continued to write by dictating to one of his daughters. At the time of his death, his family did not have enough money for his funeral and appealed to the academy for assistance. Lamarck's possessions, including his books and scientific collections, were later sold at a public auction.

Lamarck's study and classification of invertebrates and theories of evolution preceded and influenced Darwin. Lamarck also made significant contributions in botany and paleontology.

*invertebrate animal without a backbone

*evolution historical development of a biological group such as a species

*naturalist one who studies objects in their natural settings

*meteorology science that deals with the atmosphere, especially the weather and weather predictions; also known as atmospheric science

*taxonomic relating to taxonomy, the orderly classification of plants and animals into groups and subgroups according to their relationships

In the early years of the nineteenth century, Lamarck had achieved recognition for his work and publications in natural history. By the time of his death, however, his critics had achieved power in the scientific establishment and he had few followers. The French naturalist Georges CUVIER, one of Lamarck's sharpest opponents, prepared the academy's official eulogy; it did little to honor Lamarck. Cuvier dismissed all of Lamarck's theories as unacceptable and gave only faint praise to his taxonomic* work. Lamarck's evolutionary theories attracted the attention of scholars and authors in the United Kingdom and were at the core of a popular work published in 1844, titled *Vestiges of the Natural History Creation*. After Darwin published his theory of evolution in 1859, the attention paid to the subject again brought Lamarck into the limelight as an early evolutionist.

Scientific Contributions

Like many naturalists of his day, Lamarck devoted his attention to a series of scientific fields rather than specializing in one area. Meteorology and chemistry were among his earliest interests. He published works in both fields beginning in the 1790s. His only public success with meteorology was his suggestion that the French government establish a central data bank to collect standardized weather information from all over the country. Such a program was begun in 1800, but it ended ten years later, when Napoleon Bonaparte, ruler of France, ridiculed Lamarck's annual volumes of meteorological studies.

Lamarck also wrote an important text on geology. His *Hydrogéologie* (Hydrogeology), published in 1802, was originally intended to be a much broader work. He coined the title term to refer to a complete physics of the earth, including meteorology, geology, and biology. He believed that there was an interrelation among these fields and that all of nature worked according to similar principles—as general natural tendencies producing gradual changes over long periods of time. He also believed that local circumstances explained any irregularities in his theory. His sense of the great age of the earth was an important step in the development of new ideas of geological time that were popularized in the 1830s by the British geologist Charles Lyell.

In his studies of the earth sciences, Lamarck was mainly interested in the effects of the physical world and natural processes on plants and animals. His most significant research and writing dealt first with plants, then with animals, and finally with a theory about all life. He published detailed classifications of organisms as well as broad theories, but he was always more interested in the wide view of nature than in the finer details. He sometimes expressed scorn for those who were devoted to the collection of little facts.

Botany. Lamarck's earliest recognition by the French scientific community was based on his 1779 book titled *Flore françoise* (French Flora), a three-volume work on the plants of France. Its most original feature was a new system of plant classification that he had created. It

Extinction or Evolution?

Until the late 1790s, Lamarck believed that species are unchanging, but in 1800 he made his first public statement about evolution. What made him change his mind? One possible explanation concerns fossils of extinct creatures. Lamarck could not accept that these organisms were extinct because it violated his view of nature. It was easier for him to believe that organisms had changed or evolved into new forms over time.

104

enabled him to organize the information so that the reader could easily identify a plant. The work sold out within a year and was reprinted many times. When it was ready to be reprinted in 1802, Lamarck was busy with other things and gave the task of preparing a new edition to another scientist, who replaced Lamarck's system of classification.

A second major botanical work was Lamarck's contribution to the eight-volume *Dictionnaire de botanique* (Dictionary of Botany). He wrote the first three and a half volumes, contributing articles on all aspects of botany, including classification, the structures of plants, and descriptions of particular species. In addition, he identified several new genera* and species of plants.

Many of the general ideas that Lamarck demonstrated in his botanical writings reappeared in later works. One of these was the belief in a chain of being—the notion that every large group of natural objects, such as plants, animals, and minerals, can be arranged in stages ranging from simple to complex. Another theme was his awareness of the influence of the environment, especially climate, on the development of plants.

*genus category of biological classification; class, kind, or group of organisms that share common characteristics; *pl.* genera

Zoology and Paleontology.

During his tenure as professor of zoology at the Muséum National d'Histoire Naturelle, Lamarck was in charge of insects and worms, creatures lacking spinal cords, which he called invertebrates (animals without vertebrae, or backbones). He also took on the tasks of teaching courses on invertebrate zoology and organizing the museum's collection. He classified the specimens in the museum using a system he developed based on Cuvier's anatomical studies.

Although invertebrate zoology was a sharp change from botany, Lamarck was not unhappy because he had been interested in invertebrates since his days as a shell collector. He befriended his colleague Jean-Guillaume Bruguière, who was an expert on invertebrates, and when Bruguière died in 1798, he finished Bruguière's study on invertebrate animals. Soon Lamarck came to be regarded as an expert in conchology, or the study of arthropods (animals living in shells). He made important contributions to the classification of arthropods, including the fossil forms of extinct species. His texts on this subject included *Mémoires sur les fossils des environs de Paris* (Studies of the Fossils in the Regions Surrounding Paris), which was published between 1802 and 1806. His most important contributions to the field were contained in his seven-volume work, *Histoire naturelle des animaux sans vertèbres* (Natural History of Animals without Vertebrae), published between 1815 and 1822.

Lamarck's investigation of living and fossil arthropods revealed a number of similarities. He explained that the differences between past and present forms existed because organisms had changed over time. He developed his ideas on this subject in the years that followed.

Lamarck's Theory of Evolution.

Lamarck never used the term *evolution* to refer to changes in plant or animal forms. He spoke instead of transformation, or the path or order that nature followed to produce forms. The term *evolution,* which became popular in the 1860s and 1870s, included the meaning expressed by Lamarck's longer phrases.

Lamarck first publicly presented his theory of evolution in the opening lecture for his museum course on invertebrates. He stated that nature had originally crafted the simplest plants and animals. With the passage of time and because of variations in circumstance, more complex forms from those originals were produced. He also suggested that animals, in addition to their inborn tendency to develop greater complexity, also formed new habits based on their changing circumstances and physical needs. These habits, which helped strengthen certain parts or organs of the animal, were then passed on to future generations. Gradually new organs or parts formed, resulting in new species.

By 1802 Lamarck's ideas about evolution had expanded greatly, and he had realized the need to explain the mechanism of change. He defined life in physical terms, as the result of a particular kind of organization in matter. He argued that life began when heat, sunlight, and electricity acted on small amounts of unorganized moist matter to produce the simplest animals and plants. Organized into structures according to their chemical properties, these simple organisms came under the influence of something that Lamarck saw as a natural tendency of living things: the movement toward increasing complexity.

Lamarck also cautiously suggested that human beings were formed as a result of the same processes that had produced all other living organisms. In an important work, *Philosophie zoologique* (Zoological Philosophy), published in 1809, he gave his views on how such mental qualities as intelligence and feeling might also have evolved.

Philosophie zoologique is the best-known presentation of Lamarck's theory of evolution. It consists of three sections. In the first section, he presents evidence for increasingly complex generations of organisms and discusses the environment as the factor that produced those variations. In the second, he discusses the physical nature of life and his theories about how life originated. The third section contains a detailed explanation of how physical processes might have cause higher mental faculties to arise. Lamarck argued that higher mental processes were a product of increased complexity in living structures. He stated that the most important event in the evolutionary process was the development of the nervous system, because it enabled organisms to form ideas and control their movements. It also enabled them to respond to sensations and to circumstances in their environments in ways that affected their structure, which would then be passed to their children.

In the introduction to his seven-volume *Histoire naturelle des animaux sans vertèbres* (Natural History of Invertebrates), Lamarck summarized his evolutionary views in four laws. Published in 1815, the laws state that there is a natural tendency toward complexity; that new organs evolve because of environmental influences; that new habits produce changes in the body during the lifetime of an individual; and that these changes (acquired characteristics) could be passed on to offspring.

Most people at the time—including scientists—accepted the inheritance of acquired characteristics, rarely feeling the need to offer any proof. The broader ideas of evolution of organisms and the formation of new species posed a greater challenge to the established beliefs of the time than any idea about its particular mechanism.

Lamarck's theory of evolution had some supporters in France but was challenged by the conservative naturalist Cuvier. It received some attention in England. A generation later, Darwin's theory of evolution through natural selection* ensured Lamarck's fame. Although Darwin adapted segments of Lamarck's ideas, some of his critics promoted Lamarck's theory as an alternative to Darwin's. Those who revived Lamarck's theory in the later nineteenth century were called Neo-Lamarckians, and their views had influence for a time, especially in the field of paleontology, or the study of fossils. However, the wide acceptance of Darwin's theory, modified by modern knowledge of genetics*, had the effect of eclipsing Lamarckism.

*natural selection theory that within a given species, individuals with characteristics best adapted to the environment survive and successfully produce more offspring than other individuals, resulting in changes in the species over time

*genetics branch of biology that deals with heredity

Paul
LANGERHANS
1847–1888
ANATOMY, PATHOLOGY

Paul Langerhans was a German physician best known for his discovery of cells in the pancreas* that were later shown to be the source of insulin, a chemical that controls the level of sugar in the blood. Langerhans also conducted research into the anatomy of the skin and other tissues, as well as the bodily system that attacks foreign objects such as bacteria.

Langerhans was born in Berlin, Germany, to a medical family; his father and two of his stepbrothers were physicians. He studied medicine at the University of Jena in Germany and received his M.D. from the University of Berlin. A year after graduating, Langerhans traveled to Egypt and Palestine, where he conducted anthropological* studies, including taking measurements of the skulls of local Palestinians. In 1870 he returned to Europe and joined the German army as a physician and served in the Franco-Prussian War. After the war he accepted a position as professor of pathology* at the University of Freiburg.

At age 37, Langerhans contracted tuberculosis, which interrupted his academic career. Thereafter he moved to the healthier climate of the Mediterranean island of Madeira, where his condition improved. He practiced medicine in the island's capital until he developed a kidney infection that led to his death in 1888.

Langerhans did his most important work in the laboratory of the respected German physician and researcher Rudolf VIRCHOW, with whom he had developed a close friendship while still at the University of Berlin. Langerhans was among the early successful researchers to explore and use novel methods and staining techniques to study animal cell and tissue structures. He employed these techniques to locate nerve endings in the epidermis*. Using similar techniques to study tissue from the pancreas, he discovered smooth irregular cells in an area that normally contains granulated (rough and grainy) cells. Although Langerhans did not propose an explanation of their function, the cells were

*pancreas gland that controls the production of insulin and produces the juices (chemicals) that enable the body to digest and absorb fats

*anthropological related to the study of human beings, especially in relation to origins and physical and cultural characteristics

*pathology study of diseases and their effects on organisms

*epidermis outer layer of the skin

named for him; the "Islands of Langerhans" were eventually found to be the body's source of insulin.

In later experiments he and a colleague showed that when a red dye derived from mercury was injected into the veins of rabbits and guinea pigs, it was absorbed by white blood cells, bone marrow, capillary tissues, and liver tissues. However, it was never absorbed by the red blood cells. Later researchers built on the work to try to understand the workings of one of the systems that attacks foreign matter, such as bacteria, in the body—the reticuloendothelial system. Langerhans also investigated microscopic cardiac* muscle fibers, and while on Madeira he studied the causes of tuberculosis and published a book outlining the healing properties of the island's climate.

*cardiac of or relating to the heart

Antoni van
LEEUWENHOEK
1632–1723
NATURAL SCIENCES, MICROSCOPY

*microorganism tiny living thing that generally can be seen clearly only through a microscope

Antoni van Leeuwenhoek discovered a world of tiny microorganisms* that he called "animalcules," meaning "little animals," by observing parts of plants and animals through magnifying lenses, or microscopes. Grinding lenses began as a hobby but soon developed into a lifelong pursuit of microscopic investigation. Leeuwenhoek became a legend in his own time, receiving awards from scientific societies and academies and visits from foreign researchers.

Born in Delft in the Netherlands, Leeuwenhoek was the son of a basketmaker, who died when Leeuwenhoek was six. After attending grammar school, Leeuwenhoek became an apprentice to a cloth merchant in Amsterdam. Later he opened a shop of his own. Then, in 1660, he began a new career as a civil servant in the service of the city of Delft, becoming chief warden of the city in 1677. The pension he received from his civil service positions gave him financial security for life. Leeuwenhoek died in Delft in 1723.

Leeuwenhoek's scientific work began about 1671. Already familiar with the special glasses used by drapers to inspect the quality of cloth, Leeuwenhoek took the idea further and constructed his first simple microscope. It consisted of a tiny lens, ground by hand from a small piece of glass, and clamped between two metal plates. A special holder attached to this apparatus enabled Leeuwenhoek to view plant and animal specimens through the lens.

During his lifetime Leeuwenhoek made about 550 lenses. The quality of his lenses improved over time, making greater magnification possible. Moreover, because he was always secretive about his technique and refused to take on apprentices who might become proficient in his craft, his instruments were unsurpassed until the 1800s. Through his lenses Leeuwenhoek observed particles of skin, hair, and bone; insects; parts of plants; microorganisms; and many other objects. Carefully, he recorded his observations, always in Dutch, for he knew no other language.

Leeuwenhoek made his most important discovery in 1674, when he observed tiny moving objects—the one-celled animals known as protozoa. He recorded his observations and two years later communicated them to the Royal Society of London. The findings caused a sensation, and Leeuwenhoek felt obliged to obtain written testimony about his findings from ministers, judges, and medical professionals. Leeuwenhoek's observation was considered sensational because of his claim that these little animals were a naturally occurring phenomenon and not the by-product (as contemporary wisdom would have it) of the decomposition of organic material.

In the years that followed, Leeuwenhoek observed and described many kinds of microorganisms, including bacteria. He also became interested in the process of reproduction in animals and humans. He observed spermatozoa* and suggested that for reproduction to occur, the sperm would have to penetrate the ovum (egg). He was unable to detect the human egg with his microscope and so mistakenly took the ovum to be the nucleus of the egg. Because Leeuwenhoek knew that the ovum could not pass through the fallopian tubes of the female, and that the spermatozoa swam rapidly through the male's semen, he concluded that the spermatozoa were the principal agent in animal reproduction. The scientists who adopted Leeuwenhoek's view became known as "animalculists," and their view was strongly opposed by followers of the English physician William HARVEY (known as "ovists"), who believed that the ovum was the principal agent in animal reproduction.

Leeuwenhoek took particular interest in the blood and blood vessels. He observed corpuscles (blood cells) and capillaries (small blood vessels) and investigated the walls of blood vessels. Because he spoke and read only Dutch, he was unaware of the work of another microscopist, the Italian Marcello MALPIGHI, who had made similar observations of the blood earlier. Another area of interest to Leeuwenhoek was plant anatomy. Through his microscopic observations, he brought remarkable insight to the three-dimensional structure of the root, stem, and leaf. Leeuwenhoek illustrated his findings with detailed drawings from many angles and perspectives.

Leeuwenhoek continued to share his findings with the Royal Society, and as the importance of his work became more widely appreciated, the society prepared English translations of his letters and encouraged him to investigate new fields. From 1684 onward Leeuwenhoek published his own works, first in Dutch and then in Latin. In recognition of his achievements, he was elected a fellow of the Royal Society in 1680 and a correspondent of the Académie des Sciences in Paris in 1699. As his fame spread, scientists and scholars from around the world, including kings and princes, came to visit him.

*spermatozoon male reproductive cell; *pl.* spermatozoa

Leonardo da Vinci was one of the towering figures of the Renaissance, the era of new ideas in scholarship, art, science, and technology that began in Europe in the 1300s. He also won lasting fame as an artist, the painter of such well-known masterpieces as the *Mona Lisa* and *The Last Supper*. Throughout his life Leonardo was interested in scientific theory and the practical uses of science. For instance, his thorough study of human anatomy may have reflected his desire to portray

Leonardo
DA VINCI
1452–1519
ANATOMY, TECHNOLOGY

*mechanics science that studies how energy and force affect objects

the body accurately in painting and sculpture. He had many scientific concerns, ranging from pure mathematics to military engineering and problems in mechanics*, such as the question of how birds fly—and how humans might be able to do the same.

Although Leonardo has been recognized as one of the most extraordinary minds of all time, his place in the history of science is unusual because he did not contribute directly to the development of scientific thought. His ideas circulated orally, but they were not published during his lifetime. For three centuries after Leonardo's death, his scientific work, in spite of his artistic notoriety, lay buried in notebooks that were overlooked or lost in museums, libraries, and archives throughout Europe. Except for some aspects of his mechanical and engineering activities and the tradition that he knew much about anatomy, Leonardo was not well known as a scientist. For this reason some modern historians of science, rather than regarding Leonardo as the discoverer of a principle or the inventor of a device, focus instead on what he knew and how he knew it. In Leonardo's work they find a window into the possibilities of scientific knowledge during the Renaissance.

Leonardo as a Scientist

Leonardo da Vinci's life and scientific work illustrate what some scholars have seen as the spirit of the Renaissance—curiosity about the world, interest in a wide range of matters, knowledge or expertise in more than one subject, and the crossing of the traditional boundaries of knowledge.

Life and Career. The illegitimate son of a peasant girl and a citizen of the Italian city of Florence, Leonardo was born in Vinci, near Empolia, Italy. He received an ordinary education in reading and writing, but his gifts for music and art led his father to apprentice him to a sculptor in Florence. In the artist's workshop the young Leonardo studied painting, sculpture, and mechanics.

Leonardo had already produced impressive paintings when, at the age of 30, he left Florence to enter the service of Ludovico Sforza, the duke of Milan, a city in northern Italy. During the 17 years that Leonardo was part of the duke's household, he painted, produced a clay model for a statue of one of the Sforzas on horseback, and planned books on painting, architecture, mechanics, and the human figure.

After the French captured Milan in 1499, Leonardo moved to Venice and then back to Florence. For about a year he served as military engineer and chief inspector of fortifications in the northern Italian region called the Romagna. While living in Florence, Leonardo began his systematic study of human anatomy.

In 1506 Leonardo returned to Milan, where the city's French governor befriended him. There he produced most of his brilliant anatomical drawings. By this time Leonardo had come to believe that mathematics held the key to understanding nature, a view he shared with other Renaissance intellectuals. Leonardo moved again in 1513, this

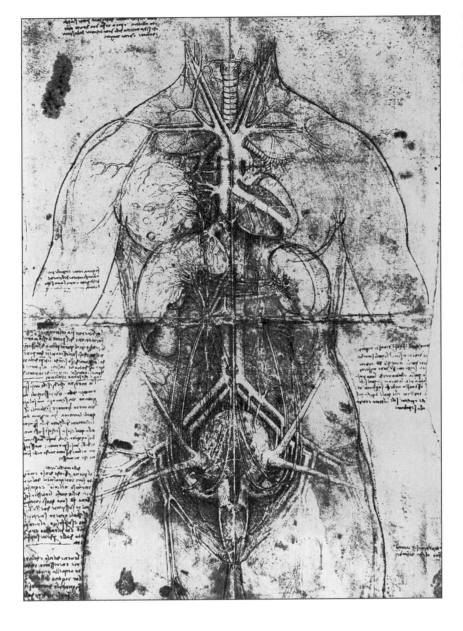

Many scholars believe that Leonardo da Vinci was the first to accurately portray human anatomy, as seen in this detailed drawing from one of his notebooks.

time going to Rome in the hope that Pope Leo X would offer him encouragement, a good working environment, and large commissions for artworks. Disappointed in this hope, three years later Leonardo and one of his pupils, Francesco Melzi, left Italy for Amboise, France. There Leonardo spent the final years of his life as the honored guest of King Francis I.

The Notes. Throughout his life Leonardo recorded his thoughts, observations, experiments, and designs in notes. In these notes he frequently mentions books that he had completed on various subjects, including anatomy, but the manuscripts of these books, if produced, have been lost. The only books published under Leonardo's name are *Treatise on Painting* and *Treatise on the Movement and Measurement*

Leonardo da Vinci

Decoding the Secrets of Trees

Leonardo studied plants as well as animals. In his early years he took great trouble to reproduce the outward forms of flowering plants accurately. Later he explored growth processes of plants. Experimenting on a gourd plant, he discovered that a single root, if well supplied with water, could nourish 60 fruits. Studying tree growth, Leonardo discovered that the rings in branches and trunks indicate how many years a tree has lived and whether each year was wet or dry. He originated the science of dendrochronology, or dating trees by their rings.

of Water, both of which were compiled from his notes by two of his followers after his death.

Masses of other notes remain—some 6,000 sheets of them, although scholars believe that many more sheets have been lost or destroyed. The surviving pages are laid out in great confusion. Leonardo made no attempt to organize them, and after his death they were disarranged, spread out among various owners, and even cut up and pasted together in new ways. They are like mixed-up pieces of a jigsaw puzzle, with a large part of the puzzle lost. As the notes have become known in recent times, they have been published and studied, but the full scope of Leonardo's genius is still unfolding. As recently as 1967 two large collections of his notes were found in Madrid, Spain. Others may await discovery.

Leonardo's notes have several distinctive features. One is his "mirror writing." Leonardo, who was left-handed, wrote normally on many occasions, but in his notes he wrote backward, from right to left, in a script that can easily be read when a mirror is held to the page. A more significant feature of the notes is Leonardo's creative but sometimes confusing way of expressing himself. He often presented his thoughts visually, in the form of drawings or designs. A single page, for example, might contain many examples of aspects of the study of curves—grass curling around a flower, an old man with curly hair, billowing clouds, rippling waves in a pool, geometrical exercises, and notes developing each image in detail. It is dangerous to dismiss any drawing as a mere doodle. Some of Leonardo's most interesting scientific concepts appear in the form of casual, small sketches.

Leonardo's habit of returning to subjects after long absences is another source of confusion. A note made in 1500 or 1510 may disagree with one made in 1490. Leonardo himself recognized that his ideas had grown and changed over the years. In 1508 he called his notes "a collection without order taken from many papers . . . blame not me because the subjects are many, and memory cannot retain them . . . because of the long intervals of time between one writing and another."

Scientific Philosophy and Methods. Leonardo saw no opposition between art and science. Both, he claimed, followed universal laws, and the key to both lay in the careful observation of the material world.

Leonardo believed that the natural world was created by God to obey laws. Human senses could perceive these laws, and human intelligence could understand them through mathematics and logic. Understanding entered the mind through the senses, especially vision—Leonardo called the eye "the window of the soul," through which a person could best see and appreciate "the infinite works of Nature." Humans could then interpret what they observed about the natural world by using mathematics, particularly geometry.

In Leonardo's view all phenomena in the physical world could be explained through a proper understanding of what he thought were the four basic powers of nature—force, energy, weight, and percussion.

(Leonardo included light and sound in this last category, which refers to a force striking a surface). Leonardo tried to apply this simplified view of nature to all fields of scientific research.

Interests and Achievements

Leonardo's achievements in science, as in art, depended mainly on three factors—his extremely sharp vision, his awareness of the geometrical relationships among the things he saw, and his creative power. These gifts led him to insights and inventions in several scientific fields.

Human Anatomy. Leonardo was interested in both the anatomy and the physiology, or functioning, of the human body. During the 1490s he investigated vision, attempting to discover how light affects the eye. He also studied the movement of the human body in activities such as sitting, running, digging, and pushing. He turned these simple movements into more complex studies of how the body behaves as a mechanical device (an arrangement of levers and weights) during work. These studies, in turn, led to studies of how levers, pulleys, and other devices allow people to transform human energy into the work of machines.

Later Leonardo turned his attention to the internal structure and function of the human body. Again, he regarded the body as a kind of machine that obeyed the mechanical laws of motion and force, with bones as levers and muscles as lines of force acting on them. Leonardo's anatomical studies required many dissections, and he wrote of how he disliked "passing the night hours in the company of corpses, quartered and flayed and horrible to behold."

Using the techniques of dissection and observation, Leonardo set out to demonstrate the anatomy of the human body. He placed great stress on the necessity for presenting the parts of the body from all sides. He stated that each part must be dissected specifically:

. . . you will need three [dissections] in order to have a complete knowledge of the veins and arteries, destroying all the rest with very great care; three others for a knowledge of the membranes, three for the nerves, muscles and ligaments, three for the bones and cartilages. . . . Three must also be devoted to the female body, and in this there is a great mystery by reason of the womb and its fetus.

Leonardo had hoped to reveal the whole figure and capacity of man in 15 drawings, and he was able to achieve most of his extensive program. He also used his skill of model making to study human anatomy. He discovered the true shape and size of the chambers in a human brain and came to appreciate the actions of the ventricles* of the heart.

Since his approach was primarily mechanical, Leonardo considered the bones of a skeleton as levers and their attached muscles as the lines of force acting on the levers. In the set of drawings now known as Anatomical Folio A, Leonardo systematically illustrated all the main bones and muscles of the body, often adding diagrams to show them in

Science in a Sacred Scene

One of Leonardo's most famous paintings is the Virgin of the Rocks, which depicts a meeting in the wilderness between the young Jesus and another youth. It reveals that the artist carefully observed and portrayed the natural world. The picture shows complex rock formations—layers of sandstone weathered in different degrees, volcanic lava that has cooled into columns, jagged rocks left by erosion—in accurate detail. Its botany is also accurate. No plants grow out of the volcanic rock, for example, because such rock is too hard for roots to take hold.

*ventricle muscular chamber of the heart

action. While dissecting the corpse of an old man in a hospital in Florence, Leonardo became interested in the digestive system and made drawings of the esophagus, stomach, liver, gallbladder, and intestines. He also made the first known illustration of the appendix.

Leonardo's studies of the heart and its action fill more notes than those he made of any other organ, possibly because he considered the heart the center of the body. In one of his experiments, aimed at finding out how the heart and blood vessels work, he made a glass model of the large blood vessel called the aorta. To this he attached a bag to represent the heart. Squeezing the bag forced water through the model, just as the heart pushes blood into the aorta. The water contained grass seeds as markers so that Leonardo could observe the direction of the blood flow through the valves in the aorta model. In this characteristic manner he labored to examine the smallest details of the body in action.

Comparative Anatomy. Humans were not the only subjects of Leonardo's anatomical work. Scattered through his notes are studies of oxen, pigs, dogs, monkeys, lions, and frogs. As a painter and sculptor, Leonardo was very much interested in the anatomy of horses.

His concern with the potential for human flight led to a close study of the anatomy of birds. He compared the arm of man and the wing of the bird and discovered that the muscles of a bird are more powerful than those of man because the bird's muscles and the fleshy parts of its breast increase the movement of its wings. Leonardo also compared the hands and feet of humans with those of bears, monkeys, and certain birds and concluded that all animals that walked on earth have many similar parts. Their muscles, nerves, and bones varied only in length and size but not in the mechanical actions they performed.

Botany. Leonardo's botanical studies developed along the same lines as his anatomical studies. His early studies consisted of representations of the external forms of flowering plants but that soon gave way to an interest in plant physiology. He conducted experiments on the movement of sap and compared it to the movement of blood in animals. Leonardo recognized that trees grew in thickness each year because of sap and was the first to count the age of trees in years by examining its annual growth rings.

Graceanna
LEWIS

1821–1912

ZOOLOGY

*naturalist one who studies objects in their natural settings

The American naturalist* Graceanna (also Grace Anna) Lewis made noteworthy contributions to zoology. One of her particular interests was ornithology, the study of birds, and she published a volume on the subject. She also produced a chart of the animal kingdom that reflected her ideas about the relationships among various kinds of organisms.

Lewis was born in Chester County, Pennsylvania, into a family of Quakers whose ancestors had migrated to America in the 1600s in search of religious freedom. Her Quaker upbringing, with its emphasis on justice and honesty, was a profound influence on her character. From an early age she witnessed examples of justice in action—her family home was a station on the Underground Railroad, the system that helped runaway slaves from the Southern states make their way to freedom. Later Lewis would become a supporter of the women's suffrage* movement.

At her Quaker-run school, Lewis studied chemistry, botany, and astronomy. Her interest in science grew, and she came to feel that scientific investigation was well suited to her Quaker beliefs. Her goal, as she expressed it, was to "discover God in nature." In the 1840s she supported herself by taking various teaching jobs. Later she supplemented her income by selling her family's farm. During the time Lewis was a teacher, she read a book about insects and was impressed with the way it portrayed the natural world in an orderly, organized way. She then became acquainted with a Pennsylvania ornithologist named Spencer Baird, who described the collections of Philadelphia's Academy of Natural Sciences—including 25,000 specimens of birds. Lewis moved to Philadelphia, where she could both study birds at the academy and become active in that city's Quaker community.

In 1868 Lewis published a book called *Natural History of Birds* that, unlike many natural history works of the time, contained information about birds' behavior as well as physical descriptions of various species. She intended it to be the first in a series of ten books, but it was less successful than she had hoped, and she could not afford to publish the remaining volumes. However, Lewis continued to conduct independent research and published the results of her work.

Zoologists had always been concerned with understanding how the various parts of the plant or animal kingdom are related to one another, and many had presented plans or charts to illustrate their ideas about those relationships. Lewis also prepared a Chart of the Animal Kingdom showing the various races of human beings as well as plant, animal, and bird species. She considered this and her other charts her most important scientific contribution. One of her charts was displayed at the 1876 Centennial Exhibition in Philadelphia. It reflected Lewis's familiarity with the fairly new notion of evolution* and her belief that nature was symmetrical, balanced, and orderly.

Lewis was undoubtedly a serious and well-informed scholar of natural history. The Academy of Natural Sciences elected her a member—only the ninth woman to receive that honor. After she retired from teaching in 1885, she continued to publish articles and to exchange letters with scientists at universities and museums. Lewis died in Media, Pennsylvania, where she had spent her final years living with her sister and compiling a history of her family.

Justus von Liebig was the foremost German chemist of the mid-1800s. During the first phase of his career, he helped establish the discipline of organic chemistry, the branch of chemistry that deals with carbon compounds, including those found in living organisms. During the second phase, he made notable contributions to the practical uses of chemistry in agriculture and industry. He added to his legacy a new method of teaching chemistry through laboratory practice.

Justus von
LIEBIG
1803–1873
CHEMISTRY

When Justus von Liebig went to study in Paris, he encountered a rigorous, quantitative, experimental approach to the study of chemistry, unlike any that he had experienced in Germany. When he returned to Germany to teach, he incorporated these methods into his own teaching style.

Life and Career. Liebig was born in Darmstadt, Germany. His father sold drugs and painting materials, making some of them himself in a small laboratory. As a child Liebig learned to perform chemical operations in that laboratory, and he carried out experiments described in chemistry books he borrowed from the town library. He continued experimenting at home until 1820, when he entered the University of Bonn.

Liebig received his doctoral degree in chemistry 1822 and spent the next two years studying in Paris, supported by a grant from the government. He then returned to Germany to teach chemistry at the University of Geissen, where he remained for 27 years. By 1851 Liebig had become famous in his field and had tired of teaching. He moved to the University of Munich, where he did not formally teach but permitted a few selected assistants and students to work in the research laboratory that the university had built for him. Liebig's later years were spent writing and arranging public lectures on scientific topics. He died in Munich at the age of 69.

Teaching Methods. At the beginning of his teaching career, Liebig launched an important new way of teaching chemistry. He was deeply grateful that he had been able to study under one of the leading French chemists in Paris, and he wanted to make similar opportunities available to a greater number of students. The University of Geissen allowed him to set up a research institution in vacant military barracks. Liebig had to buy most of the supplies and pay his assistants from his own pocket. Still, he created the first institution where students progressed systematically from elementary operations to independent research under the guidance of an established scientist and following a carefully planned program of exercises.

Liebig's institution was the model for a new style of scientific education and research. Soon it was copied throughout Germany, helping make that country a leader in chemistry in the late 1900s. The new method of teaching benefited Liebig as much as his students. By having his students carry out chemical analyses using his systematic method and the improved laboratory equipment he designed, Liebig could analyze more chemical compounds faster than ever before.

Organic Chemistry and Contributions to the Field. From 1829 until 1838, Liebig's research focused on organic chemistry. He was involved in an issue that occupied many chemists of his time: the effort to determine the number and arrangement of atoms in molecules of chemical compounds containing carbon and hydrogen, and to determine how those atoms changed as the compounds were altered or combined in laboratory processes. After developing an analytical method to answer these questions for carbon and hydrogen, he did the same for halogen.

Liebig's contribution to organic chemistry had more to do with method than with theory. Few of his theories were actually original, and none of them survived unchanged as the field matured. He did, however, discover and describe many compounds and reactions. Beyond that,

Liebig encouraged his fellow scientists to pursue chemistry in a systematic fashion. His analyses were reliable, his examination of problems was thorough, and his judgments were sound. His new way of training chemists was as important as the many excellent chemists he trained.

As much as anyone else, Liebig brought about the era of modern, large-scale research, in which the ability to organize people became as important as the ability to invent and carry out experiments. In 1832 he helped set new standards for chemistry when he founded the *Annals of Chemistry and Pharmacology*, which became one of the most important journals in the field. For a decade he was at the center of a rapidly growing and changing area of research, and he set in motion trends that continued long after he had moved to other fields of investigation.

Agricultural, Animal, and Industrial Chemistry. In 1828 Liebig began to consider how organic chemistry related to farming and to physiology*. The following year he published *Organic Chemistry in Its Application to Agriculture and Physiology*, an influential book in the history of scientific agriculture. In it, Liebig presented the results of experiments that showed that plants take carbon dioxide, and nitrogen contained in ammonia, and other necessary compounds from both the air and soil. Previously, farmers and scientists alike had thought that growing plants obtained all their nourishment from humus, decomposing plant and animal material in the soil. Liebig argued that farmers should apply minerals to fertilize their fields. The key to successful agriculture, he claimed, lay in analyzing the soil and then enriching it by supplying the minerals it lacked.

Liebig became deeply involved in the practical applications of his ideas to actual farming practices. Some of his students arranged to test his theories on farms in England, Europe, and the United States, and Liebig himself issued instructions for making chemical fertilizers. In 1862 he published the seventh edition of his 1840 book that contains a complete statement of his views, backed with extensive analyses and the results of many experiments. It was his last major scientific work.

During this second phase of his career, Liebig also investigated animal chemistry, with special attention to how nutrients provide the elements found in blood and how nutrients change within the body. He also contributed to industrial chemistry, although he did not participate as actively in this field as in agricultural chemistry. Many of his students founded or worked in Germany's new, large-scale chemical factories, and Liebig worked with some of them to develop or refine industrial processes, such as making chemical dyes.

*physiology science that deals with the functions of living organisms and their parts

The Swedish naturalist* Carl Linnaeus is perhaps most famous as the inventor of modern systems of classification for plants, animals, and minerals (taxonomy). Linnaeus also established binomial nomenclature—a system of naming plants and animals by using two names. His achievements in classifying, ranking, and naming organisms earned him deep respect and a lasting reputation. Because he

Carl
LINNAEUS
1707–1778
BOTANY, ZOOLOGY

Linnaeus was an enthusiastic and devoted teacher. He delighted in sending his students on expeditions to collect plants and other natural specimens from the far reaches of the world.

---

*naturalist one who studies objects in their natural settings

wrote many of his works in Latin, he is sometimes referred to by the Latin form of his name—Carolus Linnaeus; his original Swedish name was Carl von Linné.

Life and Career. Carl Linnaeus was born in Råshult, a small town in southern Sweden. His father, Nils, was a Lutheran pastor who had a great love of flowers and introduced the young Linnaeus to the mysteries of botany at a very early age. Consequently, by age eight he had acquired the nickname "the little botanist."

In 1716 Linnaeus was sent to school in the nearby city of Växjö, where he pursued his interest in botany and natural history. An average student, he spent much of his time studying and learning about plants. Linnaeus's father hoped that Carl would become a clergyman like himself, but Carl's interest in science drew him away from that career path. In 1727 the young Linnaeus entered the University of Lund to study medicine. At that time botany was part of the curriculum for medical students. Because the medical instruction at Lund was mediocre, Linnaeus made many trips to surrounding areas to study and collect plants on his own. After only a year at the university, he left Lund and enrolled at the University of Uppsala, near the city of Stockholm, the most prestigious university in Sweden.

Linnaeus again spent his time at Uppsala collecting and studying plants. He found the school's botanical garden especially interesting because of the many rare foreign plants it contained. He met Olof Celsius, a veteran botanist with whom he studied the plants of the surrounding region. Soon Linnaeus began to formulate the basic features of a new classification system for plants, which he based on plant sexuality. He classified flowering plants according to their stamens (male structures) and pistils (female structures).

In 1735 Linnaeus enrolled at the University of Harderwijk in Holland, where he rapidly received a degree in medicine. He also met some of Europe's best-known botanists and gained wealthy patrons. Linnaeus's reputation as a botanist was firmly established after he published much of his research while still in Holland. The most important of these was *Systema naturae* (The System of Nature), which contains a detailed explanation of his system of classification for plants, animals, and minerals.

Returning to Sweden in 1738, Linnaeus worked as a physician in Stockholm and became one of the founders of the Swedish Academy of Science. Three years later he accepted a position as professor of medicine at the University of Uppsala, and the following year he became professor of botany at that school. In 1747 Linnaeus was appointed official physician to the royal court, and he was granted a title of nobility as Carl von Linné 15 years later. Linnaeus remained at Uppsala for the rest of his life, but his fame as a botanist spread throughout the world. Forced to retire from teaching in 1774 because of illness, he died of a stroke four years later.

Work and Accomplishments. A successful teacher, Linnaeus gave lectures filled with humor and unusual ideas. The excursions he led to collect plants were popular among his students. Many foreign students came to Sweden to study with Linnaeus, and they helped spread his ideas. His students also enriched Linnaeus's studies by sending him specimens that they collected during their own travels in many parts of the world. He also maintained contact with many botanists and naturalists, sharing his ideas with them. Like his students, these scholars sent Linnaeus specimens from around the globe, helping him in his work.

Linnaeus's mission during his years at Uppsala was to complete his reform of botany. Although his early work had established the basic principles, they still had to be developed and put into practice. In 1751 he published his most influential work, *Philosophia botanica* (Philosophy of Botany), which dealt with the theory of botany. The work also discussed the laws and rules that a botanist must follow to describe and name plants correctly and to organize them into their proper categories.

Linnaeus also struggled with the enormous goal of cataloging all the world's plant and animal species and giving each its correct place in his system of classification. This was especially important since a steady stream of new and unknown plants was arriving in Europe in the 1700s from Africa, Asia, and the Americas. Linnaeus began with his native Sweden, publishing *Flora suecica* (Swedish Plants) and *Fauna suecica* (Swedish Animals) in 1745 and 1747. By 1753 he had already cataloged about 8,000 plant species from around the world and described them in *Species plantarum* (Plant Species). He also continued to update and revise his *Systema naturae,* which became the bible of natural history.

Linnaeus catalogued every plant and animal specimen he came across, and he sorted and classified them into groups and subgroups. His need for order contributed to another major accomplishment—fixed rules regarding the distinction between genus* and species and a system of binomial nomenclature based on these two classifications.

*genus category of biological classification; class, kind, or group of organisms that share common characteristics; *pl.* genera

Although Linnaeus was not the first to use a two-name system for classifying organisms, systems developed before his time had not been applied uniformly. For instance, the name of a particular organism might differ from one source to another, resulting in confusion. Linnaeus's system, on the other hand, was simple, uniform, and easy to use. According to his system of binomial nomenclature, which he first introduced in 1747, every plant or animal received two names (in Latin or Greek)—one for the genus and the other for the species.

The consistent use of this system made it easy for scientists to recognize a particular plant or animal, no matter what common name it might have. For example, *Canis familiaris* is the scientific name for dog, while *Canis lupus* is the name for wolf. Linnaeus recognized three other levels of scientific classification—order, class, and kingdom. (Later scientists added two more—family and phylum.) Each of these could be divided into subgroups, providing a very specific system by which to classify all organisms.

Linnaeus's classification system worked more easily for plants than for animals and minerals. Nevertheless, his work marked a considerable advance over earlier classifications. The first to recognize whales as mammals, he also noted the link between man and the apes. He also made important contributions to paleontology* and historical geology, describing many fossils and accurately classifying various fossil species.

His work was accepted by scientists throughout the world, and his ideas influenced generations of future biologists. Although modern scientists have devised more accurate systems of classification, Linnaeus's accomplishments laid the foundation for their work.

Joseph LISTER
1827–1912
SURGERY

The English surgeon Joseph Lister developed antiseptic procedures that dramatically reduced the likelihood of infection during and after surgery. Before the advent of Lister's antiseptic practices, an alarmingly high percentage of hospital patients died from infection even when the surgery itself was successful. Because of Lister's efforts, surgery was transformed from a frightening and risky experience to one that held the strong probability of recovery and renewed health. At the time, however, his ideas were greeted with skepticism, and it was many years before they were universally adopted.

Early Life and Career
Born in Upton in Essex County, Lister grew up in a prosperous London household with parents who supported and encouraged his efforts and ambitions. His father was an artist, a Latin scholar, and an accomplished mathematician, despite having had little formal education. When Lister was five years old, his father was elected to the Royal Society of London for inventing a new type of microscope lens. The son was destined to surpass his father's scientific accomplishments.

Education and Early Work. Lister attended private schools, including a Quaker school where he studied natural science, mathematics, and modern languages. When required to write formal essays, he chose such topics as chemistry and osteology (study of the bones), indicating an early interest in a medical career. His father encouraged his interests by introducing him to microscopy and natural history* at home. The young Lister also dissected animals and reconstructed their skeletons, and declared his intention to become a surgeon. After graduating from secondary school, he enrolled at University College of London, which had a modern hospital and an outstanding medical faculty. He earned his bachelor's degree in three years, and shortly thereafter began to study medicine but contracted smallpox. Lister tried to return to school too soon and suffered a bout of depression that forced him to leave college for an extended period. When he recovered, he returned to school and immersed himself in his studies. He received his M.D. at age 25 and joined the Royal College of Surgeons.

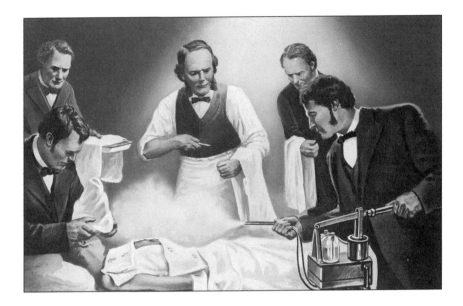

Lister (third from right) is seen here directing the use of carbolic acid spray before an "anti-septic" surgical operation. He believed that the spray would kill airborne germs in the operating room and prevent infection. The spray was eventually proven ineffective, but Lister developed other methods to ensure the prevention of infection during surgeries.

In his later years at medical school, Lister undertook his first investigations into histology, the study of tissues. In one study on the eye, he confirmed that the iris is comprised of involuntary muscle and showed that two muscles control the size of the pupil. Another report dealt with involuntary muscles of the scalp. His first love was still surgery, and in 1846 he attended Britain's first major surgery performed when the patient was under ether* anesthesia.

In 1853, at the urging of one of his professors, Lister traveled to the University of Edinburgh to study under the eminent surgeon James Syme. He lived in Edinburgh for the next seven years. During this time he developed a close relationship with Syme, who appointed Lister house surgeon and permitted him to assist in Syme's own practice. Two years after arriving in Edinburgh, Lister became engaged to Syme's eldest daughter, whom he married the following year.

*ether light, volatile liquid used mainly as solvent and anesthetic

Researches in Scotland. About this time Lister began to give lectures in surgery and surgical pathology* at Edinburgh's Royal Infirmary. Named assistant surgeon in 1854, he conducted public surgeries that students could observe and intensified his studies of inflammation that were a first step to his antiseptic procedures. In papers he read to the Royal Society of London, Lister described the vascular (blood vessel) and tissue changes in the early stages of inflammation. He noted that inflammation was characterized by blood clotting and investigated that phenomenon as well. His work resulted in election to the Royal Society at the early age of 33, and helped him secure the professorship of surgery at the University of Glasgow the same year. In 1861 he was elected to take charge of the surgical wards at Glasgow's Royal Infirmary, where he studied the use of anesthesia and invented a wide range of surgical devices and procedures.

Although Lister loved his profession, he was appalled by the high rate of mortality due to infections such as septicemia, pyemia, and gan-

*pathology study of diseases and their effects on organisms

grene. About 40 percent of amputation patients died from these infections, and many procedures, such as chest or brain surgery, were almost never performed because of the risk of deadly infection. When Lister took charge of the infirmary, his wards were much healthier than those in most other hospitals because of his insistence on cleanliness, good air circulation, and lack of crowding. Still he found the conditions unacceptably unhealthy. It was at this time that he began to claim that wound suppuration (formation of pus) was a form of tissue decomposition. The accepted view was that when oxygen combined with moist tissue, it caused a kind of combustion that led to suppuration. Lister, however, doubted this was true. He showed that applying carbolic acid (phenol) to a wound, even in the presence of oxygen, could stop an infection such as gangrene. This was the first step to his antiseptic theory.

Antiseptic Theory and Practice

In 1865 a chemistry professor at the University of Glasgow told Lister of the work done by Louis PASTEUR on tissue decomposition. Pasteur had claimed that some microorganisms* carried in the air could cause decomposition and that these organisms could be destroyed by various means, such as heat and filtration. He also showed that bodily fluids, such as blood and urine, would not decompose if collected and stored under sterile conditions. This gave Lister the key to understanding wound sepsis* and enabled him to eliminate hospital infection.

Early Success and Resistance. Lister learned that the city of Carlisle treated its sewage with carbolic acid, and that this destroyed a type of bacteria that had infected cattle grazing in nearby fields. He began experimenting with the substance and developed a solution of carbolic acid dissolved in olive oil or linseed oil. When treating patients with compound fractures, Lister cleansed their wounds with the carbolic acid solution and protected the wounds from airborne germs by covering them with a dressing soaked in the acid. He also covered the site with a sheet of molded tin to prevent the solution from evaporating. He changed the dressings daily, using the solution to wash the crust of blood that formed over the wounds. His results were remarkable; 9 out of 11 patients recovered, a survival rate much higher than normal. He refined his procedure by developing an antiseptic "curtain" of rags soaked in linseed oil (four parts) and carbolic acid (one part) that enabled him to prevent infection from developing while he drained open abscesses (wounds with pus). Lister published his results in the prestigious medical journal *The Lancet*, noting that wounds treated with his antiseptic procedures healed without infection.

Despite Lister's successes (his ward was entirely free from sepsis for nearly a year), many fellow surgeons expressed doubts about these methods. They criticized Lister's constant updating of his procedures and complained that they took too much time and trouble to develop. Many dismissed the idea that infection was due to germs carried in the air. Other surgeons tried to perform operations without spending the

*microorganism tiny living thing that generally can be seen clearly only through a microscope

*sepsis toxic condition resulting from the spread of infectious bacteria

Lister the Inventor

In addition to antiseptic procedures, Lister invented several surgical procedures and medical devices still in use. He was the first to perform radical mastectomy for breast cancer and he pioneered the use of wires and steel pegs to join fractured bones that had separated completely. Among the tools he devised were a needle for silver-wire sutures, a screw clamp to close off blood flow to the aorta (a large artery in the chest), and various types of dressings and drains for removing pus from wounds. The "hot box" that he invented to sterilize instruments evolved into today's autoclave, an apparatus that is an indispensable part of modern surgical practice.

time and effort to follow the procedures correctly, with fatal results for their patients. One of Lister's opponents even claimed that Lister had stolen the ideas of a French surgeon who had described the use of carbolic acid for surgery some years earlier. This attack was printed in *The Lancet*, but in a letter to the journal, Lister denied that he ever claimed to be the first to use carbolic acid in surgery. He also pointed out that his procedures were very different from those developed in France, which he noted had showed no appreciable results.

Growing Support and Final Success. Initial resistance gave way to increasing support as more and more surgeons began to experiment with Lister's methods. His techniques were supported enthusiastically in Europe, particularly in Germany. In 1868 Lister performed experiments in which he showed that urine, when exposed to air, decomposes rapidly and becomes infested with microorganisms, convincing many skeptics that airborne germs were a source of infection. His efforts occurred around the same time that Pasteur's germ theory of disease gained increasing acceptance.

At age 42, Lister was named professor of clinical surgery at the University of Edinburgh after his mentor Syme died of a stroke. The next eight years were happy and triumphant ones, as Lister established a prosperous medical practice and continued to refine his antiseptic techniques. He had some false starts, including the development of a carbolic acid spray that he pumped into the air during surgery. He believed this would kill the airborne germs in the room, but it proved ineffective and led to some troublesome side effects such as carbolic acid poisoning in some cases. He also had great successes and invented a number of novel devices to make his methods more effective. One of these was a "hot box" that reached temperatures up to 300°F in which he sterilized surgical instruments.

As Lister's procedures were adopted in more and more countries, he gained worldwide recognition. At age 50 he became professor of surgery at King's College in London, where he eventually convinced many London physicians of the merits of his ideas. Lister remained active in developing refinements to antiseptic procedures, experimenting with substances other than carbolic acid, which he was concerned might hinder the body's natural healing processes. In 1893, when his wife of 40 years died, he almost gave up his private practice and laboratory work and made few social engagements. However, he kept his commitments to the college and continued to promote and defend his work.

Lister received many awards and honors, including membership in 60 scientific and medical societies around the world and the presidency of London's Royal Society. England's Queen Victoria gave him the title of baronet, and later baron, and Lister served as Sergeant Surgeon to Victoria and her successor, King Edward VII. Lister suffered a stroke at age 76 from which he partially recovered, but four years later he went into a decline that ended in his death at age 85. By this time his procedures were widely accepted and practiced by surgeons worldwide. As the man who made surgery safe, he left behind a legacy as one of the most influential figures in modern medicine.

François MAGENDIE

1783–1855

PHYSIOLOGY, MEDICINE

A firm believer in facts rather than speculation, Magendie, in his first published scientific article, wrote, "[The] majority of physiological facts must be verified by new experiments and this is the only means of bringing the physics of living bodies out of the state of imperfection in which it lies at present."

*physiology science that deals with the functions of living organisms and their parts

*vivisection practice of dissecting or cutting into the body of a living animal for the purpose of scientific investigation

A physician and a professor of medicine, François Magendie's most notable contributions were in physiology*. By insisting that facts—such as the results of his experiments on animals—were more important than unproved theories or philosophical notions, Magendie helped place physiology on a foundation based on practical experimentation and shaped the way it was taught to generations of French scientists. His approach became known as "medical positivism." Landmarks in his research include the demonstration of the differential functions of the spinal nerves and the discovery of anaphylaxis, a strong reaction in a body that has absorbed proteins from another animal.

Background and Career. Magendie was born in Bordeaux, France. His father admired the French philosopher Jean-Jacques Rousseau and raised his children according to Rousseau's ideals, giving them personal freedom and paying little attention to the instruction they received. As a result, Magendie reached the age of ten without ever attending school or learning to read or write. By that time his family had moved to Paris, and Magendie, at his own request, entered elementary school. He made rapid progress and at age 14 won a national essay contest.

In 1799 Magendie began working as an assistant to an anatomist at a Paris hospital, and four years later he became a medical student at the Hôpital Saint-Louis in Paris. He received his medical degree in 1808 and a year later, in his first published article, wrote that physiological facts must be verified by new experiments. Throughout his career Magendie acted on this belief, refusing to engage in speculation and relying on facts, usually through vivisection*. Later he visited Great Britain and demonstrated some of his experiments on live animals, provoking an antivivisection campaign there.

For several years early in his career, Magendie taught anatomy and surgery at a medical school in Paris. In 1813 he resigned to practice as a physician and teach private courses in physiology. These courses became quite successful, and Magendie wrote a textbook called *Précis Élémentaire de physiologie* (Introduction to Basic Physiology), which was later translated into German and English. It had great influence on physicians and biologists until the mid-1800s. In 1821 Magendie founded the *Journal de physiologie expérimentale* (Journal of Experimental Physiology), the first scientific periodical devoted to the subject. He also instilled his experimental approach into his students, including Claude BERNARD, who became a noted physiologist in his own right.

In 1830 Magendie became the director of a hospital department, and throughout that decade he delivered influential lectures on the physical phenomena of life. He retired from both duties in the mid-1840s and moved to his country estate in Sannois. There he began to experiment on plant physiology with the goal of improving agriculture, but he made no notable contributions in this area before his death.

Experimental Physiology. Between 1813 and 1821 Magendie made a great many discoveries in almost all the fields of research then included in the science of physiology. He demonstrated the mechanics of vomiting, experimented on nutrition and proved that mammals need protein and that the lack of vitamins can produce disease, studied the role of pancreatic* juice in digestion, and proved that the liver plays a key role in removing harmful substances from the body. Magendie also showed that the body absorbs liquids through the walls of blood vessels. He demonstrated this in a classic experiment using a dog. He prepared the animal so that one of its legs was connected to its body by a single blood vessel. He then injected a toxin into the leg, poisoning the dog.

Magendie's most noteworthy achievement in physiology concerned the spinal nerves. A Scottish anatomist named Charles Bell had claimed that one set of spinal nerves controls movement and another set controls the senses. Without any detailed knowledge of Bell's work, Magendie conducted his own experiments and his results, published in 1822, were a clear statement and proof of what Bell had earlier suggested. This basic physiological principle of the differential action of the spinal nerves, known as the Bell-Magendie law, was one of the foundations of neurophysiology, the study of how the nervous system operates.

Another important discovery was the phenomenon that later came to be called anaphylaxis. Magendie discovered that rabbits could tolerate a single injection of egg white, but that a second injection killed them. This was a stepping-stone in the study of the toxic effects of animal proteins on other animals.

Contributions to Medicine. Because Magendie was a doctor and a scientist, his physiological researches had medical significance. One of his earliest series of experiments was influential in the beginning of modern pharmacology*. Magendie and a colleague studied the effects that poisonous plants had on animals. Magendie believed that the toxic or medical action of natural drugs depended on the active chemicals they contain, and he discovered some of these active chemicals, including strychnine (a bitter substance that is used both as a poison and as a stimulant). Magendie pioneered the medical use of such chemicals and favored their use over natural or botanical drugs. He had great confidence in the results of his pharmacological experiments on animals. If animal experiments showed a substance to be harmless, he did not hesitate to test it on himself.

In Magendie's day, medicine was taught by discussing cases at the patients' bedsides. When he became a professor of medicine in 1831, he substituted these discussions with demonstrations of his experimental method. He also focused on the medical concerns of his day, such as the deadly disease cholera. When an epidemic of this disease broke out in Paris, Magendie fought it courageously and developed treatments for its

A Literary Portrait

Magendie liked to think of himself as a collector of facts. He told his student and disciple Claude Bernard, "I compare myself to a ragpicker: with my spiked stick in my hand and my basket on my back, I traverse the field of science and gather what I find." Honoré de Balzac, one of the best-known French authors of the 1800s, knew of Magendie's preference for facts over theories. In his 1831 novel *La Peau de chagrin* (The Wild Ass's Skin), Balzac described a doctor— thinly disguised under the name "Maugredie," who "believed only in the scalpel" and "claimed that the best medical system was to have none at all and to stick to the facts."

pancreatic of or relating to the pancreas, the gland that produces the juices (chemicals) that enable the body to digest and absorb fats

pharmacology science that deals with the preparation, uses, and effects of drugs

*quarantine to isolate someone who suffers from or has been exposed to a contagious disease, in the hope of limiting the spread of the disease

symptoms. However, he mistakenly concluded that the disease was not contagious, and he opposed the practice of quarantining* people with cholera, yellow fever, or other diseases that he also believed were not contagious. This error had serious consequences for Magendie's career, especially after his appointment to head a committee on public health. It was not until Pasteur's germ theory of disease became widely accepted in the 1870s that contagion was fully accepted.

The many medical advances based on Magendie's physiological work far outweigh this error, however. His work greatly influenced the intellectual development of many scholars of the time. Magendie was honored by membership in many scientific societies, including the Académie des Sciences in Paris.

Marcello
MALPIGHI
1628–1694

MEDICINE, ANATOMY

The Italian physician and biologist Marcello Malpighi, considered one of the founders of the science of plant anatomy, made many valuable observations on the structures of animals and plants. Using different types of lighting and degrees of magnification, he developed techniques in microscopic observation that revolutionized the field of anatomy. Malpighi also pioneered the study of abnormal tissues as a tool to gather an understanding of normal tissues by comparing the two.

Early Life and Career. Born in Crevalcore, Italy, Malpighi entered the University of Bologna in 1646. On the advice of his tutor, the philosopher Francesco Natali, he began to study medicine. He attended various private schools in pursuit of his medical education and was one of a select group of students allowed to attend dissections and vivisections*.

*vivisection practice of dissecting or cutting into the body of a living animal for the purpose of scientific investigation

Malpighi received doctoral degrees in both medicine and philosophy in 1653. Three years later he began teaching as a lecturer in logic at the University of Bologna. At the end of the first year, however, he accepted a position as professor of medicine at the University of Pisa. The three years that Malpighi spent in Pisa were crucial to the formation of his scientific pursuits. Influenced by the mathematician and naturalist* Giovanni BORELLI and the ideas of the astronomer Galileo Galilei, he began to question many of the traditional medical and scientific teachings at the university.

*naturalist one who studies objects in their natural settings

In 1659 Malpighi left Pisa and returned to Bologna to teach medicine and continue his research. At that time Malpighi made one of the major discoveries in the history of medicine. While studying frogs under a microscope, he identified a network of tiny tubes in the lungs that connected the arteries and veins. Malpighi published his findings in *De pulmonibus* (On the Lung), one of his most important works. His discovery not only added to current knowledge of the lungs but also confirmed the theory first proposed by the English anatomist William HARVEY concerning the circulation of blood through the body.

Further Discoveries. Malpighi's discoveries and growing fame led to jealousy on the part of many of his colleagues. Frustrated at the increasingly hostile environment at Bologna, he left there in 1662 and took a position as professor of medicine at the University of Messina, Sicily. There he enthusiastically continued his researches on anatomical structures, including studies of various marine animals.

Some of his most important studies during this period focused on the nervous system and the blood. Malpighi discovered that the central nervous system and the nerves are composed of the same type of fibers. He pictured these fibers as long, fine channels filled with a liquid—the nerve fluid—produced by glands in the brain. From his observations, Malpighi described the entire mechanism of the central nervous system, from the brain to the outer or peripheral nerve endings.

In his study of blood, Malpighi discovered that it contains tiny red cells, known today as red blood corpuscles. The first to see these cells, Malpighi also correctly attributed the red color of blood to them. Another of his discoveries at Bologna involved the tongue and the sense of taste. While closely examining the surface of the tongue, he noticed that it has many small bumps. He speculated that these were sensory receptors that were stimulated by particles in saliva and produced the various sensations of taste. These receptors became known as the taste buds.

Later Life and Career. Malpighi returned to Bologna in 1667 and spent most of his remaining career there, continuing to make important discoveries. He discovered microscopic subdivisions in the liver, spleen, kidneys, and other organs and concluded that all organs are composed of tiny glands that separate or mix different types of bodily fluids.

Around this time Malpighi also began to study plants. He concluded that plants have anatomical structures similar to those of animals. He published his findings in a work titled *Anatome plantarum* (Anatomy of Plants), which earned him acclaim as one of the founders of plant anatomy.

Malpighi also became interested in animal embryology*. He studied the development of chickens in eggs and observed the stages through which a silkworm is formed. He helped to clarify the structural development of higher life-forms. In later studies Malpighi observed abnormal tissues, such as warts. His investigation of the breakdown of these tissues showed the effect of such disturbances on the organism as a whole.

In his final years Malpighi struggled with declining health and personal problems. Many of his colleagues still refused to accept his work, and the climax to this opposition came in 1684, when his home was burned and all his books, manuscripts, and other possessions were destroyed. In 1691 Pope Innocent XII invited Malpighi to Rome to become his personal physician. Malpighi died there three years later.

*embryology branch of biology that deals with embryos, organisms from the first division of the fertilized egg through the early stages of development before birth or hatching

Through his plant breeding experiments, Johann Gregor Mendel discovered laws or rules of heredity that came to form the basis of the science of genetics*. Despite its revolutionary nature, Mendel's work remained largely unknown at the time and went unrecognized by the scientific community. It would be more than 30 years before three scientists independently and simultaneously rediscovered Mendel's writings.

Johann Gregor
MENDEL

1822–1884

GENETICS, METEOROLOGY

Mendel's contemporaries were largely ignorant of his work and its implications for future scientific discoveries. Because he failed to receive recognition for his work, he stopped publishing his findings.

*genetics branch of biology that deals with heredity

*theological referring to theology, the study of religion

*pomology scientific study and cultivation of fruit

*viniculture cultivation of grapes

*hybridization process of creating a hybrid, an offspring produced by crossing two or more varieties or species of plants or animals

Life and Career

Family background and personal temperament played important roles in shaping the path Mendel took. Coming from a family of farmers and gardeners, he acquired an early knowledge of and appreciation for horticulture.

Early Life and Career. Mendel was born in Heinzendorf, Austria, in the present-day Czech Republic. His father was a farmer, his mother's father a local gardener, and many of his ancestors were professional gardeners. In addition, the director of his primary school taught natural sciences and encouraged the cultivation of fruit trees at the school. An exceptional student, Mendel was sent to nearby secondary schools to continue his education. When he was 16, however, financial difficulties in the family forced him to become a tutor to earn a living. The strain of this forced Mendel to interrupt his studies for several months for health reasons.

In 1840, after he recovered he prepared to enter the University of Olmütz for higher studies, but his failure to find private pupils renewed his psychological stress and he once again fell ill. This time he spent a year at home, but he still refused to give up his studies. He accepted his sister's offer of part of her dowry so he could return to school, and he subsequently completed the university's two-year course in philosophy. His physics teacher at Olmütz recommended that Mendel be admitted to the Augustinian monastery in the town of Brno (in the present-day Czech Republic) so he could continue his studies there.

Although Mendel felt no religious calling, the monastery proved to be an ideal place for his academic work. As a monk he had no financial worries, and the monastery itself was a center of scientific activity. The abbot, a board member of the Moravian Agricultural Society, had established a tradition of experimenting with plants in the monastery's garden. The monk in charge of the garden when Mendel entered the monastery was studying plant variation, heredity, and transformation. He gave Mendel his first introduction to these topics and placed him in charge of the garden. In addition to his scientific work and his theological* studies at the monastery, Mendel also attended courses in agriculture, pomology*, and viniculture* at the local Philosophical Institute. There he learned about artificial pollination and hybridization* as means of breeding and improving plants.

Later Life and Career. After his theological studies, Mendel was named chaplain to the local parish and among his duties was visiting the sick in the local hospital. However, he was unable to bear the sight of so much suffering, and he once again suffered depression bordering on illness. The abbot relieved him of the duty and sent him as a substitute teacher to a grammar school. Mendel so excelled at teaching that the headmaster of the school recommended that he take the university exam for natural science teachers. Although he passed parts of the test, Mendel failed others due to his lack of a university education. The abbot then sent him to the University of Vienna to work on his weak areas so he could try to take the exam again.

At Vienna, Mendel took courses in experimental physics, botany, paleontology*, zoology, chemistry, and plant physiology*. He also took a course on organizing botanical experiments. One of his professors at Vienna, Franz Unger, supported ideas of evolution* and believed that the great variety in cultured plants was because of sexual reproduction. Unger argued that new plant forms arose from different combinations of "elements" in the plant cell, but he could not prove the existence of these elements. During this time Mendel discovered a book that described breeding experiments using peas, which later became the subject of his own historic research.

When he retuned to Brno, Mendel was named substitute teacher of physics and natural history* at the town's technical school, a job at which he excelled. However, when he went to retake the natural sciences teaching exam he broke down during the written portion of the test and withdrew from the examination process. Once again he became very ill, and afterwards attempted no more academic degrees. After his return to Brno, Mendel had also begun experimenting with peas. This work, which he began in 1856, took up most of his time during the next seven years.

In 1868, at the age of 46, Mendel was named abbot of the monastery. He also became active in the Agricultural Society, the Horticultural Society, and the Society of Apiculturists (Beekeepers). Mendel also supported liberal political views, backing the Liberal Party in the elections of 1871. When the liberals won, though, they passed a law requiring a large contribution by the monastery to the religious fund. Mendel refused to pay the tax, however, leading to a dispute with the government and ultimately the seizure of monastery lands. The long battle took its toll on Mendel, who died in 1884 of complications from chronic diseases of the kidney and heart. No one at his funeral was aware that a scientific giant was being buried.

Scientific Accomplishments

Mendel's name is forever linked to his work on heredity, but he was also a pioneer in the field of meteorology. In both fields he drew on his powers of observation and statistical analysis of the data he collected.

Meteorology. At the age of 41, Mendel published his first paper in meteorology. He used statistical methods to compare weather data from Brno during a 15-year period. He later expanded this work to include data from the surrounding region of Moravia. In 1877 he helped produce the first weather forecasts for farmers in central Europe. He also studied unusual storm phenomena and observed sunspots, which he correctly believed had some bearing on the weather. An example of his scientific approach to meteorology was his description and analysis of a tornado he witnessed at Brno. He was the first to suggest that tornadoes were vortices (whirlpools) of air caused when

*paleontology study of extinct or prehistoric life, usually through the examination of fossils

*physiology science that deals with the functions of living organisms and their parts

*evolution historical development of a biological group such as a species

*natural history systematic study of animals and plants, especially in their natural settings

No Meeting of the Minds

Mendel was familiar with *On the Origin of Species,* the book in which Darwin set forth his theory of evolution by natural selection. Notes in his copy of the book show that Mendel accepted the theory and agreed with Darwin that one cannot draw sharp lines between species. For his part, Darwin searched in vain for the causes of variations that would provide support for his theories. Although Darwin could have had access to Mendel's work, which was reprinted in a book with which Darwin was familiar, he, like the other leading scientists of his day, either never read the material or did not understand its meaning and significance.

conflicting air currents came together. Like his hybridization experiments, this finding too was largely overlooked for many years because Mendel was living and working in a monastery and was outside the more professional scientific circles.

Plant Hybridization. Mendel's experiments on plants were based on his belief that heredity is passed on through "factors" or "elements" such as those described by Professor Unger. Mendel stated that each parent contributes one of a pair of factors to its offspring, and that each factor corresponds to a hereditary trait. Thus, one parent might contribute a factor that produces round seeds while the other contributes a factor that produces angular seeds. The first generation of hybrids produced by breeding are all alike; all have one parental trait (such as round seeds) in its unchanged form. He called such traits "dominant." The other trait in the pair (angular seeds), which only appears in the next generation, he called "recessive." Mendel felt that these factors are transmitted through the reproductive cells of the plant, so that every pollen cell and every egg cell contains a factor that produces one or the other trait in each pair.

Mendel was not the first to study heredity, but he was the first to express his results in a formal manner and to subject them to statistical analysis. An example of this is the algebraic notation he used to describe his findings. He expressed each dominant trait as a capital letter and the matching recessive trait as a lowercase letter. For example, the trait for round seeds was A and for angular seeds it was a. Mendel found that each offspring contained some mixture of both traits. Thus, a hybrid could either be AA (having only the factors that produced the dominant trait), aa (having only the factors that produced the recessive trait), or Aa or aA (having both factors). Whenever the dominant factor occurred—$AA, Aa,$ or aA—the offspring showed the dominant trait. Whenever only the recessive factor occurred—aa—the recessive trait appeared. He extended this statistical analysis to cover seven different pairs of traits, which yielded 128 different possible combinations of factors.

To obtain his results, Mendel bred and tested some 28,000 pea plants, continually crossing hybrids with constant dominant and recessive traits. He chose peas based on his study of the literature as well as from careful experiments he performed before beginning his major research program. He also chose only very pure varieties of plants that differed in only a few, well-defined characteristics. In this manner he could be sure of the accuracy of his results. Mendel found that his hybrid plants produced egg and pollen cells containing all the possible combinations of factors found in the parent plants. He also extended his findings to plants other than peas, concluding that the diversity in the color of garden flowers was also due to the laws of heredity that he had uncovered. During the course of his work, he became convinced that, through hybridization, a species can change dramatically and even change into different species.

In 1865 Mendel presented his paper to a meeting of the Moravian Natural Sciences Society and sent it in manuscript form to more than 130 scientific institutions around the world. He even corresponded with several authorities on hybridization. No one, however, grasped the significance of his work. Mendel followed up his work on peas with studies of other plants and of bees. His work received little or no recognition or encouragement although reports of his experimental results did make their way into the literature of plant hybridization. He eventually stopped publishing the results of his experiments.

Rediscovery of Mendel. In 1900 three researchers, all of them working independently on hybridization experiments, discovered in the literature that Mendel had presented important studies more than 30 years earlier. The researchers were Hugo de Vries, Carl Correns, and Erich von Tschermak, who were each working separately in Amsterdam, Tübingen, and Vienna.

Their rediscovery of Mendel's work had a profound influence on the study of hybridization and heredity. Initially it seemed to conflict with the Darwinian theory of evolution, but it took scientists two decades before they recognized that Mendel's theory provided an explanation of the main source of variability in plants and animals, which is the mechanism on which natural selection* operates. Instead of merely speculating on how heredity worked, scientists were now able to subject it to mathematical and experimental analysis. This led to the establishment of a recognizable field of genetics, which has linked the study of heredity to mathematics and later, chemistry. Mendel's ideas, as they were developed in the years immediately after their rediscovery, became an essential part of experimental biology and critical for the practices of plant and animal breeding.

*natural selection theory that within a given species, individuals with characteristics best adapted to the environment survive and successfully produce more offspring that other individuals, resulting in changes in the species over time

Franz Anton
MESMER
1734–1815
MEDICINE, HYPNOSIS

Franz Anton Mesmer is known for his practice of mesmerism, in which he put patients into a trancelike state to cure their illness. Although mesmerism was later shown to have no clear scientific basis or curative value, it did lead to the development of hypnosis as a tool in medicine and psychoanalysis*.

Mesmer, one of nine children of an Austrian forester in Iznang, Germany, studied law before switching to medicine. He began his career as a member of the highly regarded faculty at the University of Vienna medical school. His doctoral thesis concerned the theory of animal magnetism, in which he claimed that all living beings contained fluids that moved in harmony with the movements of the planets. Illness was said to be a result of imbalances in the body's fluids, and Mesmer began using magnets to restore the balance of fluids within his patients' bodies. He later gave up magnets in favor of other devices such as a "tub" that stored fluid and transmitted it through iron bars placed on diseased areas of the patient. Using his technique, Mesmer apparently achieved some marvelous cures, particularly in a young

*psychoanalysis method of treating emotional disorders in which the patient is encouraged to talk freely about personal experiences

woman suffering from hysteria. However, Mesmer's theatrics offended Vienna's mainstream physicians, and he left for Paris under a cloud of suspicion and hostility.

In Paris, Mesmer attracted many followers and adopted exotic practices such as running his hands over the bodies of his patients and transmitting fluid through ropes, trees, and other objects. These demonstrations captured the imagination of the public but again angered prominent French physicians and scientists, who considered Mesmer a fraud. In 1784 a royal commission set up to investigate mesmerism found that Mesmer's magical fluid did not exist and that his treatments were worthless. This dealt a harsh blow to supporters of mesmerism, who then split into different camps that developed their own techniques.

Mesmer himself traveled throughout Europe for a time, until he finally settled in Switzerland, where he spent most of the last 30 years of his life in seclusion. He died in 1815 in Meersburg, Germany. Although mesmerism was based on flawed ideas, it appeared to have some effect on nervous disorders, which may have been due to the close bond developed between the patient and the doctor. One group of Mesmer's followers developed a form of hypnosis that was based on his practices. Many years later this hypnosis became an accepted medical treatment and influenced the ideas of the famous Austrian psychologist Sigmund Freud in the early 1900s.

Élie
METCHNIKOFF
1845–1916
ZOOLOGY, MICROBIOLOGY

*immunology science that deals with the immune system, which protects the body from foreign substances, cells, and tissue by causing the body to produce substances to counteract the infectious materials

*physiology science that deals with the functions of living organisms and their parts

*natural history systematic study of animals and plants, especially in their natural settings

*embryo organism from the first division of the fertilized egg through the early stages of development until birth or hatching

*evolution historical development of a biological group such as a species

The Russian scientist Élie Metchnikoff (also Ilya Ilyich Mechnikov) is best known for discovering that certain cells in the blood, which he called phagocytes, surround and fight off foreign bodies such as bacteria that invade the organism. This discovery marked an important advance in the developing science of immunology*. In recognition of his work in this field, Metchnikoff shared the 1908 Nobel Prize in physiology* or medicine with the German immunologist Paul EHRLICH.

Metchnikoff was born in Ivanovka, Russia. His mother, a writer, encouraged him to pursue a career in science, while a family tutor introduced him to the wonders of natural history*. An excellent student, Metchnikoff devoted most of his attention to biology. He later focused on zoology and physiology.

In 1864, after completing his university education, Metchnikoff studied marine animals on an island in the North Sea. The following year he went to Naples, Italy, where he began to study the embryos* of invertebrates (animals without backbones). He devoted years to studying the development of the embryonic layers of different types of lower animals or invertebrates. His aim was to show that lower animals develop along a path similar to that of higher animals and to provide support for the theory of evolution*. In 1867, Metchnikoff went to St. Petersburg, Russia, where he obtained his doctoral degree. The same year he was hired at the University of Odessa, and the following year he accepted an appointment at a university in St. Petersburg.

While teaching in St. Petersburg, Metchnikoff suffered a personal tragedy, when in 1873 his wife died of tuberculosis. Shortly after his wife's death, Metchnikoff swallowed a large dose of morphine in an unsuccessful suicide attempt. After this period of tragedy and exhaustion, Metchnikoff returned slowly to his scientific work. However, his eyesight had begun to deteriorate and he was unable to use a microscope, which was essential to his work. Instead he planned an anthropological* expedition to an area north of the Caspian Sea, where he observed the region's indigenous peoples. He made comparative physical measurements and concluded that their development was arrested in comparison to the Caucasians. He attributed the growth lag to their habitual consumption of fermented milk. During this time, Metchnikoff recovered from his hardships and his eyesight improved as well. In 1875 he returned to Odessa, and shortly thereafter he remarried.

In 1880, personal pressures and illness led Metchnikoff to attempt suicide a second time. While recuperating on a farm belonging to the family of his second wife, he studied an infestation of beetles that was destroying grain fields. Metchnikoff discovered that some of the insects had died from a fungal infection, and he began to experiment with the idea of introducing the infection to kill the beetles. This study was the starting point for his interest in infectious diseases.

By 1882 the unrest in Russia had become so great that Metchnikoff moved to Messina, Italy, where he made his greatest discovery—the role of phagocytes in the defense of the animal body. He concluded that, in higher animals and humans, these cells were responsible for ridding the body of foreign invaders, especially bacteria. Over the next several years, Metchnikoff continued his studies of this phenomenon and defended his theory against critics.

By 1886 Metchnikoff had returned to Odessa and had become well known as a biologist, microbiologist*, and pathologist*. He again left Russia in 1888, this time to work in Paris at the invitation of Louis PASTEUR. He remained at the Pasteur Institute for the rest of his life, becoming a revered member of the institute and attracting many students to his laboratory. The period between 1895 and 1905 was the happiest time of his life. He continued his research on immunity (the body's self-defense mechanism), the nature of fevers, and the mechanisms of infection. In 1901 he published a comprehensive book, *L'immunité dans les maladies infectieuses* (Immunity of Infectious Diseases), in which he reviewed the entire field of comparative and human immunology.

After completing this book, Metchnikoff turned his attention to the problems of aging and the idea of death. In thinking about how to prolong life, he stressed the importance of proper hygiene and diet, which along with the suppression of diseases, he thought could enable individuals to live to a very old age. During these later years, Metchnikoff also studied syphilis, discovering that the sexually transmitted disease was not restricted to humans and that it responded well to early treatment.

In 1908, in recognition of his work in understanding immunity, Metchnikoff received the Nobel Prize in physiology or medicine, which he shared with Paul Ehrlich. The outbreak of World War I several years

*anthropological related to the study of human beings, especially in relation to origins and physical and cultural characteristics

*microbiologist scientist who studies microscopic life-forms, such as bacteria and viruses

*pathologist one who specializes in pathology, the study of diseases and their effects on organisms

later was a profound shock to Metchnikoff; it not only interrupted his work, but also made him realize that science had not yet brought humans to a stage of civilization where the atrocities of warfare could be avoided. Metchnikoff became ill and progressively weaker and he died in 1916 at the Pasteur Institute in Paris.

Johannes Peter MÜLLER

1781–1858

ANATOMY,
PHYSIOLOGY, ZOOLOGY

Müller's importance to science exceeded the discoveries he made in his investigations of human and animal bodies. He also influenced an entire generation of German scientists, many of whom later became leading scientists in their own right.

physiology science that deals with the functions of living organisms and their parts

Johannes Müller taught and conducted research in anatomy and physiology* at several German universities. Müller made important discoveries about the senses and the nervous system and introduced a new era of biological research in Germany. At a time when medicine was dominated by philosophical and speculative theories, he pioneered the use of experimental methods, and insisted that physiological research, with its many applications to medicine, be based on laboratory experimentation and careful observation. He was also the teacher of many of the important physiologists of nineteenth-century Germany.

Life and Career. Müller was born in Coblenz, Germany, and attended school there. His methodical work habits and thirst for knowledge made him an exceptional student; Müller was ambitious, with a strong desire to succeed in any activity in which he participated. He received his medical degree from the University of Bonn in 1822 and then went to Berlin for additional study. There he was influenced by Carl Rudolphi, Germany's foremost anatomist, who sought to make scientific research less mystical and more exact.

After several years of advanced study, Müller began lecturing on anatomy and physiology at the University of Bonn. By 1830 he had become a full professor. When Rudolphi died in 1832, Müller wanted to take over his post at the University of Berlin. He took the unusual step of writing to the government's minister of education to emphasize his qualifications for the job. Müller convinced the minister of his brilliance, and the Berlin professorship was his. In the years that followed, he turned down offers from other institutions so that he could remain at Berlin, where he twice served as rector, or head of the university.

Müller's career was interrupted by periods of depression during which he was unable to work. His depression and anxiety may have been related to the growing realization that he could not forever remain a leader in physiology. He was also obsessed by fears that his field of research was exhausted and that he could no longer be productive. He was plagued with insomnia (the inability to sleep), and he sometimes wandered the streets of Berlin at night, driven by anxiety. When he died suddenly in 1858, many suspected that he had committed suicide. Müller left a double legacy—his scientific achievements and his influence on many students, including Hermann von HELMHOLTZ, Emil Dubois Reymond, and Ernst HAECKEL, who became leading scientists.

Achievements in Physiology. Some of Müller's earliest physiological research, undertaken while he was still a student, involved the study of animal movements. He also studied embryology, the study of how organisms develop as embryos before birth. In 1820, when the medical school at Bonn offered a prize to the scientist who could answer the question, "Does a fetus breathe in its mother's womb?" Müller determined that it does. To solve the question he experimented on live cats and sheep, although later in life he rejected vivisection*, which he considered crude and "knife-happy."

In 1826 Müller attracted considerable scientific attention by publishing a lengthy book about his interests and studies. The work contains a wealth of new findings on human and animal vision, insightful analyses of human sight, and brilliant investigations into the multipart eyes of crabs and insects. The most important achievement revealed in the book was Müller's discovery that each sensory system responds to sensations in a fixed and definite way—the eye always with a sensation of light and the ear always with a sensation of sound. Müller's great insight was that human beings do not really perceive things in the external world, only the alterations that these things produce in the sensory systems. As Müller expressed it, "In our intercourse with the external world we continually sense ourselves."

Thereafter Müller entered a period of extraordinary productivity, becoming the most famous member of Bonn's medical faculty. Often involved in several projects at once, he investigated the glands and the spinal and cranial* nerves. He studied how nerve impulses travel from sensory nerves to the brain and then to the motor nerves that control movement, which helped explain such phenomena as hiccuping, vomiting, and sneezing.

Müller studied specimens of tumors and deformities in the university's anatomical museum. He realized that further study of tumors demanded chemical analysis and microscopic examination, and he encouraged students to study tumors and healthy tissue at the cellular level. In this way, Müller helped establish pathological histology, the study of cells present in diseases such as cancer. His student Rudolf VIRCHOW went on to fully develop this area of pathology. Soon these procedures became useful to doctors as tools in diagnosing patients' diseases.

Throughout the 1830s Müller published various sections of his *Handbuch der Physiologie* (Handbook of Physiology), an influential work that became a milestone in European medicine by linking physiological research to medical treatment. It inspired new physiological research for years. By the time it was completed, however, Müller had lost interest in experimental physiology and turned in new directions.

Other Scientific Contributions. After about 1840 Müller devoted his time to research in zoology, anatomy, and paleontology*. He was especially interested in marine animals and gathered specimens for his research during expeditions to the North and Mediterranean Seas. He focused on classifying amphibians and reptiles and on comparing the anatomies of various types of creatures.

Müller published research on sharks, rays, sea slugs, sea urchins, and other animals. He was also interested in the Cyclostomata, a class of primitive, jawless fish. According to Müller the lancelet, a member

*vivisection practice of dissecting or cutting into the body of a living animal for the purpose of scientific investigation

*cranial of or relating to the skull (cranium)

*paleontology study of extinct or prehistoric life, usually through the examination of fossils

*vertebrate animal with a backbone

of this class, provided the simplest model of the anatomy of vertebrates*. He was the first to realize the lancelet's significance to studies of vertebrate anatomy in general.

These zoological studies brought Müller great recognition, including prizes from English and French scientific societies. His last research was devoted to single-celled marine animals and was continued after his death by Haeckel, his student.

PARACELSUS

ca. 1494–1541

MEDICINE, CHEMISTRY,
NATURAL PHILOSOPHY

*Renaissance period that marked the beginnings of modern science and the rebirth of interest in classical art and literature that occurred in Europe from the late 1300s through the 1500s

Paracelsus was one of the most controversial scientific figures of the Renaissance*. He barged into the medical profession, outraging doctors and delighting students with his bold—sometimes obscene—rants against the reigning practices of the day. Finally forced out of several respectable academies, Paracelsus took to wandering through Europe, spreading his knowledge, ideas, and treatments where he could. His thought and practice were a remarkable mix of the rational and the mystical. He was a keen observer and experimenter who made important progress in medicine, and at the same time he developed complex theories about spiritual essences linking human health to the cosmos.

Family Background. "Paracelsus" is a nickname given in later life to the man born Theophrastus Philippus Aureolus Bombastus von Hohenheim. Scholars are uncertain about the origin and meaning of the nickname, but it probably meant "surpassing Celsus," a reference to the ancient Roman scholar Aulus Cornelius Celsus, whose works on illness, surgery, nutrition, and drugs made him an important authority on classical medicine.

Paracelsus's father was William of Hohenheim, of the Bombast family of Swabia, a region in present-day Germany. William had an affair in Switzerland—with a slave who worked as a servant at an abbey there—resulting in the birth of a son. William was a practicing physician, and he took charge of Paracelsus's early education in mining, mineralogy*, botany, and natural philosophy*. Paracelsus also studied with an abbot who introduced him to mystical theological* ideas. He found time as well to practice basic medicine in the mines of central Europe.

*mineralogy study of the properties of minerals

*natural philosophy set of theories or ideas about the natural world; theoretical basis for research in the natural sciences

*theological referring to theology, the study of religion

A Turbulent Career. Paracelsus probably studied medicine at various Italian universities, but it is uncertain whether he actually received a degree. He traveled often and found jobs as a military surgeon in Venice, Scandinavia, the Middle East, and the Greek island of Rhodes. During his early 30s he drifted through the Germanic states of central Europe. During this time he practiced medicine and narrowly escaped trouble for sympathizing with the Peasants' War, in which rural laborers took up arms to demand the abolition of serfdom* and their right to hold common land.

His break came in Strasbourg (in present-day France), where he set up a practice. In 1527, called to Basel for a consultation, Paracelsus cured an important citizen's infected leg, for which local physicians had

*serfdom form of slavery in which medieval European peasants were bound to work on the lands owned by aristocrats

t afbeeldfel ten halven lyve, met het geveft van zyn zwaard
en knop van 't zelve bewaarde hy zeker algemeen Geneesm:
genaamd, 't welke hy alom met zich droeg; en, dewyl d
nen dood gemaakt is, vindtmen in den binnen en buitenkrin

TORIS THEOPHRASTI PARACELSI ÆTATI

Like the ancient Greek physician Galen, Paracelsus believed that plants had medicinal properties. Applying the notion of "signatures," he selected herbs that resembled the affected organ in shape and color. For example, he used a yellow plant to treat the liver.

recommended amputation. He won the post of physician to the city of Basel and professor of medicine at the university, despite the disapproval of university officials. They refused to accept him as a colleague because they believed that he showed disrespect by not swearing a required oath or submitting documents to prove his qualifications. Moreover, he lectured in German instead of Latin and allowed unlicensed doctors, known as barber-surgeons, into his classes. Paracelsus also spoke and wrote mightily to attack the traditional medicine taught by the other physicians. Rejecting the official doctrines and textbooks, he promised a new set of lessons based on his own firsthand experience as a researcher and physician.

A loud, rude, and imposing man, Paracelsus offended and alienated many people. He was angry, resentful, and uncompromising. He was often seen in lower-class taverns, drinking heavily and gathering knowledge about folk medicine. He would treat the poor for free but charged high fees to the rich. He criticized organized religion, attacked academic medicine as wasteful, and called on the world to follow his new ways of thinking. In 1528 he denounced a church official who refused to pay one of his enormous bills for treatment, and the authorities of Basel decided that they had had enough. Paracelsus was forced to leave the city, and he never again received a professorship or even steady employment.

He moved on to other cities, finding work and patrons and writing *Opus paramirum* (A Work Beyond Wonder). His stays were always tumultuous and brief. When he was able to set up a laboratory or lodge with prominent aristocrats who requested his help, Paracelsus continued his research and wrote papers about his findings. His own health failed him in 1541, and he died in Salzburg, Austria.

A Medical Revolution. In Paracelsus's time the medical profession was based on the work of the ancient Greek physician GALEN, who held that the body had four natural humors, or fluids, that had to be in balance for an even temperament and good health. Treatments were usually attempts to restore this balance—for example, by draining blood from a patient.

Paracelsus was one of the first physicians to reject the authority of ancient medical texts. Rather than search for a cause of an illness within the body's supposed natural state, he looked for external causes that had entered the body. He also looked outside the body for treatments, administering prepared doses of medicine. Paracelsus took a careful, conservative approach to treatment, emphasizing the body's natural ability to heal with little intervention. A dedicated chemist, he often prescribed chemically prepared drugs in preference to the herbal medicines of ancient times. He invented laboratory techniques and chemical substances and was the first to attempt to organize chemicals according to their medicinal properties.

Paracelsus's influence on the development of science in the 1600s was his chemical philosophy, which was based on three fundamental elements—salt, sulfur, and mercury. This *tria prima* represented the principles of solidity, combustibility, and liquidity, which he held are inherent in all substances. However, Paracelsus was not really a scientist in the modern sense of objective inquiry and logical reasoning; he was a visionary, a spiritual mystic who developed a complex philosophy of matter and of the universe. He believed that all matter and living things had a vital spirit, a force of existence that was related to the light of stars. He found links of essence between each star and specific herbs, minerals, body organs, diseases, and remedies. Many of Paracelsus's ideas were influenced by folk rituals, certain early Christian philosophies, and other ways of thinking that were shunned by the religious and medical establishment.

Although Paracelsus was a fine doctor and an able chemist, resistance from authorities and his own uncompromising attitude prevented him from accomplishing much in his lifetime. However, he helped revive and reinterpret parts of scientific tradition that the authorities had previously suppressed. In doing so he made important progress in medicine and chemistry, and his influence on future scientists was profound. His ideas attracted naturalists* and physicians including Johannes Baptista van Helmont, Robert Boyle, and Georg Ernst STAHL.

Ambroise PARÉ
ca. 1510–1590
SURGERY

Ambroise Paré, the son of an artisan, rose to become chief surgeon to the kings of France. Born in Laval, France, Paré served as an apprentice to a barber-surgeon, a physician who lacked a university degree in medicine. Paré continued his studies in Paris and, when still in his 20s, became a master barber-surgeon and entered the French army, serving in Italy for two years.

During this tour of duty, Paré revolutionized the treatment of gunshot wounds. Until then doctors believed that bullet wounds were poisonous and had to be cauterized* with hot oil. But during one battle Paré ran out of oil, so he used a dressing made of egg yolk, oil of roses, and turpentine. The next day he realized that the soldiers who had received the dressing were healing better than those who had been cauterized. His paper on the subject, published in 1545, made him instantly famous.

*cauterize to seal and numb a wound by burning with high heat

Paré's other pioneering work included a new device for closing off blood vessels during amputations, as well as techniques for surgical births. His understanding of contagious infections and public health measures was crude by modern standards but advanced for his time.

During his career Paré encountered great resistance from the French academic medical profession, which tried to exclude and humiliate barber-surgeons. However, Paré's skills were so great that he won the support of his aristocratic clients, and he was appointed chief surgeon to the kings Charles IX and Henry III. During the great religious and civil struggles that wracked France in his lifetime, Paré remained a Roman Catholic and a member of the royal court, but his concern for those who suffered always rose above politics.

James PARKINSON
1755–1824
MEDICINE, PALEONTOLOGY

James Parkinson was a surgeon by profession, but he was also a humanitarian and was interested in chemistry, geology, and fossils. Born in London, he became a surgeon in 1784. His medical practice flourished, and during the early years of his career, he devoted much energy to social and political issues. Parkinson supported universal voting rights and reform of England's House of Commons to better represent the people. Although his political activism had waned by 1800, his crusading spirit remained alive. His humanitarianism reappeared in 1811, when he campaigned for better regulation of asylums for the mentally handicapped and for legal protection of their patients.

Parkinson wrote on medical topics, including a work on gout* and a report on a punctured, severely diseased appendix. In 1817 he published an important essay, *The Shaking Palsy*, which contains a description of the symptoms of the condition known today as Parkinson's disease.

*gout disease marked by painful inflammation of the joints

A collector of fossils, Parkinson wrote *Organic Remains of a Former World*, a three-volume introduction to the subject. The first volume covers plant fossils, and the others deal with fossils of large and small animals. The work, which also contains a summary of geological discoveries of the time as well as theories and information about British fossils, was considered a milestone in British paleontology*. Parkinson also contributed further to the development of British paleontology and geology when he helped found the Geological Society of London. He died in London at the age of 69.

*paleontology** study of extinct or prehistoric life, usually through the examination of fossils

Louis
PASTEUR

1822–1895

CHEMISTRY, MICROBIOLOGY, IMMUNOLOGY

*immunology** science that deals with the immune system, which protects the body from foreign substances, cells, and tissue by causing the body to produce substances to counteract the infectious materials

*rabies** disease of the nervous system usually transmitted to humans through the bite of infected animals, often dogs

Louis Pasteur's contributions to human well-being made him a national hero and brought him international fame. An experimental chemist and biologist, he directed his energies toward work that had practical benefits, both economic and medical. He was also strongly patriotic, with a great desire to aid French industry, and some of his major research products were undertaken to help the nation's producers of vinegar, wine, beer, and silk. His studies of food decomposition led him to develop pasteurization, a method of protecting food from decay.

Much of Pasteur's 50-year scientific career was devoted to the study of microorganisms, living plants and animals that are invisible to the naked eye. His discoveries about their biology helped settle many long-standing controversies in the life sciences. Above all, his work led to breakthroughs in the understanding and treatment of disease and in immunology*. Pasteur produced vaccines for several animal diseases and developed one medical treatment for human use—the first known treatment for rabies*. He also played a major role in establishing the germ theory of disease, which claimed that microorganisms cause infectious diseases. He also inspired lifesaving changes in medical and surgical procedures.

Life and Career

Pasteur rose from a modest background to become one of the best-known scientific figures of his day. Ambitious, proud, and quick to defend his ideas, Pasteur was a powerful personality who aroused envy and hostility in some of his critics and inspired great loyalty in many of his assistants and colleagues. He was honored as a "benefactor of humanity," a reputation that cannot be seriously challenged.

Background and Education. Pasteur was born in Dole, in the Jura region of France. When he was five years old, the family moved to the town of Arbois, where Pasteur grew up and which he regarded as his home. Pasteur's was a working-class family with little education. He absorbed the values of hard work and respect for financial security from his parents. Pasteur's father dreamed of his son becoming a teacher at a local school, little suspecting that one day the school in Arbois would be renamed in his son's honor.

Fame lay far in the future. Pasteur was an unremarkable student, notable only for the artistic talent he showed in sketches of his family

Because Pasteur found vivisection personally repugnant, he asked his assistants to perform the animal experiments he designed. Here, an assistant experiments on a rabbit while Pasteur (first from left) and another man observe.

and friends. But his enthusiasm for study awakened in his last year of high school, and he decided to study science at the École Normale Supérieure, then a teachers' college in Paris.

Before he could enroll in the École, Pasteur had to obtain bachelor of arts and sciences degrees, which required four years of study at the Royal College of Besançon. Ironically, in view of Pasteur's later accomplishments, his instructors rated him "mediocre" in chemistry. In 1843, he entered the École Normale. Pasteur served as an assistant to one of the chemistry professors there and graduated with doctoral degrees in chemistry and physics in 1847.

Professional Career. Even before his graduation from the École, Pasteur had begun the research that would soon establish his reputation. In the years that followed, his career unfolded in phases, each devoted to a particular area of research or practical problem. From 1847 to 1857 he worked in crystallography*, concentrating on the structure of organic crystals and the ways they affect light as it passes through them. From 1857 to 1865 he was involved in two of the most hotly debated issues of the time in the life sciences: the related questions of fermentation* and the spontaneous generation of life. During this time Pasteur conducted studies on vinegar and wine. He then spent five years researching two diseases that were affecting silkworms and threatening France's economically important silk industry. From 1871 to 1876 he returned to the topics of fermentation and spontaneous generation, with the practical aspects of his research directed at beer making. During the final phase of his scientific career, from 1877 until his death 18 years later, Pasteur investigated infectious diseases in animals and humans and searched for ways to combat them.

Throughout his career Pasteur was associated with various schools and institutes. His first position as a chemistry professor after receiving

crystallography study of the properties of crystals

fermentation process of change in organic substances in which microorganisms called enzymes cause compounds such as carbohydrates to break down into alcohol or acids

his doctoral degrees was at the University of Strasbourg. In 1849, soon after taking the post, he married Marie Laurent, the daughter of a Strasbourg school official. Devoted to her husband and his career, Pasteur's wife not only tolerated his intense concentration on his work but also sometimes helped him in the role of secretary.

Five years later Pasteur moved to the University of Lille, where he served as chemistry professor and head of a new science department. Lille was located in the heart of a flourishing industrial region, and the department was intended to promote scientific support for industry. Pasteur approved of this goal and tried to link the university to industry in his courses by teaching the principles and techniques of industrial processes, such as bleaching, refining sugar, and manufacturing beet-root alcohol, an important local industry.

In 1857 Pasteur became director of scientific studies at the École Normale in Paris. He also lectured at the École des Beaux-Arts, a school of fine arts in Paris, where a professorship in the relation of the sciences to the arts was created for him. He introduced laboratory procedures connected with the materials and techniques of art. The most exhausting demand on his time, however, was his silkworm research, which took him from Paris to southern France for many months each year.

In 1867 Pasteur was relieved of his duties as head of scientific studies at the École because of his rigid and unpopular stand against a student free-speech movement. For the next seven years, he held a professorship in chemistry at the Sorbonne, a prominent university in Paris. Between 1867 and 1888, Pasteur also directed a research laboratory at the École, with financial support from the government.

Honored Life, Honored Death. For the last seven years of his life, Pasteur directed the Pasteur Institute, founded in 1888 with donations from the government and from donors around the world. The institute's mission was to administer the rabies treatment that Pasteur had invented. So many people came to the institute to receive the treatment that branches in other nations were soon opened.

For his services to science, industry, and medicine, Pasteur received a pension from the French government. He also earned a long list of prizes, awards, and honors from the governments and scientific organizations of many countries. One cherished honor was his 1882 election to the Académie Française, the nation's most prestigious scholarly organization.

On Pasteur's seventieth birthday, the Sorbonne held a public celebration in its grand amphitheater. However, he was so frail at the time that he had to be led by Sadi Carnot, then president of the French Republic, to receive the thanks of an enormous crowd of students, colleagues, government officials, and foreign dignitaries. Pasteur's son delivered his father's brief speech of appreciation, in which the great scientist advised students to "live in the serene peace of laboratories and libraries." He also told of his "invincible belief that Science and Peace will triumph over Ignorance and War, that nations will unite, not to destroy, but to build, and that the future will belong to those who have done most for suffering humanity."

Pasteur's first health crisis had come in 1868. In the midst of his silkworm studies, he suffered a stroke that paralyzed his left side. Although his condition later improved somewhat, his speech and movement were impaired for the rest of his life. He continued to design and direct experiments with great care and ingenuity, but he often relied on assistants or collaborators to execute them.

Pasteur's health worsened in 1886, when he began to suffer from heart trouble. A second stroke the following year left him significantly weakened, and after a third in 1894, he was almost completely paralyzed. He died the following year, and received a state funeral at the Nôtre Dame cathedral in Paris. He was buried in a splendid crypt in the Pasteur Institute. His wife, who died in 1910, was buried there with him.

Crystallography and Chemistry

Some of Pasteur's most original and important contributions to science came from his early work in crystallography, but this research is less well known than his work on immunology and germ theory. His work established that the properties of chemical compounds depend not just on the specific atoms that combine to form the molecules of those compounds but also on the manner in which the atoms of each molecule are arranged in space. His papers on this subject helped found stereochemistry, the science that deals with the chemical effects of the spatial arrangement of atoms.

Pasteur's interest in crystallography was sparked by the work of scientists who had investigated the way light was polarized* when it was passed through a liquid containing organic crystals. Pasteur turned his attention to two types of crystals, tartaric and racemic acids. Tartaric acid comes from tartar, a by-product of winemaking, and was used in medicines and dyes. Racemic acid has the same composition as tartaric acid, but its properties are different—tartaric acid polarizes light, but racemic acid does not, for reasons unknown at the time.

In a series of papers in the late 1840s and early 1850s, Pasteur announced the results of his study of the two acid crystals. He found that the molecular structures of optically active crystals (those that polarize light) were asymmetrical. He had expected optically inactive ones to be perfectly symmetrical, but he discovered that optically inactive racemic acid formed two types of crystals. The molecular structures of both were asymmetric, and they were mirror images of each other. This was Pasteur's first great discovery—that some chemical compounds exist in "right-handed" and "left-handed" forms. The right-handed crystals polarized light to the right, while the left-handed ones polarized it to the left. Together they canceled each other out, making the compound optically inactive. From this discovery arose "Pasteur's law," which declared optical activity to be linked with asymmetrical crystalline structure, although later researchers proved that there are some exceptions to this rule.

Making Milk Safe

Pasteur's studies of fermentation and microorganisms led to the discovery that some microorganisms can cause food to decay or decompose. He developed a process of sterilizing vinegar and wine by heating them to a temperature high enough to kill the microorganisms and sealing them for protection from airborne microbes. The process, known almost immediately as pasteurization, enabled manufacturers to store and ship food products without spoilage. It also made milk safer to drink, and it remains in use today, supplemented by new sterilizing techniques such as the use of radiation to kill microbes.

*polarize to cause light to vibrate in a pattern

*microorganism tiny living thing that generally can be seen clearly only through a microscope

Pasteur had originally separated the left- and right-handed racemic acid crystals by hand, a difficult and time-consuming process. He later developed a more efficient method to separate the left- and right-handed parts of other compounds. Next, while studying a compound called ammonium paratartrate, he discovered that the right-handed forms of the compound could be used as food by microorganisms*. This discovery led Pasteur to a lifelong belief that life was connected in some profound way to molecular asymmetry. He was convinced that someday life would be created, or at least altered, in the laboratory through the asymmetrical application of some force such as light or magnetism.

Fermentation and Spontaneous Generation

At Lille, Pasteur turned his attention to beetroot alcohol. At first he was interested in its optical properties and structure, but soon he began to examine a subject of considerable scientific interest: fermentation. This led to investigations into another controversial topic, the question of whether life arises spontaneously in matter.

Fermentation. For thousands of years people had used fermentation to make all sorts of products, from yogurt to wine, but scientists did not know exactly how the process worked. There were two main theories. The dominant theory was that fermentation was a chemical reaction, but around the 1830s, some scientists began to argue that it was a biological process that depended on the activity of living microorganisms, such as those found in brewer's yeast.

Pasteur favored the biological theory and he devoted years of research to confirming it. Because much research had already been done on alcoholic fermentation without overturning the chemical theory, Pasteur focused on lactic fermentation, or the process that causes milk to go sour. He published his results in 1857, claiming that fermentation is the activity of live microorganisms that eat substances in the medium that is fermenting. Different microorganisms cause different types of fermentation, and chemical properties of the medium can encourage or discourage the growth of different microorganisms. He also introduced the idea that air (composed mainly of nitrogen and oxygen and some trace gases) might be the source of these organisms.

By the time Pasteur published his next paper on alcoholic fermentation in 1860, he had developed techniques for cultivating microorganisms and producing fermentation in a medium that contained no nitrogen. However, because many supporters of the chemical theory believed that nitrogen was essential to the process, Pasteur's experiments were considered a strong criticism of that theory.

"Life Without Air." The same year Pasteur discovered that one type of ferment (microorganism that causes fermentation) died when exposed to air, leading him to investigate how air affected other ferments. He found that the yeast microorganism thrived but did not ferment in air. After a series of experiments on various microorganisms,

he concluded that fermentation was a form of nutrition that occurred only in the absence of oxygen and when microorganisms had to break down chemical compounds to obtain the oxygen necessary for life.

Pasteur also studied organic decomposition in the absence of air and determined that it, like fermentation, was caused by the activity of anaerobes, microbes whose nutritional processes do not require oxygen. Pasteur usually receives credit for discovering "life without air," but scholars have shown that earlier scientists, including the Dutch naturalist* Antoni von LEEUWENHOEK, had already proposed the existence of anaerobic microorganisms.

*naturalist one who studies objects in their natural settings

In the early 1860s Pasteur began to study acetic fermentation, the process by which vinegar is produced. He demonstrated that microorganisms, not chemical reactions, cause the fermentation. He also showed manufacturers that vinegar could be reliably produced by sowing cultivated microorganisms into a mixture of alcohol, ammonia, and mineral salts. He then turned his attention to the wines of his native Jura region, identifying the microorganisms responsible for various "diseases" or imperfections in wine, which is also a product of fermentation. He invented methods to pasteurize both wine and vinegar to protect them from diseases or spoilage. (Pasteurization is the process by which a substance is heated to a temperature high enough to kill objectionable organisms, but not so high that the chemical composition of the substance is altered.) Later he developed a similar process for beer, and it was also extended to milk.

Spontaneous Generation. Because of Pasteur's involvement in studying fermentation, he became embroiled in the debate on the related topic of spontaneous generation. Proponents of this concept held that living microorganisms could arise independently of a living parent, especially in decaying organic matter such as food. Scientists were divided on the issue. Pasteur believed that the microscope, by revealing a formerly hidden world of teeming, unfamiliar life-forms, was responsible for strengthening the notion of spontaneous generation. His work on fermentation and microorganisms, however, suggested that what seemed like the spontaneous appearance of life might simply be the growth of microbes carried by the air.

Pasteur set out to determine whether airborne microbes were responsible for what appeared to be spontaneous generation. He showed that boiling a liquid decreased the likelihood that microorganisms would appear in it, and in a well-publicized series of experiments conducted high in the mountains of Jura, he showed that liquids exposed to mountain air developed less microbial activity than those exposed to air at sea level or elsewhere. He concluded that microbes or germs are distributed unevenly in the air, depending on locality, altitude, and other environmental circumstances. In 1863, when Pasteur successfully prevented microbial growth in blood and urine that had not been boiled, he claimed that these experiments "carry a final blow to the doctrine of spontaneous generation."

Keeping It Clean

Before the germ theory of disease gained acceptance, Pasteur outraged physicians and surgeons by claiming that they often produced disease by touching patients with hands or instruments contaminated by microbes. Pasteur wrote, "Had I the honor of being a surgeon, I would never introduce any instrument into the human body without having passed it through boiling water, or better yet through a flame, immediately before the operation." Pasteur's work eventually brought such practices into use. In his private life, Pasteur guarded against germs—he was cautious about shaking hands and wiped his silverware before eating.

145

The question of spontaneous generation was of interest to more than scientists. The public was deeply interested because of the possible religious significance of the concept. In an 1864 lecture at the Sorbonne, Pasteur expressed an idea shared by many—that spontaneous generation threatened belief in God as the sole creator of life. Despite Pasteur's insistence that he had conducted his experiments with an open mind, it is clear that he was opposed to spontaneous generation from the start. His position was correct, however, and a committee of experts from the French Académie des Sciences, after reviewing the arguments and experiments conducted by Pasteur as well as leading supporters of spontaneous generation, agreed with Pasteur. The scientific debate continued, especially in Germany and England, but by the 1880s, the theory of spontaneous generation had lost much of its strength, largely due to the steady stream of experiments and arguments directed against the notion by Pasteur and his colleagues.

The Silkworm Problem

Pasteur's work on fermentation and spontaneous generation was interrupted by his five-year project to save France's silk industry. Silk makers were desperate because a disease called *pébrine* was ravaging populations of silkworms, the insect larvae that produce silk.

The work was slow, partly because it took a year to see how the results of his experiments affected silk production and partly because he suffered from personal troubles, including the deaths of his father and young daughter. At first Pasteur concluded that *pébrine* was a condition that certain silkworms had inherited at birth. However, he reversed this position once his experiments yielded convincing evidence that the disease was caused by parasitic* microorganisms. He also determined that another silkworm ailment, which most experts believed to be part of *pébrine,* was actually a second, independent disease.

Pasteur recommended that sericulturists* examine all newly laid silkworms and reject those that showed signs of infection, and control the temperature, humidity, and ventilation of the silkworm nursery. Many sericulturists adopted his methods, with considerable success. Pasteur recognized that this work had raised important questions about how the parasite, host, and environment interact to produce disease. The final and most famous phase of his career would deal directly with disease and medicine.

Medicine and the Germ Theory of Disease

Pasteur often stated that his work on fermentation and spontaneous generation might relate to medicine. At the time, many scientists believed that fermentation and disease operated in the same way. Having demonstrated that germs, or microbes, cause fermentation, Pasteur naturally supposed that the germs could cause disease as well.

Earlier scientists had proposed the germ theory, but it was not widely accepted because most doctors and researchers believed that the

*parasitic relating to a parasite, an organism that lives on or within another organism from whose body it obtains nutrients

*sericulturist one who practices sericulture, the process of raising silkworms for the manufacture of silk

microorganisms often seen in cases of disease were by-products of the disease, not their causes. The notion that invisible microbes could kill much larger organisms seemed strange to many. They argued that diseases were caused by imbalances or inborn conditions in an organism, not from an external living agent. Pasteur's work became a highly influential part of this debate.

Experimental Study of Disease.

As early as the mid-1860s Pasteur began to speak of plans to study anthrax, an infectious disease that affects cattle and sheep and can be transmitted to humans. He started the work a decade later in a laboratory built for him by the government at the École Normale. Confirming the conclusions of some earlier researchers, notably Robert KOCH of Germany, Pasteur showed that anthrax was caused by bacteria. He established that bacterial spores* were transmitted to livestock when the animals grazed on grass growing above the bodies of animals that had died of anthrax. In his most original contribution to the problem, he showed that earthworms carried the spores from the dead animals to the surface in their intestines.

*spore single-celled, environmentally resistant body produced by plants and some microorganisms and capable of development into a new individual directly or after mixing with another spore

Pasteur next focused on cowpox and fowl cholera. Nearly a century earlier Edward JENNER had shown that it was possible to immunize a person against smallpox by administering an inoculation*. Pasteur tried to identify the microbes responsible for other diseases, with the goal of developing vaccines. He created an effective vaccine against fowl cholera, and in 1881 he developed a new vaccine against anthrax.

*inoculation introduction of a disease agent into an animal or plant to produce a mild form of the disease and render the organism immune

The Rabies Treatment.

Pasteur's most dramatic success, at least to the public eye, was his development of a treatment for rabies, the disease caused by bites from infected animals. The disease was rare in France, but he was determined to conquer it—some later scholars believe that he had a particular horror of rabies because a rabid wolf had terrorized the people of Arbois during his childhood.

Neither the blood nor the saliva of rabid animals was a reliable source of the disease. Pasteur and his assistants discovered, however, that injections of brain matter from a rabid animal always produced rabies in a healthy animal. By transmitting the disease to several animals of different species, Pasteur created progressively weaker forms of it, until he arrived at a form weak enough to serve as a vaccine that would immunize without causing the disease. By 1885 he had begun administering the treatment to dogs bitten by infected dogs, and he was able to prevent some of those dogs from developing the disease.

The same year a woman brought to Pasteur's laboratory her nine-year-old son, Joseph Meister, who had been mauled by a rabid dog two days earlier. Two experts on rabies had given up on the boy and urged Pasteur to try his experimental method on him. For ten days, Pasteur administered 13 injections of weakened rabies virus extracted from the bones of infected rabbits. The boy remained healthy, as did a second boy whom Pasteur treated a few months later.

The day Pasteur announced the results of these treatments to the Académie de Médicine, a leading rabies expert predicted that the date

would "remain forever memorable in the history of medicine and forever glorious for French science." In the years that followed, Pasteur's rabies treatment and preventive vaccination were hailed as among the chief medical triumphs of the time, despite occasional tragic failures. By the time of Pasteur's death, about 20,000 people had undergone the treatment at Pasteur Institutes around the world.

Pasteur and the Revolution in Medicine. Pasteur's rabies vaccination was an important achievement not only because it was the first known protection against rabies but also because it laid the foundation for the campaign to extend the practice of vaccination to other diseases. Much of Pasteur's impact was indirect and lay in the changes and new developments his work inspired.

Pasteur's work on anthrax, for example, had established anthrax as the first major killer disease of large animals known to be caused by microorganisms. This achievement ushered in the golden age of bacteriology. In less than 20 years, the microbial theory was extended to cholera, tuberculosis, diphtheria, typhoid, gonorrhea, syphilis, pneumonia, tetanus, and plague—diseases that had ravaged humankind for thousands of years. Koch and other German scientists did much of the work of isolating and studying the disease-causing microorganism, while Pasteur and the French concentrated on the question of immunity from disease and on disease prevention through vaccination.

Through his work on the germ theories of fermentation and disease, Pasteur brought about a medical revolution. He presented compelling evidence that many diseases are transmitted by germs, and that those germs can exist invisibly in the air and on surfaces. Joseph LISTER, an English surgeon who became Pasteur's friend and a follower of his ideas, used Pasteur's germ theory as the basis for developing antiseptic procedures for surgery. Although the medical profession was slow to adopt antiseptic surgery, eventually it gained acceptance along with the germ theory of disease.

Jan Evangelista
PURKYNĚ

1787–1869

PHYSIOLOGY,
HISTOLOGY, EDUCATION

*physiological of or relating to physiology, the science that deals with the functions of living organisms and their parts

The investigations of the Czech scientist Jan Evangelista Purkyně (also spelled Purkinje) produced breakthroughs and stimulated a great deal of research in many fields. Among the areas that Purkyně studied were the physiological* basis of sensory stimulation, the workings of the eye, and early microscopic investigations into the structure and functions of plant and animal tissues and cells (histology). In his later years, he led an effort to expand scientific education in his homeland.

Early Life and Studies. Purkyně was born in Libochovice, Bohemia (now Czech Republic). He grew up on the estate of a Bohemian prince that was managed by his father, and at age ten he began formal schooling at a monastery near the Austrian border run by Piarist Monks. An excellent student, Purkyně decided to join the order and taught for a short time at a Piarist school. In 1806 he enrolled in the Piarist Philosophical Institute to prepare for enrolling in university. After a year, however, he gave up the idea of a religious vocation and became a private philosophy tutor in Prague.

At this time Purkyně began his scientific research; he studied sound waves using homemade equipment. Although he achieved few results, he gained experience that helped in his later scientific work. For a time he worked as a tutor to the son of a nobleman, but he ultimately decided on a scientific career. In 1818 he enrolled as a medical student at the University of Prague, giving his dissertation on the topic of subjective visual phenomena. This would also be the subject of some of his most fascinating later discoveries.

Hoping to gain a professorship at Prague, Purkyně served as an assistant to the professor of anatomy, but his educational and scientific ideas were too radical for the faculty there. A colleague recognized his skills and persuaded the University of Breslau to appoint him as professor of physiology. Initially Purkyně encountered hostility, but he soon became one of the most well-liked and respected faculty members at Breslau, where he remained until his death in 1869.

Purkyně's work in the last years of his life was influential in the Czech national revival and exerted a lasting effect on the subsequent development of science in his country.

The Physiology of Perception. Before Purkyně's research, scientists could not explain many unusual perception-related phenomena. They believed that visual errors in perception or sensations produced without an external cause were the result of chance or violations of nature's laws. Purkyně, however, believed that each subjective sensation corresponds to a particular physiological process. By carefully analyzing his own perceptions, he was able to make many discoveries about those processes.

Purkyně studied visual phenomena such as the spots produced when pressure is applied on the eyeball when the eye is closed, and the way the eye perceives color. Among his many findings were the "Purkyně shift," in which the brightness of colors appears to change under different lighting conditions. He also discovered that the outer parts of the retina are unable to distinguish colors, something no previous researcher had noticed. His findings led later scientists to fix the true location of the retina at the back of the eye, and to discover the rods and cones that perceive black-and-white and color vision. Purkyně's work also produced many breakthroughs in ophthalmology*, and some of his practices are still a routine part of eye examinations.

In addition to visual perception, Purkyně examined the vestibular sense, which controls the body's equilibrium. His work indicated that the portion of the brain known as the cerebellum plays a major role in posture and balance. It would be another 50 years before his successors built on these findings to determine that the inner ear contains the special organs that control balance.

*ophthalmology medical specialty focusing on the structure and function of the eye, as well as diseases of the eye and their treatment

Studies of Cells. Purkyně's first important discovery in histology was the discovery of a small structure in the yolk of a bird's egg from which the embryo* develops. Later identified as the cell nucleus, this breakthrough led to the later discovery of egg cells in mammals including humans. Purkyně also studied the structure of plant cells, pointing out

*embryo organism from the first division of the fertilized egg through the early stages of development until birth or hatching

how their different structures led to the development of different types of plant tissues.

Purkyně's histological work accelerated in 1832, when he received a powerful new microscope that enabled him to make new discoveries and become expert at preparing materials for viewing. For example, he found that treating samples with acetic acid (vinegar) makes the cell nuclei visible. By exploiting such techniques, he made advances in the study of the structure of the skin and its glands; bones, teeth, and cartilage; and the arteries and veins.

The microscope also enabled him to discover "Purkyně's network," fibers that form bridges between muscle cells in the heart. The fibers were later shown to have an important role in conducting the contraction during a heartbeat to all parts of the heart. He revealed many details of the nervous system, including the facts that cells are responsible for carrying nerve impulses and that nerve fibers were not hollow tubes as previously believed. Purkyně also examined the number of nerve fibers and their distribution, one of the first efforts in a field now known as quantitative neurobiology.

Advancing Scientific Education. In 1839, at age 52, Purkyně opened the world's first independent physiological institute in Breslau. Until that point, physiology was underappreciated as an independent field and treated inferiorly in medical schools. Purkyně's institute was very successful and prompted universities across Europe to establish similar facilities at their medical schools.

After 1850 Purkyně spent his time promoting scientific education among his countrymen. He began publishing a scientific review in the Czech language and worked to have Czech accepted as a teaching language at the University of Prague. He worked to standardize the writing of all Slavic languages by adopting the Roman alphabet. His efforts were influential in the growth of Czech culture and science.

John
RAY

1627–1705

NATURAL HISTORY

*naturalist one who studies objects in their natural settings

*taxonomy orderly classification of plants and animals into groups and subgroups according to their relationships

*herbalist person who collects or deals in herbs, especially medicinal herbs

One of the leading naturalists* of the 1600s, John Ray spent a lifetime studying and writing about nature. Ray made important contributions to the study of biology and botany, particularly in the area of taxonomy*. The first to fix the species as the fundamental unit in the taxonomic hierarchy, Ray established systematic methods for classifying plants and animals that helped make possible the work of Swedish botanist Carl LINNAEUS in the 1700s.

Early Life and Career. Born in Black Notley in Essex, England, Ray was the son of the village blacksmith. His mother was well known in the local area as a skilled herbalist* and medical practitioner. In his later writings Ray recalled that he had become very much interested in botany from an early age.

Ray attended grammar school in nearby Braintree, and in 1644 he entered Trinity College at Cambridge University on a scholarship. Four years later he graduated with a bachelor's degree and accepted a fellowship at the college. During the decade that followed, Ray lived quietly in Cambridge, teaching Greek, mathematics, and humanities. However, his life was interrupted suddenly in 1662 by the Act of Uniformity, a law that required people to take an oath that they would conform to the beliefs and practices of the Church of England. Ray's refusal to take the oath lost him his fellowship, and he was forced to leave Cambridge.

Ray then found a wealthy patron named Francis Willughby, also a student from Cambridge, who became his student and colleague. For more than a decade, Willughby's various estates at Middleton Hall, Warwickshire, and Wollaton Hall, Nottingham, served as Ray's bases for scientific expeditions throughout England. Ray and Willughby also undertook expeditions through parts of Europe to study plants and animals. Their most ambitious expedition, which lasted from 1663 to 1666, took them through Germany, Italy, France, Switzerland, and the Low Countries (present-day Netherlands, Belgium, and Luxembourg). The year after they returned to England, Ray was elected a Fellow of the Royal Society of London, the new center of scientific activity. He rarely attended the society's meetings, however, and even refused the position of secretary of the organization when it was offered to him.

Willughby died suddenly in 1672, but he left sufficient money in his will to Ray so that he could complete the work they had started together. Ray married the next year and eventually returned to Black Notley. He remained there for the rest of his life, engaged in his writing, studies, and correspondence. In addition to his own work, which focused on plants, Ray undertook to complete Willughby's work on animals. Together their goal had been to produce a systematic study of nature based on firsthand observations and critical evaluation of the works of other scientists and scholars. Ray died in Black Notley in 1705.

Studies and Research. Ray's primary interests were botany and plant anatomy. While at Cambridge he took frequent walks in the countryside to study plants. His studies led to the publication of two catalogs of English plants. The catalogs, which contained descriptions of hundreds of different plants, set new standards for the composition and classification of plants. They marked the first phase of Ray's botanical work. Thereafter, he turned his attention to plant physiology*, morphology*, and taxonomy.

In 1668 Ray composed tables of plants for a book by another scholar, John Wilkins. In attempting to complete this task, he began searching for consistent principles for the classification of plants. His work on classification continued, and in 1682 Ray published a work that summarized his ideas on taxonomy. In this work, *Methodus plantarum* (Systematics of Plants), Ray became the first botanist to make a distinction between monocotyledons (plants with one seed leaf) and dicotyledons (plants with two seed leaves).

Ray's masterwork, *Historia plantarum* (History of Plants), a three-volume work, was published between 1686 and 1704. It represented Ray's contribution to his and Willughby's goal of producing a systematic study of nature. The aim of *Historia plantarum* was to classify, list,

The variety of plants that Ray observed during peaceful country walks in Cambridge sparked his interest in botany. Wanting to further study the local flora, Ray and some friends established small botanical gardens at their college.

*physiology science that deals with the functions of living organisms and their parts

*morphology branch of biology that deals with the form and structure of plants and animals

and describe all known plants in Europe. In addition to information gained from his own observations, Ray compiled material from a wide range of sources. He derived his discussion on plant anatomy and morphology from the writings of scholars such as the Italian biologist Marcello MALPIGHI and the English botanist Nehemiah GREW.

For each plant species in *Historia plantarum,* Ray not only provided names, classifications, and descriptions; he also gave details of the habitat, distribution, and medicinal uses of each plant. However, unlike some earlier books on plants, *Historia plantarum* contained no illustrations. This was probably due largely to the financial and technical difficulties of adequately illustrating such a comprehensive work.

Attempting to complete Willughby's survey of the animal kingdom, Ray published *Ornithologiae* in 1676. An important feature of this work was Ray's pioneering attempt to classify birds according to habitat and anatomy. Ray also completed books on fish, reptiles and quadrupeds (four-footed animals), and insects. The book on insects was the first such work published on this subject in nearly 100 years.

In addition to his work in science, Ray published several books on religion. The most popular of these, *The Wisdom of God,* discussed science from a religious perspective. Beginning with the solar system, it included discussions of the theory of matter, geology, the plant and animal kingdoms, and human anatomy. Ray argued that the fundamental relationship that is found between form and function throughout nature is proof that God created everything in the universe.

Francesco REDI

1626–ca. 1697

ENTOMOLOGY,
PARASITOLOGY, TOXICOLOGY

*tourniquet tight bandage that restricts the flow of blood

*physiologist one who specializes in physiology, the science that deals with the functions of living organisms and their parts

Francesco Redi was a pioneer of experimental toxicology (the study of poisons) and also made significant contributions in entomology (the study of insects) and parasitology (the study of parasites). The son of a famous Italian physician named Gregorio Redi, Francesco was born in Arezzo, Italy. He studied at the University of Pisa, graduating with a degree in medicine in 1647. Thereafter he served as the head physician and counselor to the powerful Medici family of Florence.

During this time Redi also served as the superintendent of the family's pharmacy, where snakes were widely used in the preparation of antidotes (remedy) to poisons. Working with poisonous snakes, Redi identified the source of their venom and discovered that the venom is harmful only when it enters the bloodstream. Knowing this he recommended applying a tourniquet* above a snakebite wound to prevent the venom from circulating and infecting the blood. He also recognized that it is safe to suck the venom from a wound because swallowing the venom is not harmful. These were the first investigations into experimental toxicology and were published in his 1664 letter titled *Osservazioni intorno alle vipere* (Observations on Vipers).

Redi is best known for designing a series of experiments to test the English physiologist* William HARVEY's theory that flies are not generated spontaneously but develop from eggs too small to be seen. Using a microscope, Redi identified the egg-producing organs in insects, proving that they reproduced like many other animals. He then argued that decaying matter was an ideal source of food for insect larvae and that maggots only appear there because insects use such material as a source of nourishment and lay their eggs in it. He then proved his theory by placing decaying organic matter in containers that could not be penetrated by insects. When no maggots appeared on the organic matter, Redi's theory was proved correct, and he published his findings in 1668 in *Esperienze intorno alla generazione degli insetti* (Experience in the Generation of Insects). Redi nevertheless supported the idea of spontaneous generation in the case of intestinal worms and gallflies. The doctrine of spontaneous generation was successfully challenged in the nineteenth century by the French microbiologist* Louis PASTEUR.

microbiologist scientist who studies microscopic life-forms, such as bacteria and viruses

Walter
REED

1851–1902

MEDICINE

Walter Reed is perhaps best known from the army hospital in Washington, D.C., that is named after him. He achieved that honor because of his outstanding work in studying and combating malaria, typhoid fever, and yellow fever. Reed's efforts during the late 1800s greatly reduced the serious toll that these diseases took on military personnel.

Born in Belroi, Virginia, Reed did not begin formal schooling until age 14. He enrolled in the University of Virginia the following year and earned a medical degree by age 17. He earned a second M.D. from Bellevue Hospital in New York the following year, but it was not formally awarded to him until he reached age 21.

Early in his career Reed practiced medicine in New York and served as a health inspector for the then-independent city of Brooklyn. In 1874 he joined the army as an assistant surgeon and spent most of the next 20 years on obscure military bases. In 1893 he was named curator of the Army Medical Museum and professor of bacteriology* and clinical microscopy at the Army Medical College in Washington, D.C.

Reed's first important breakthrough occurred during the Spanish American War, which began in 1898. He was appointed chair of a board that had been established to study the causes of typhoid fever in Cuba. Reed and his colleagues on the board found that the disease was caused by a bacillus (rod-shaped bacteria) spread by mosquitoes, and that some people could carry the disease without becoming ill themselves. Their work helped end the typhoid epidemic that cost thousands of soldiers their lives during the war.

In 1900 Reed was ordered to study the yellow fever epidemic in Cuba. Earlier investigators had identified a particular bacillus and mosquito as possible causes of the disease. Reed, who concluded that the mosquito was the culprit, designed experiments that led to the development of a vaccine made from the blood of infected victims. Within a year Reed successfully eliminated a disease that had plagued Cuba for years. Reed died a year later from complications during surgery to remove a ruptured appendix.

bacteriology science that deals with bacteria, microscopic organisms that can cause infection and disease

153

Royer, Clémence

Clémence
ROYER

ANTHROPOLOGY,
SCIENCE WRITING

Royer's strong feminist views and her anticleri-
cal beliefs were the underlying themes of her
work. They were repeated in the articles she
wrote for scientific, economic, and feminist
journals, as well as in the introduction to her
translation of Darwin's *On the Origin of Species*.

evolution historical development of a
biological group such as a species

anthropology study of human beings,
especially in relation to origins and physical and cultural characteristics

naturalist one who studies objects in
their natural settings

Clémence Royer played an important role in educating the public
about scientific issues. She translated into French the English biologist Charles DARWIN's groundbreaking book *On the Origin of Species*
and published her own works on evolution* as it applied to humans
and societies. She also wrote on anthropology* and on the structure of
matter. Her career was shaped by her feminist views and by her belief
that the basis of philosophy and morality was science, not religion.

A Self-Educated Scientist. Royer was born in Nantes in western
France, in the region known as Brittany. Two years after she was born,
her father, an army captain, took part in a political uprising that failed.
His involvement in this venture caused him to flee France for Switzerland, where the Royer family lived for the next four years.

When the family returned to France, Royer attended school briefly
before completing her education at home. Her father tutored her in
mathematics. Later she trained as a schoolteacher, earning certificates
that qualified her to teach French, music, and mathematics. At age 23
she went to Wales to work as a teacher and to learn English.

By that time Royer's political views had already turned toward
republicanism, or government by elected officials. She found that her
ideas about religion were changing as well. No longer a believer, she
was becoming critical of the role of religion in public and private life.
To escape the distress this created, Royer left France and settled in Lau-
sanne, Switzerland. There she turned to science and spent two years
reading books on scientific and philosophical topics in the town's public library. By 1859 she had become so well informed that women in
the community encouraged her to give scientific lectures to female
audiences. Royer's lectures went beyond scientific subject matter as she
urged women to accept and welcome scientific knowledge and to
become involved in the sciences.

Achievements and Publications. Shortly thereafter Royer began writing articles on economics for a political science journal. She also continued to lecture on topics that included the life sciences. While preparing to talk about Jean Baptiste LAMARCK, the noted French naturalist*,
she read Darwin's recently published *On the Origin of Species*, which
introduced the subject of biological evolution.

Royer saw at once that Darwin's work was important. Eager to
introduce the *Origin* to French readers, she began to translate the work
into French with the help of a naturalist and added some material—
lengthy notes explaining the text and an introduction that set forth
ideas of her own, including an attack on the authority of the church.
Royer also argued that certain practices, such as marriage choices that
favored unintelligent women and social programs that protected the
weak and sick, tampered with the natural process of human evolution.

Darwin disagreed with some of Royer's notes, and he found her
introduction surprising. In the second edition of Royer's translation, he
changed some of her wording. In the third edition Royer included a criticism of pangenesis, Darwin's theory about how parents passed their

physical characteristics to their offspring. This offended Darwin, who rejected Royer's work and turned over the work to another translator. However, Darwin changed his mind in 1882, a few years before his death, and allowed Royer to publish a new edition of her translation.

Royer's translation of Darwin's work caused a sensation in French scientific circles—much later, a colleague would say that Royer had "shattered the windows" with it. Yet her work won her a membership in the previously all-male Société d'Anthropologie, a scientific society for anthropologists and others interested in human biology. In the late 1880s, during a society conference on evolution, Royer delivered lectures on the historical development of the mind. She also wrote articles for the society's journal and received an award for an essay on the history of atomism, the philosophical and scientific concept that the universe is made up of tiny, invisible particles.

By this time Royer was living in Paris. Supported only by a small grant from the Ministry of Public Education, Royer faced growing financial distress in the 1890s until journalists publicized her plight and friends stepped in to help.

Resettled in a retirement home in suburban Paris, Royer became acquainted with a new group of feminist admirers. At their urging she helped found a feminist newspaper called *La Fronde,* and she wrote a column for the paper, covering both political and scientific subjects. Royer also published scientific articles, continued to discuss the structure of matter, and exchanged letters on the topic with philosophers and mathematicians. In 1900 she published a large volume on matter and the possible structures of atoms. That same year she received the Legion of Honor, one of the French government's most distinguished awards, for her services to learning. She died two years later, having achieved recognition as a pioneering feminist in the scientific community.

Ahead of Her Time

Royer's feminist views and independent mind often led her to explore subjects considered unsuitable for women in the 1800s. Even the Société d'Anthropologie, which published many of Royer's articles, found some of her work too advanced or controversial. Royer once wrote about the birth rate, discussing the role of women in French society and their decision to bear fewer children. Because it was a sensitive topic, the society did not publish the article and its existence was unknown until recently.

Santorio
SANTORIO
1561–1636
MEDICINE, PHYSIOLOGY, SCIENTIFIC INSTRUMENTATION

Santorio Santorio, also known as Sanctorius, was noted for his experimental approach to medicine at a time when most physicians relied unquestioningly on the medical doctrines of the ancient Greek physicians and philosophers HIPPOCRATES and GALEN and the great philosopher ARISTOTLE. Although Santorio supported many of the accepted ideas on anatomy and medicine, he stressed the importance of reaching conclusions based on observation and reasoning. He said, "One must believe first in one's own senses and in experience, then in reasoning, and only in the third place in the authority of Hippocrates, of Galen, of Aristole, and of other excellent philosophers."

The son of a Venetian nobleman, Santorio was born in Justinopolis in the Venetian Republic (present-day Koper, Yugoslavia). He received a classical education in languages and literature before he left to study medicine at the University of Padua in 1575. He graduated in 1582, set up a private medical practice, and almost immediately began to study the change in weight that occurred in his own body as a result of eating and eliminating waste. This work resulted in the publication of his most famous work, *De statica medicina* (Medical Statics), in which he argued that health was dependent on a balance of substances ingested by an organism and those expelled by it. His measurements indicated that a large part of excretion takes place invisibly, through the skin and lungs. He studied the size of this excretion, its relationship to visible excretions, and its dependence on diet, sleep, and exercise. He concluded that invisible excretion varies according to several internal and external factors. Although Santorio's ideas about the relationship of health to the balance of material taken in and expelled were later modified, his emphasis on quantitative experimentation introduced an important new approach in medicine. He developed scales and other measuring devices to carry out his experiments. His approach was called iatrophysics (medical physics). He published his findings in *De statica medicina* in 1614 and the work rapidly became popular and was translated into many European languages.

Santorio modified traditional medical ideas according to his findings. For example, the accepted authorities did not differentiate between different ailments produced by the same causes, but Santorio defined a continuum of illness from mild to severe. He also attempted to deduce the total number of possible diseases, which according to his calculations was about 80,000. Santorio published his arguments in 1602, in a book in which he examined the methods a doctor should follow to avoid making mistakes in medical practice. The work also contains descriptions of many diseases and examples of diagnoses for different illnesses.

Santorio invented other scientific measuring instruments, including a thermometer, a device for measuring atmospheric humidity (a hygrometer), a pendulum for timing the pulse rate, an instrument for making precise incisions (a trocar), and a special syringe for extracting bladder stones.

In 1611, Santorio took up a professorship at the University of Padua and remained there until 1624. Thereafter, he retired from this post and moved to Venice, where he lived until his death from a disease of the urinary tract. In 1630 he was given the task of organizing efforts to deal with an epidemic of the plague. The same year he was elected president of the Venetian College of Physicians. Santorio is known in the history of medicine for his work on quantitative experimentation.

Mathias Jacob
SCHLEIDEN
1804–1881
BOTANY, NATURAL SCIENCE

Jacob Schleiden's contributions to science involved the microscopic studies that led to his theory of cell formation. His observations, based on the study of plant cells, formed the basis of a textbook that fundamentally changed the way the subject was taught. Just as important as his research were his successful efforts to popularize science.

The son of a physician, Schleiden was born in Hamburg, Germany. He studied law at the University of Heidelberg and began a law practice in Hamburg. However, he cared little for the work and left the practice after several years. Inspired by an uncle, he began to study botany, receiving his doctorate from the University of Jena in 1839.

Early in his career as a botanist, Schleiden worked with the German physiologist* Theodor SCHWANN to study cell formation. Making extensive use of microscopes, Schleiden examined the structure of plant tissues. He concluded that cells form only in liquids that contain sugar, gum, and mucus. The mucus condenses into spheres and the liquid on the surface of each sphere is transformed into jelly. The jelly forms a wall around the remaining liquid and eventually becomes the membrane that separates the cell from other cells.

Three years after graduating from Jena, Schleiden published a botany textbook, introducing teaching methods that dominated the field for many years. He rejected the practice of philosophical speculation, in which one proposes a theory of how things work and then sets out to find evidence to support it. He favored the inductive method, in which one first collects data and observations and then comes up with a theory to explain the facts. Consequently the book begins with a treatment of the structure of plants and plant cells and then moves on to cover broader topics. Schleiden's text revolutionized how botany was taught and aroused great interest in the field among young scientists.

Schleiden lived during an era in which many leading scientists devoted their attention to presenting their ideas to the public. He established a career as a traveling lecturer, attracting large audiences. He published studies in scientific periodicals, and printed collections of his lectures sold well. He did not confine his writing to botany. His publications include a detailed work on the economic, social, and historical importance of salt to human life; and scholarly studies of the fate of Europe's Jews during the Middle Ages*.

These latter works, which established Schleiden as a liberal thinker, were the object of much interest and debate in Germany, whose universities at the time were experiencing a wave of anti-Semitism (discrimination against Jews). Schleiden, no stranger to controversy, engaged in public debates with many scientific figures of his time. Although his untraditional ideas put him at odds with many scientists and thinkers, they never diminished his popular appeal. Schleiden died in Frankfurt at the age of 77.

*physiologist one who specializes in physiology, the science that deals with the functions of living organisms and their parts

*Middle Ages period between ancient and modern times in western Europe, generally considered to be from the A.D. 500s to the 1500s

During a very active research career that lasted only five years, Theodor Schwann unlocked the secret of how complex life-forms develop from individual cells. His ideas formed the basis of cell theory and laid part of the foundation for histology*. Due to the scorn of his professional colleagues and his own temperament, however, Schwann's contributions to science ceased while he was still a young man.

Education and Early Career. Schwann was born in Neuss, Germany. As a child, he was an ideal student; cooperative and hard working, yet quite shy, he devoted himself to his studies, family life, and religion.

Theodor Ambrose Hubert
SCHWANN
1810–1882
PHYSIOLOGY, HISTOLOGY

*histology branch of anatomy that deals with the minute structure of animal and plant tissues, observable only through a microscope

157

Theodor Schwann founded modern histology by defining the cell as the basic unit of animal structure.

*theological referring to theology, the study of religion

*physiologist one who specializes in physiology, the science that deals with the functions of living organisms and their parts

*fermentation process of change in organic substances in which microorganisms called enzymes cause compounds such as carbohydrates to break down into alcohol or acids

*putrefaction decay of living matter

*satire literary work that uses humor or wit to make fun of a person or idea

Because he did not show an interest in the outside world, his family planned for him a career in the Church. At age 16 he left home to enter the Jesuit College of Three Crowns in Cologne.

There Schwann met a gifted teacher named Wilhelm Smets who argued that spiritual growth comes through personal perfection and that reason plays a great role in achieving such perfection. Schwann was so taken with Smets's emphasis on reason that he abandoned his theological* studies and took up medicine. He transferred to the University of Bonn, where he attended lectures by the physiologist* Johannes MÜLLER, in whose laboratory he would make his most famous later discoveries.

Schwann graduated from Bonn in 1831 and continued his studies in Berlin, where he earned his M.D. three years later and then went to work for Müller. Although Schwann was a devoted follower of Müller, he disagreed with Müller's belief that a "vital force," acting intelligently, created live tissues and gave them their energy. He believed instead that living tissues conform to the same physical forces and natural rules that apply to all matter. This conviction led him to his most important discoveries.

Early Researches. Schwann designed his first formal experiments to test his ideas about vital force. He believed that he could measure and express in mathematical terms the physiological properties of living organs and tissues. Doing so would help prove that living tissues operate according to predictable natural laws and not because of the powers of a special living force. He created a device that measured how much a muscle contracts when pulling different loads. The device also enabled him to compare the intensity of contraction to the size of the load. This was the first time that anyone had measured a so-called vital force (in this case muscle contraction) and expressed in mathematical terms the laws by which it operated.

Schwann's belief in a set of universal physical forces underlying all of nature led him to another breakthrough. The subject at issue was the role that heat plays in the processes of fermentation* and putrefaction*. Some scientists believed that when air is heated, it loses oxygen, which is necessary for these processes to occur. Schwann, however, was convinced that it was not the act of heating itself but the destruction of live germs in the air caused by heating that prevented the two processes from occurring.

Schwann first proved that heating did not destroy oxygen by showing that frogs could breathe previously heated air. He then investigated fermentation and found that the process is not related to heat or oxygen but to the multiplication of yeast cultures. In this manner he proved that a living organism causes fermentation as well as putrefaction. Other researchers agreed with him, but parts of the scientific establishment rejected his arguments. In 1839 Justus von LIEBIG and Friedrich WÖHLER, two of the most respected scientists of the day, published a vicious satire* of Schwann's findings in a prestigious journal. The attack made it almost impossible for Schwann to continue his scientific career in Germany and was probably a major factor in his decision to abandon his active research at such an early age.

The Cell Theory. Schwann's conviction that the same natural forces act on all things was echoed in his ideas on the structural organization of living organisms. For many years scientists had debated whether all organisms develop according to the same basic principles or patterns, or whether each organism grows according to its own unique plan. Earlier researchers advanced the notion that all things are comprised of some type of basic particle that contained cells. However, no one had yet suggested that living organisms consisted entirely of cells or products of cells.

The debate progressed little until the perfection of the microscope in the 1830s. Using one of the new microscopes, Schwann found that the cells in the spinal cord of frog larvae appeared to have nuclei on the inner surface of their walls like those in plant cells. He also found evidence of nuclei in cartilage cells, and he saw that those cells also have the same structure as plant cells. Finally, he noted that new cells formed within the organism's existing cells.

These findings led Schawnn to conclude that the structure of animal cells was similar to those of plant cells; both cells contained a nucleus, a membrane (cell wall), and a vacuole (the cavity between the cell wall and the nucleus). In further studies he found that different types of tissue, such as muscle, bone, and nerve, all develop from the same basic cellular material. All tissues begin as cells, and during development they become differentiated or specialized into distinct tissues, organs, and parts.

These results convinced Schwann that the idea of "vital force" was invalid. He concluded that because the same force unites both animal and plant molecules into cells, that force must reside in matter itself and cannot be supplied by an outside intelligence. Although later scientists found that Schwann's theory contained a technical error in his explanation of how cells formed, he was correct in his notion that the cell is the basic structure from which all organisms develop.

Later Life. After the attack by his colleagues, Schwann left Germany for Belgium where he taught anatomy, physiology, and embryology* at two separate universities. However, he spent most of his time after 1850 in religious studies and inventing practical devices for the mining industry such as water pumps and breathing apparatus. He also began work on a theory that would extend his cell theory to a general system of organisms that included principles of religion and psychology. However, he suffered a stroke before he had the opportunity to publish this final work. He died in Cologne at the age of 71.

*embryology branch of biology that deals with embryos, organisms from the first division of the fertilized egg through the early stages of development before birth or hatching

Ignaz Philipp Semmelweis is best known for his brilliant work in determining the cause of , and devising effective preventive measures for, puerperal fever (also called childbed fever). Before Semmelweis appeared on the scene, the disease, whose symptoms include infection of some part of the female reproductive organs following childbirth or abortion, was a major cause of death among newborn infants and their

Ignaz Philipp
SEMMELWEIS
1818–1865
MEDICINE

mothers. By instituting a regimen of hand washing and antiseptic procedures, Semmelweis was able to dramatically reduce the incidence of the disease. Unfortunately, his ideas were rejected by most of his fellow physicians for many years.

Born in Buda, Hungary, Semmelweis was the son of a wealthy shopkeeper who wanted his son to enter government service. Thus, Semmelweis began his academic career at the University of Vienna law school, but he soon switched to studying medicine at the Vienna Medical School. He received his doctoral degree in 1844. He remained in Vienna after graduation and earned a master's degree as a midwife, underwent surgical training, and received additional medical instruction. Two years later he became house officer of the Vienna General Hospital's First Obstetrical* Clinic.

*obstetrical referring to obstetrics, the branch of medicine dealing with pregnancy and childbirth

At the time the clinic was experiencing very high mortality due to puerperal fever; one in every eight mothers and newborns died of the disease. However, in the hospital's Second Obstetrical Clinic, only about 1 in 50 succumbed to the disease, but no one understood why there was such a large discrepancy in the mortality rates between the two clinics. The only difference between the two was that the first clinic was used for teaching medical students while the second was used for teaching midwives. In 1847, when Semmelweis was on vacation, an incident that occurred gave him the clue to crack the mystery.

A good friend of Semmelweis's had died after a knife accidentally punctured the friend's finger when he was conducting an autopsy. When Semmelweis's friend's corpse was examined, it showed symptoms very similar to those of puerperal fever. Based on this observation, Semmelweis concluded that medical students who conducted autopsies were bringing contamination from the corpses into the clinic and passing them along to the patients they examined. He then instituted a program in which students were required to thoroughly wash their hands in a chlorine solution after they had observed or conducted autopsies.

The students and medical staff at the hospital resisted at first, but when they adopted Semmelweis's methods, the results were impressive. Mortality from puerperal fever dropped to less than 3 percent. Notwithstanding this success, Semmelweis continued to experience great difficulty in convincing his colleagues to adopt his practices. Frustrated by his inability to convince doctors or government officials of the use of his procedures, he left Vienna abruptly in 1850 and moved to the town of Pest.

In 1861 Semmelweis published his findings in book form, but the work received unfavorable reviews. He reacted by lashing out at his critics, which did little to help his cause. Four years later he suffered a form of mental illness that led to his committal to an insane asylum in Vienna, where he died. It was only through the work of Louis PASTEUR many years later that scientists were finally convinced of the effectiveness of the methods that Semmelweis had introduced.

Michael Servetus practiced as a doctor and is remembered in the history of science for his insight into the roles of the lungs and heart in the circulation of the blood. Theology*, however, was his first subject of study and a lifelong concern. At a time when heresy* was punishable severely, Servetus paid the ultimate price for disagreeing with the religious authorities of his day.

Servetus's date and place of birth are not known, but he was probably born in 1511 in Villanueva de Sixena in Spain's Huesca province. His parents were nobles, and one of his brothers was a priest. The young Servetus learned Latin, possibly at the University of Zaragoza, which was not far from his home. At age 15, Servetus entered the service of Juan de Quintana, a friar of the Franciscan religious brotherhood who was also a learned and influential man. Quintana became confessor to Emperor Charles V of the Holy Roman Empire, whose coronation Servetus witnessed. In 1530, however, Servetus left Quintana's service because his studies of the Bible had raised doubts in his mind about the rightness of Roman Catholic religious doctrine, especially the idea that God is a Trinity, or threefold deity. Servetus moved to Switzerland, where he published works that denied the Trinity, outraging both Catholics and Protestants.

Assuming the name Michel de Villeneuve, Servetus then moved to France. As an employee of a publishing house in Lyons, he prepared several new and successful editions of *Geography*, written by Ptolemy, a Greek scientist of the ancient world. Servetus also read many medical books and developed an interest in the subject. In the late 1530s, he published two books on the topics of healing herbs, medicinal syrups, and diet, both considered noteworthy contributions to modern pharmacology*. Servetus spent several years studying medicine in Paris, where he lectured on geography, astronomy, and the use of astrology in medicine and in forecasting the future. However, he was charged before the Faculty for Medicine for teaching astrology.

Although he lived outwardly as a Catholic, Servetus had not abandoned his beliefs or his theological studies. In 1553 he published his major work on theology, *Christianismi restitutio* (Christianity restored), which contains Servetus's lasting claim to scientific fame. To explain how the divine spirit enters the blood and is spread through the body, Servetus described the limited circulation as blood traveling from the right to the left side of the heart via the lungs—not through minute holes in the dividing wall of the heart (the septum) as the ancient Greek physician GALEN had argued. Servetus's religious ideas, however, caused such protest that the authorities seized and burned nearly all copies of his book. Not until 1694 was Servetus's scientific discovery recognized and accepted. Long before that time, however, the Italian anatomist Realdo COLOMBO had made the same discovery and published his findings. In fact, an Arab physician named Ibn al-Nafis had described circulation through the lungs in the 1200s, but it is unlikely that either Servetus or Colombo knew of his work.

The publication of *Christianismi restitutio* was the undoing of Servetus, who had been living under an assumed name since the publi-

Michael
SERVETUS

---

ca. 1511–1553

BIOLOGY, PHILOSOPHY

*theology study of religion

*heresy belief that is contradictory to church doctrine

*pharmacology science that deals with the preparation, uses, and effects of drugs

cation of his works denying the Trinity. He was arrested and imprisoned for heresy, but he escaped. As he fled through Switzerland toward Italy, he was recognized and turned over to the authorities, who burned him at the stake.

Lazzaro SPALLANZANI

1729–1799

NATURAL HISTORY,
BIOLOGY, PHYSIOLOGY

In addition to his accomplishments in biology and physiology, Spallanzani also made an important discovery regarding food preservation. He sealed meat extracts in glass containers and heated them for an hour, becoming the first to have success with canning foods.

*natural history systematic study of animals and plants, especially in their natural settings

*naturalist one who studies objects in their natural settings

The Italian scientist Lazzaro Spallanzani is considered one of the founders of experimental biology. Famous throughout Europe for his experiments in animal reproduction, Spallanzani also made important contributions to the study of bodily functions, such as blood circulation, digestion, and respiration. His work challenged the theory of spontaneous generation—the idea that living organisms could be produced from inanimate, or lifeless, matter. Spallanzani also was a pioneer in the science of vulcanology, the study of volcanoes and volcanic phenomena.

Early Life and Work. Born in Scandiano, Italy, Spallanzani was the son of a distinguished and successful lawyer. He attended local schools until age 15, at which time he went to a Jesuit college in the nearby town of Reggio Emilia, where he studied philosophy, languages, and the classics. Invited to join the Jesuit religious order, Spallanzani chose instead to study law at the University of Bologna. There he became interested in science and mathematics through the influence of his cousin Laura Bassi, who was also a professor there. Spallanzani broadened his education and began studying physics, chemistry, natural history*, and other subjects. With Bassi's support he also gained permission from his father to abandon law and pursue his scientific interests.

Around 1753 Spallanzani earned the degree of doctor of philosophy. Soon afterward he also was ordained a priest and became attached to churches in the city of Modena. Although he performed his priestly duties irregularly, he remained attached to the church throughout much of his life. At various times financial assistance from the church enabled him to pursue his scientific investigations. Early in 1755 Spallanzani began teaching at the College of Reggio Emilia, and two years later he was appointed lecturer of mathematics at the recently founded University of Reggio Emilia. In 1761 he set out on the first of many scientific excursions to various parts of Italy. Such trips became a regular part of his scientific research because they enabled him to investigate unexplained natural occurrences and collect numerous specimens of plants and animals, which he later donated to museums.

Early Discoveries and New Directions. While teaching at Reggio Emilia, Spallanzani was introduced to the work of the French naturalist* Georges-Louis Leclerc BUFFON and the British biologist John Turberville Needham. Buffon and Needham believed that all living things contained both inanimate matter and special particles called animalcules that serve as the elementary building blocks of life. They argued that when an organism dies, the animalcules play a role in the spontaneous generation of new life from nonliving matter.

Equipped with a microscope, Spallanzani began to conduct experiments to investigate spontaneous generation. Scientists had long held that simple living things, such as the microorganisms* revealed by the Dutch naturalist Antoni van LEEUWENHOEK's research with a microscope, could be generated spontaneously through the reorganization of nonliving material. Spallanzani showed that the solutions in which microorganisms ordinarily reproduce prevented breeding when boiled for 30 or more minutes and then placed in a sealed flask. Proponents of spontaneous generation dismissed Spallanzani's work, arguing that prolonged boiling merely destroyed a vital principle in the air. In 1765 Spallanzani reported his findings to the Bologna Academy of Sciences.

Spallanzani's work on spontaneous generation led to new avenues of research. He began to study the ability of some lower, less complex animals to regenerate, or regrow, lost parts of their bodies, such as tails or legs. By studying earthworms, salamanders, toads, and frogs, he discovered that lower animals have a much greater capacity to regenerate than higher, more complex animals, that the ability to regenerate decreases with the age of the organism, and that internal organs cannot regenerate.

Further Studies. Spallanzani's scientific accomplishments and discoveries brought him fame throughout Europe. In 1768 he was elected a Fellow of the Royal Society of London, and the following year he accepted a position as professor of natural history at the University of Pavia in Italy. He remained there for the rest of his career.

A popular teacher and lecturer, Spallanzani spent much of his time conducting scientific research. He continued to study regeneration and found further evidence to disprove more of the theories of Buffon and Needham. In experimenting with the idea of transplantation, he eventually succeeded in transplanting the head of one snail onto the body of another.

Spallanzani broadened his studies to investigate the blood circulation and digestion of animals. Through his work with circulation, he established the existence of connections between the arteries and veins of warm-blooded animals. He also studied the effect of growth on circulation as well as the influence of gravity and the effect of wounds on different parts of the circulatory system. Finally, Spallanzani showed that the pulse of warm-blooded animals is caused by the pressure that the blood exerts on the walls of the arteries as it is pumped through the body by the heart.

In studying digestion, Spallanzani concluded that the basic factor in the digestive process is the action of gastric juice—a term he introduced. He discovered that gastric juice helps dissolve food in the digestive system and that the speed at which it dissolves any given food is related to the quantity of the juice. Spallanzani also found evidence that gastric juice contains chemicals that are suited to particular types of foods. Despite some errors and gaps in his work, Spallanzani successfully explained many phenomena of gastric digestion.

Spallanzani also studied fertilization in both plants and animals. In his work with animals, he showed that contact between a female ovum

*microorganism tiny living thing that generally can be seen clearly only through a microscope

Dressed for Results

Spallanzani and other scientists knew that semen stimulated, in some way, the development of an organism within a female egg. However, they did not fully understand the function of semen and sperm or know if actual contact between egg and semen was necessary.

In one of his experiments, Spallanzani fitted tight pants on male frogs and brought them into contact with frog eggs. When no tadpoles developed, he then manually brought the eggs in contact with semen, concluding that contact between egg and semen was essential for the formation of a new organism.

(egg) and a male sperm is necessary for fertilization. Spallanzani also performed the first successful experiments in artificial insemination, in which he used artificial means to cause a dog to become pregnant.

Other Accomplishments. Early in his career at the University of Pavia, Spallanzani was placed in charge of the Museum of Natural History there. Charged with acquiring new exhibits for the museum, he undertook many expeditions to various parts of Europe to gather new specimens of plants, animals, minerals, and other objects. Through his labors the collections of the museum became among the finest in Italy.

Spallanzani's specimen-gathering expeditions gave him an opportunity to investigate new and different life-forms and study natural phenomena. During one such trip he founded Europe's first marine zoological laboratory and conducted studies on deep-sea phosphorescence*. He also demonstrated the animal nature of corals and other tiny marine organisms.

Among Spallanzani's better-known studies of natural phenomena are those dealing with volcanoes. He visited active volcanoes in Italy, including Etna in Sicily as well as Stromboli and Volcano on islands off the Italian coast. Making perilous climbs to the craters of these volcanoes, he observed and measured lava flows and noted the gas explosions that forced up red-hot lava and ejected huge rocks. His observations of volcanic activities proved fundamental to the emerging science of vulcanology.

During the last years of his life, Spallanzani conducted further research on microscopic plants and animals. He also engaged in research that contributed greatly to the understanding of plant and animal respiration. Through his experiments he determined that the blood carried carbon dioxide through the body and that oxygen was converted to carbon dioxide in the tissues rather than in the lungs. This work played an important role in developing new ideas about respiration and demonstrating the basic uniformity of the respiratory process throughout the animal kingdom.

*phosphorescence property of some organisms to give off a natural glow or light

Georg Ernst
STAHL

1660–1734

MEDICINE

The German physician Georg Ernst Stahl is a controversial figure in the history of science. Stahl devoted much effort to developing distinctive theories about the nature of matter and of biological processes. He also had a successful medical practice and was regarded in his day as an important scientific figure. He was out of step with the intellectual trends of his time, however, and by the end of the 1800s, new research and experiments had disproved or overturned his system of medicine.

Education and Career. Stahl was born in Ansbach, Germany. Beyond the fact that his upbringing was shaped by Pietism, a movement within the Lutheran Church that called for moral reform, little is known about his background or early life. He attended the university at Jena, a city in eastern Germany, where he studied medicine. He became friendly with a fellow student named Friedrich Hoffmann, who later influenced his career. After his graduation in 1684, Stahl concentrated on his research, lectured at the university, and became a reputed scientist and teacher. He then spent seven years in Weimar as the court physician to the duke.

In 1694 Hoffmann was appointed professor of medicine at a new university in the city of Halle, and he arranged for Stahl to receive the second professorship of medicine. Stahl lectured on a variety of topics at Halle, but his favorite subjects were chemistry and the theory of medicine.

Stahl's relationship with Hoffmann weakened over time, however, and their disagreements over scientific issues became profound. The two men became rivals, even enemies. In 1715 Stahl left Halle for Berlin, where he became the court physician to Frederick William I of Prussia. Stahl spent the rest of his life in Berlin.

Major Scientific Theories. Although Stahl never prepared a straightforward overview of his theories, his work contains many recurring themes that formed the foundation of his thinking. One of these themes is the belief that living and nonliving things are fundamentally different. This belief was the basis of Stahl's difference of opinion with Hoffmann. Hoffmann adopted a view called iatromechanics, which said that the simple laws of mechanics, which explain the properties and movements of machines, were sufficient to explain how living organisms function. Stahl, however, believed that life is a nonmaterial quality that cannot be explained in purely mechanical terms.

According to Stahl, both living and nonliving things are made of matter, but living things also possess something more, a vital principle or life force that he called "anima." In fact, the term *animism* refers to this concept of a life force that cannot be studied or observed directly. Although Stahl was not the only scientist to hold such views, he was the only one who tried to explain the anima's relationship with the body. He argued that life depends on motion, such as the motion of the heart and the blood, and he concluded that motion comes from the anima, not from matter. However, he never clearly explained how motion linked the nonmaterial anima and the material body.

In his writings on medicine and in his treatment of patients, Stahl was practical. He taught that the proper study of medicine involves learning the body's functions, and he wrote about the specifics of physiology*, pathology*, and the treatment of illnesses. Stahl placed all these subjects within the framework of his theory that the body is controlled by the force of the anima.

*physiology science that deals with the functions of living organisms and their parts

*pathology study of diseases and their effects on organisms

The American biologist Nettie Maria Stevens specialized in cytology, the study of the cells found in living organisms. Her greatest achievements were in the field of cytogenetics, which is the branch of biology concerned with the relationship of cells to heredity. Stevens's research led to breakthroughs in the scientific understanding of how the sex of an organism is determined.

Nettie Maria
STEVENS

1861–1912

BIOLOGY, CYTOLOGY

*physiology science that deals with the functions of living organisms and their parts

*histology branch of anatomy that deals with the minute structure of animal and plant tissues, observable only through a microscope

Sharing the Glory

The history of science contains many accounts of discoveries made by two different researchers working independently. Nettie Maria Stevens's discovery that chromosomes determine the sex of organisms is an example. When Stevens wrote her paper on the subject, Edmund Beecher Wilson of Columbia University, a former head of Stevens's department at Bryn Mawr College, reviewed the paper. Wilson had just written a paper on insect chromosomes, announcing the same discovery. He encouraged Stevens to publish her paper, and in an example of scientific cooperation, each cited the other's work as evidence that their conclusions were correct.

Background, Education, and Research. Stevens was born in Cavendish, Vermont, and educated in public schools, where she received very high grades. After graduating from high school in 1880, she taught high school for three terms in Lebanon, New Hampshire. The subjects she taught included English, Latin, mathematics, physiology*, and zoology. In 1881 Stevens enrolled in the Westfield Normal School, a teachers' college in Massachusetts. The institution offered a four-year course of study, but Stevens completed it in two years, with excellent grades. She performed especially well in science and mathematics.

For the next 13 years, Stevens worked as a teacher and librarian in various Massachusetts towns. Details about her life are sketchy, and little is known about her decision to return to college and pursue a scientific career, but in 1896 she moved to Palo Alto, California, to attend Stanford University. Some years later her father and sister, her only living relatives, moved to California as well.

At Stanford, Stevens decided to major in physiology. Under the influence of a professor named Frank Mace MacFarland, she concentrated on cytology and histology*. For four summers, Stevens studied at a laboratory that the university maintained on the California coast at Pacific Grove, investigating marine organisms. She received her B.A. in 1899, her M.A. in 1900, and one year after that her master's thesis, a report of her studies on small marine creatures, was published.

Pursuing her interest in cytology and histology, Stevens then went to Bryn Mawr College in Pennsylvania for advanced study. Two prominent biologists, Edmund Beecher Wilson and Thomas Hunt Morgan, headed the college's biology department, and their influence shaped the course of Stevens's future work. Impressed with Stevens's abilities, the college gave her a fellowship to study at a zoological research station in Italy and at the University of Würzburg in Germany with Theodor BOVERI, a leading biological researcher. At the time Boveri was investigating chromosomes, the structures inside cells that carry the genetic information that governs heredity and the development of the organism. Stevens would later conduct research of her own involving chromosomes.

In 1903 she received her doctoral degree from Bryn Mawr, and for the rest of her life she remained connected to the college, first as a research fellow and later as an associate professor. Her position required her to teach, however, and she wanted to devote herself to research. Eventually the trustees created a research professorship for Stevens, but she died of breast cancer at Johns Hopkins Hospital in Baltimore, Maryland, before she could fill the position.

Contributions to Science. At Bryn Mawr, Stevens worked with Morgan, who was studying regeneration in various creatures. She joined in his work, focusing on how cells divided as tissue was regenerated. By about 1903, Stevens had turned her attention to the relationship between chromosomes and heredity. It was in this area that she would make her most important scientific discoveries. In 1904 she began to study the behavior of chromosomes in small insects called aphids and

After beginning scientific studies while in her mid-30s, Nettie Stevens went on to become one of the first American women to be recognized for her significant contributions to biological research.

published many papers on the topic. For one of these studies, she won a $1,000 prize for the best scientific paper written by a woman.

At the time many biologists were researching chromosomes and heredity, laying the foundations of the science known as genetics. They were fairly certain that chromosomes governed heredity, or at least that they were involved in it, but no one had demonstrated a connection between a specific chromosome and a particular characteristic passed from parents to an offspring. The characteristic that Stevens decided to study was sex determination, the factors that determine whether a particular organism will develop as male or female. For a time some scientists had thought that external or environmental causes acting on a newly fertilized egg or an embryo determined the organism's sex. By 1903, Morgan had reported in a paper that internal factors, not external ones, determined sex. Neither Morgan nor other scientists knew what those factors were, but a biologist named Clarence McClung had suggested that there is an extra chromosome in the male and that the presence of this extra chromosome determines that the organism is male.

Stevens set out to investigate the theory that chromosomes determine sex. Funded by the Carnegie Institution of Washington, she studied five insect species. In her examination of the common mealworm, she found that females have 20 large chromosomes, while males have 19 large chromosomes and one small chromosome, which she called the Y chromosome. This strongly suggested that the sex of an individual organism is determined by the chromosomes it inherits from its parents. Male mealworms, Stevens discovered, produce two kinds of sperm—one with the Y chromosome and one without it. When a sperm cell with a Y chromosome fertilizes an egg, the result is a male organism.

Stevens published her findings in an important paper titled "Studies in Spermatogenesis with Especial Reference to the 'Accessory Chromosome.'" Although not all scientists accepted Stevens's conclusion at the time, her work proved to be a milestone in genetics, confirming the role of chromosomes in heredity. In the years that followed, she continued her research on chromosomes, publishing more than 30 papers. Years later her mentor and colleague Thomas Hunt Morgan, who received the Nobel Prize for his work in genetics, declared, "Stevens had a share in a discovery of importance and her name will be remembered for this, when the minutiae of detailed investigations that she carried out have become incorporated in the general body of the subject."

Eduard Adolf
STRASBURGER

1844–1912

BOTANY, PLANT CYTOLOGY

*cytology branch of biology that deals with the structure, function, and life history of cells

*chromosome threadlike structure in the cell that contains the DNA (genes) that transmit unique genetic information

*naturalist one who studies objects in their natural settings

*evolution historical development of a biological group such as a species

Eduard Adolf Strasburger was one of the leading botanists of his day and a pioneer in the field of plant cytology*. His work answered many long-standing questions about cell division and the role of the nucleus and chromosomes* in heredity. By drawing attention to the similarities of plant and animal tissues, he also gave support to the English naturalist* Charles DARWIN's theory of evolution*.

Strasburger, the son of a merchant, was born in Warsaw, Poland. He received his education at the Sorbonne in Paris and the University of Bonn in Germany. In Bonn he became skilled in using the microscope, an ability that proved invaluable to his later discoveries. Strasburger later transferred to the University of Jena, where he worked with the famous zoologist Ernst HAECKEL, who had a major influence on his work. In 1881 he returned to Bonn, where he established what became the world's leading center of plant cytology.

Strasburger had witnessed the nucleus of a fern cell dividing during cell division very early in his research career. Later as he studied and described the stages of cell division in plants, he noted that the same phenomena occurred in the same sequence in animal cell division. This suggested to him that animal and plant cells have a common origin.

Strasburger had also observed the splitting of "filaments" (chromosomes) within the nucleus. Studies by other scientists had revealed that the division of these filaments played an important role in heredity. At the same time, other researchers had witnessed a sperm cell entering an egg cell and concluded that fertilization occurred when the nuclei of the two cells fused. Based on these findings and his own work, Strasburger concluded that the nucleus was responsible for heredity. Around the same time, other scientists, including August WEISMANN, independently arrived at the same conclusion.

Strasburger also determined that the filaments within the nucleus contained the material that passed characteristics from parents to offspring. He argued that the splitting of the filaments ensured that the material was equally divided between the two cells produced during cell division. He also proposed that the cytoplasm (the cellular material surrounding the nucleus) exerted some influence on heredity, but that the nucleus controlled metabolism*, growth, and other cellular processes.

*metabolism set of chemical reactions in organisms that convert food into energy and tissue

From his studies of plant reproduction, Strasburger concluded that asexual reproduction was the earliest form of reproduction and that sexual reproduction evolved later. He pointed out that asexual reproduction had certain advantages under favorable environmental conditions and that it led to a rapid increase in the number of organisms. However, sexual reproduction enabled species to adapt to meet unfavorable conditions.

In addition to his research, Strasburger was a popular professor who attracted students from around the world. He was also the author of several important botany textbooks and a member of most of Europe's leading scientific societies. He was still actively teaching and researching at the time of his death at age 68 in Poppelsdorf, Germany.

Thomas SYDENHAM
1624–1689
MEDICINE

The English physician Thomas Sydenham earned a reputation for his ability to devise therapies that effectively relieved suffering and restored his patients to health. His observations of epidemic diseases such as smallpox enabled him to formulate a set of fundamental principles concerning the development and treatment of disease. His efforts helped later physicians to conduct better bedside observations that ultimately improved their abilities to diagnose and treat illnesses effectively.

Sydenham was baptized in Wynford Eagle in Dorset County, but it is not known if he was born there. His father was an English nobleman who supported the Parliament against King James I during the English Civil War. Sydenham himself fought in the war and was nearly killed on more than one occasion. The war interrupted his education, but he returned during breaks in the fighting and earned his bachelor of medicine degree from Oxford University in 1648. Sydenham probably served additional time in the military after graduation, and he was later nominated but not elected to Parliament. He began to practice medicine around 1655, a profession he pursued until his death at age 65 in London. During his last years, he suffered from kidney-related problems and gout*.

*gout disease marked by painful inflammation of the joints

Sydenham believed that human knowledge was limited to observations of the physical world and reasoning based on experience. He placed little value on book learning, or reliance on the authority of written sources that had not been subjected to critical examination. This put him at odds with many of his contemporaries, but earned him the support and friendship of the eminent scientist Robert Boyle and the philosopher John Locke. In fact, the manuscripts for some of Sydenham's works are in Locke's handwriting. Some have suggested that Locke was the author, but the ideas in the texts are almost certainly those of Sydenham.

Sydenham developed a method for treating fevers, in the hope that his method would improve the uncertain and often bad effects of treatment current in his day. However, the Great Plague of London in 1865 and subsequent epidemics of smallpox showed that his ideas were ineffective. He noted that the fevers produced during these outbreaks showed puzzling variations, and he decided to study them more carefully. He kept a notebook of clinical observations over a five-year period that formed the basis of his major work on therapy.

In his book, Sydenham stressed the need for further knowledge about the seasonal variations in each disease. He also raised the possibility of developing treatments based on the observable symptoms of a disease and championed the practice of repeating treatments several times before declaring them effective. In the text he also suggested that diseases, like plants, have particular species, each with its own symptoms and variations.

Following his own prescriptions, Sydenham developed a more moderate treatment for smallpox. He also developed medicine from cinchona (quinine, which was later used to treat malaria) and invented liquid laudanum (preparation of opium) for use as a pain reliever. Sydenham's contributions to therapy earned him the title "English Hippocrates."

THEOPHRASTUS
ca. 371 B.C.–ca. 287 B.C.
BOTANY

The ancient Greek philosopher Theophrastus made important contributions to the field of botany. A person of remarkable learning and accomplishment, he also wrote on history, law, literature, music, and politics.

Student and Teacher. Born on the island of Lesbos in the Aegean Sea, Theophrastus met the great philosopher ARISTOTLE either on Lesbos or in Asia Minor. He accompanied Aristotle to Macedonia in 342 B.C., and later joined him in Athens. Around 322 B.C., he replaced Aristotle as the leader of the Lyceum, the famous school founded by Aristotle.

During the 35 years that Theophrastus headed the school, enrollment reached its peak and he taught nearly 2,000 students. He was so respected by the Athenians that an attempt to prosecute him for religious irreverence failed. On his deathbed, Theophrastus willed the Lyceum and a library of writings by Aristotle and himself to his relatives and associates.

Work and Writings. Theophrastus is generally considered a botanist, and his contributions in other fields were less important than those of

Theophrastus was a Peripatetic, or follower of Aristotle. It is believed that the term was derived from a covered walk called *peripatos* that attached to one of the buildings at the Lyceum, the school where both Aristotle and Theophrastus taught.

Aristotle. His writings include more than 200 works on the subjects of science, philosophy, history, law, literature, music, and politics, but few have survived to the present.

Theophrastus fully embraced Aristotle's conclusions on most topics. Like Aristotle he believed that there were different kinds of knowledge and that each required a different method of inquiry. The emphasis on the differences among methods of knowledge, and on the need to start from observation of the specific rather than the general, is characteristic of all of Theophrastus's scientific works.

Contributions to Botany. Theophrastus's important work on botany is contained in two long volumes—*Historia plantarum* (Inquiry into Plants), which contains descriptions, classifications, and analyses of various plants; and *De causis plantarum* (Growth of Plants), which deals with the life cycle of plants.

Historia plantarum consists of several smaller books, each dealing with a different group of plants—wild and domestic trees, shrubs, herblike plants, and others. The work also contains a discussion of the parts and composition of plants, their differences, and an analysis of plants that are peculiar to certain regions. The main subjects of *De causis plantarum* are plant growth and reproduction, sprouting and fruiting, the effects of natural factors and cultivation on plant growth, seeds, plant juices, and plant degeneration and death.

In these two lengthy works, Theophrastus described and discussed nearly 550 plant species and varieties in regions stretching from the

Walking About

Theophrastus and other followers of Aristotle are known as Peripatetics. The term comes from a Greek word meaning "walking about" or "traveling on foot from place to place" and refers to Aristotle's style of teaching. Theophrastus helped Aristotle found the Peripatetic school of philosophy, which was centered at the Lyceum in Athens. When Theophrastus became head of the Lyceum he played a major role in continuing Aristotle's teaching methods and in defending Aristotelian ideas against rival philosophers.

Atlantic coast of Greece through the Mediterranean coastal regions to as far east as India. He made frequent references to the beliefs and practices of farmers, physicians, and others, and he cited various literary sources, including earlier Greeks who had written about plants.

Theophrastus made no fundamental innovations in developing his plant classifications, nor did he present any new theories. In fact, Aristotle had already used similar procedures in many other subjects, including zoology. Like Aristotle, he regarded plants as living things with a life dependent on their inner heat, moisture, and relationship with the environment. He differed from Aristotle only in perspective—Aristotle considered plants as the lower members of a system of living things that culminates with humans, but Theophrastus concentrated on the plants themselves and avoided placing them within a larger system.

Theophrastus collected his data impartially, classified and discussed plants within a flexible system, and withheld judgment when the facts were not clear. In doing so he created a method for studying plants and laid the groundwork for later botanical studies. Although many of his observations and explanations were incomplete or incorrect, he accomplished more in the field of botany than anyone before him.

Theophrastus was aware that what he wrote about plants was merely the beginning, that more data were needed, and that his explanations might need to be revised in the future. But it took centuries for that to happen.

Andreas VESALIUS
1514–1564
MEDICINE, ANATOMY

The physician Andreas Vesalius was a powerful figure in the development of the practice of anatomy. Many of his new ideas about the structure of the human body challenged theories of anatomy that had been accepted for generations. Equally significant is his insistence on the importance of dissection in the study of human anatomy, which changed the conduct of anatomical research.

Life and Career
Vesalius was born in Brussels, Belgium, to a family that had been prominent in the medical profession for several generations. His father was an apothecary* to the Holy Roman Emperor Charles V.

*apothecary individual trained to make up the drugs necessary to fill prescriptions; also called pharmacist or druggist

Education and Early Work. Vesalius studied at the University of Louvain, Belgium, and later chose to pursue medicine at the prestigious University of Paris in France. At age 19 he began his medical education in the tradition developed by the ancient Greek physician GALEN, whose ideas he later challenged. In 1536 war between France and the Holy Roman Empire forced Vesalius to return to Louvain. There he successfully convinced the university administration to reintroduce anatomical dissection into the medical curriculum after it had not been taught there for many years. The following year he received his bachelor's degree, and a year later he enrolled at the University of Padua in

Italy, Europe's most famous medical school. He received his doctorate after two days of examinations, and the next day he was appointed lecturer in surgery and anatomy. It was at that time that Vesalius's new approach to anatomy became apparent.

Instead of reading from ancient texts while a barber-surgeon performed the dissection, Vesalius performed the dissections himself. He produced large, detailed anatomical charts for his students to use when no cadavers* were available for study. He also prepared a dissection manual in which he first publicly expressed ideas that disagreed with those of Galen. As he performed more dissections, Vesalius became convinced that Galen had based his ideas about human anatomy on nonhuman animals and that these ideas were often inaccurate. In a series of anatomical demonstrations in Bologna, Vesalius declared that human anatomy could be learned only by dissecting the human body. He also demonstrated that Galen's description of bones fit the bones of apes but not of humans.

*cadaver dead body, especially one intended for anatomical dissection

Later Work. Prompted by the success of his investigations, Vesalius began work on a book that presented his ideas about anatomy. The book was published in 1543, the same year as the publication of the Polish astronomer Nicholas Copernicus's great work on the revolutions of heavenly bodies. Vesalius's book *de Humani Corporus Fabrica* (On the Structure of the Human Body) immediately secured his reputation as one of the greatest anatomists of the Renaissance*. Soon after its publication Vesalius suddenly abandoned his anatomical studies to take a position as physician to Emperor Charles V. Part of his duties included serving as a surgeon on the battlefield, where he increased his knowledge of anatomy and developed several successful surgical techniques. His fame as a surgeon spread, and he was in great demand throughout Europe. After Charles gave up his throne, Vesalius took a post as physician at the court of Charles's son, Philip II of Spain. He served in this capacity for the rest of his life. In 1564 Vesalius left Spain for a trip to the Holy Land. Sometime during the return voyage, storms forced his ship to land at the island of Zákinthos, off the western coast of Greece. Vesalius died there and was buried in an unidentified site.

*Renaissance period that marked the beginnings of modern science and the rebirth of interest in classical art and literature that occurred in Europe from the late 1300s through the 1500s

Scientific Achievements

Vesalius's major treatise, *Fabrica,* was of enormous influence at the time. Before Vesalius, anatomy was based on the teachings of Galen. With the *Fabrica,* Vesalius largely replaced many Galenic ideas of human anatomy and also of the philosophy underlying teaching in that field.

In 1543, Vesalius published *Fabrica,* the first textbook on human anatomy. Because he believed that illustrations served as an aid to understanding, he incorporated several detailed and precise anatomical drawings, such as the one shown here, in his book.

Purpose. Vesalius argued that to practice medicine properly, a physician had to acquire hands-on knowledge of the human body. Until that time physicians had engaged only in research and theorizing; actual surgery and dissection were performed by surgeons, who had less training and education. Moreover, dissections were rare because there were many prohibitions against using human bodies as subjects. Vesalius

The Best Physician in the World

Best known for his revolutionary work in anatomy, Vesalius was also an accomplished physician who learned much of his art on the battlefield. While serving as an army surgeon, he developed a technique to drain pus surgically from wounds to prevent infection. He later correctly diagnosed an internal aneurysm (abnormal blood-filled dilatation of a blood vessel) and accurately predicted the course of the ailment, a remarkable feat at the time. His reputation was so great that a contemporary called him "the best physician in the world."

hoped that the *Fabrica* might convince physicians to appreciate the fundamental importance of anatomy to all aspects of their profession. He also wanted to demonstrate the errors of Galen's approach to anatomy. Vesalius stressed that animal dissection was valuable only as a way to compare animal and human anatomy, and he used the comparisons to highlight Galen's errors.

He said that a physician should perform the same dissection several times on different bodies to make sure that his observations were not based on cases that represented anatomical abnormalities. Finally, Vesalius argued that it was important for a physician to become skilled at dissection to reach his own conclusions, rather than accepting the conclusions of others. To this end he included detailed descriptions of techniques for dissecting various parts of the body.

Contents. The *Fabrica* probably gained its greatest notoriety with its detailed illustrations, particularly those that depict the skeletal and muscular systems. The illustrations, which were probably done by a member of the Titian school in Venice, were astonishingly detailed, complete, and accurate and included captions as well as numerical and alphabetic notations that referred to and clarified some of the accompanying text. This work marked the first time that a scholarly work integrated with illustrations was used as an effective teaching tool. Vesalius's muscle men illustrations, beginning with the outer skin and revealing the underlying layers of muscles, were particularly novel. The naturalistic poses of the cadavers in the illustrations represented a startling departure from the traditional schematic illustrations at the time. Few anatomical texts after Vesalius repeated these illustrative features.

Of course, the *Fabrica* does not just offer new illustrations of the human body but also incorporates the new ideas that Vesalius had formulated based on his studies. The section on bones emphasizes the importance of the skeleton as the foundation of the body's structure and demonstrates Galen's errors on this subject. In the section on the nervous system, Vesalius shows that the nerves are not hollow, as Galen had claimed. The *Fabrica*'s coverage of the abdominal organs disputes Galen's claim that the liver had several different lobes. Contrary to Galen, Vesalius argued that the cavities in the brain called ventricles had nothing to do with intellectual activities and that their function was merely the collection of fluid. He also challenged the notion that sensation and motion were controlled by a series of arteries near the base of the brain. The *Fabrica* contains descriptions of many previously unknown structures, and many of the terms that Vesalius coined for various structures remain in use.

The *Fabrica* is not without blemish. It follows Galen's physiological system and contains many traditional views. For example, Vesalius describes the supposed pores in the septum (dividing wall) of the heart, despite his admission that he could not detect them. His treatment of the female reproductive organs is inadequate largely because of the scarcity of female cadavers. Still, his true accomplishment with the *Fabrica* was to change accepted attitudes about his field. Medicine and anatomy had long depended on the uncritical acceptance of Galen's theories. Although individuals had occasionally cited Galen's errors, none had offered a way to check systematically the accuracy of his ideas. By arguing for the importance of dissection and demonstrating how it could be used to correct errors and discover new truths, Vesalius charted a new course for later anatomical investigators. His work inspired the discoveries made by Realdo COLOMBO and Gabriele Falloppio of Italy and by William HARVEY of England, as well as many physicians of the next generations.

Rudolf Carl Virchow was one of the most prominent scientific figures of the second half of the nineteenth century. Trained as a physician, he was equally interested in the scientific and social aspects of medicine. As a scientist, Virchow helped transform German medicine from a practice based on speculation and philosophy to one firmly grounded in experimentation and observation. To his particular field, pathology*, he brought a new emphasis on the study of diseased or disturbed cells. As a social critic, Virchow worked toward political and social reforms. His belief that environmental conditions and poor sanitation contribute to disease made him a public health activist. In the second half of his career, he conducted research in anthropology*.

Rudolf Carl
VIRCHOW
1821–1902
PATHOLOGY, PUBLIC HEALTH, ANTHROPOLOGY

pathology study of diseases and their effects on organisms

anthropology study of human beings, especially in relation to origins and physical and cultural characteristics

The Young Radical. Virchow was born in Schivelbein, a small town in rural northeastern Germany. As a child he showed an interest in the natural sciences, and he received private lessons in Greek and Latin. He did well in school, and at the age of 18 he received a military fellowship to study medicine in Berlin. The fellowship provided advanced education to those who could not afford it. In exchange, Virchow would be expected to serve as an army doctor.

In Berlin, Virchow studied under Johannes MÜLLER, a medical and physiological* researcher who advocated the shift from theory to experimentation that was underway in German medicine. Müller exposed Virchow to experimental laboratory methods. As Virchow's career developed, he would emphasize the importance of such methods. After Virchow received his medical degree from the University of Berlin in 1843, he was assigned to serve as a medical officer at a Berlin hospital. Within a few years he was also teaching pathological anatomy at the university.

physiological of or relating to physiology, the science that deals with the functions of living organisms and their parts

In 1845 Virchow made several forceful speeches before large and influential audiences. He rejected the philosophical and mystical concerns that had been the basis of many medical theories and claimed that progress in medicine would come from three sources: observation of patients; experimentation on animals to study disease processes and to test drugs; and research in pathological anatomy, especially at the microscopic level. Thereafter Virchow was recognized as a leading spokesperson for the new generation of German physicians. He and another pathologist launched a journal titled *Archive of Pathological*

typhus bacterial disease transmitted by body lice that causes severe fever, headache, and delirium

radical favoring extreme changes or reform

The Treasures of Troy

Rudolf Virchow's interests extended beyond medicine; he was fascinated by archaeology, the study of past human cultures, and in 1870 he began to excavate a site in northern Germany. Virchow also befriended Heinrich Schliemann, a German amateur archaeologist who was determined to find the ruins of Troy, the ancient city described in the Greek epic poem the *Iliad*. After Schliemann located Troy at Hissarlik in Turkey and began excavations there, Virchow visited the site. Because of his friendship with Virchow, Schliemann was able to bring the golden artifacts from Troy to Berlin.

Anatomy and Physiology and of Clinical Medicine. It became one of the most prominent medical journals of its time, and Virchow served as its editor until his death in 1902.

In 1848 the government sent Virchow and other physicians to study an epidemic of typhus* that was ravaging the German province of Silesia. There he saw the struggles of the uneducated and impoverished Polish minority, and the experience gave new force to his political and social beliefs, which were already liberal. Instead of returning with a new set of medical guidelines for the government, he recommended political freedom and educational and economic reforms for Silesia.

Virchow's views became more radical*, and he grew increasingly dissatisfied with Germany's social and political state. He took part in radical uprisings in Berlin in 1848 and began editing a weekly political journal. These revolutionary activities displeased Virchow's superiors at the hospital, and the failure of the liberal movement created a climate in Berlin that he found uncomfortable. The following year Virchow moved to Würzburg to teach pathological anatomy at the university there.

Pathology and Public Health. At Würzburg, Virchow entered a period of scientific successes. In his famous 1845 lectures, he had argued that life is the product of physical and chemical activities at the cellular level. Now he came to regard the cell as the fundamental biological unit of life in health and in disease. He established the concept of cellular pathology, which held that disease is the result of alterations or disturbances in cells. This concept, a new approach in medicine, relied heavily on the use of microscopic observations.

In 1856 Virchow accepted an invitation to return to the University of Berlin as professor of pathological anatomy and director of the recently created Pathological Institute. Under Virchow's direction, the institute became a famous training ground for many German and foreign medical scientists. In addition, he spent two decades in charge of a section of the hospital where he had formerly worked. This enabled him to examine patients, one aspect of the program for medical progress that he had described in 1845. Virchow also wrote and published several articles and books, including a work on tumors. His most famous book, however, was a volume on cellular pathology, the field that he had helped to create.

During Virchow's second period in Berlin, his interests turned toward public health. With the help of the mayor of Berlin, who was his brother-in-law, he was able to improve the fast-growing city's sewage system and water supply. In 1870, when France and Germany went to war, Virchow was active in organizing military hospitals and ambulance and train services for wounded soldiers.

Virchow stressed a sociological theory of disease, claiming that political, social, and economic conditions made people vulnerable to illness. Every individual had the right to be healthy, he claimed, and society should provide sanitary conditions so that all people could develop in a healthy way. Virchow did not just talk about these high ideals—he fought for reforms in school hygiene, sewage treatment,

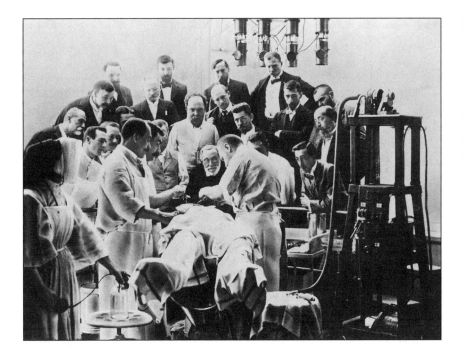

Virchow was the best-known German physician of the 1800s, his fame reaching far beyond his homeland. His eightieth birthday was the occasion for a torchlight parade in Berlin and in scientific centers as far away as Japan. In this photograph, the celebrated Virchow—seated at the center wearing glasses and sporting a beard—observes a brain operation.

water purification, and hospital construction. However, Virchow had always been argumentative, and as his career progressed he became increasingly unwilling to adopt ideas developed by the new generation. As a result he opposed some new medical ideas and practices, such as doctors washing their hands to avoid spreading infectious disease.

The Later Years. Virchow believed that medicine was the highest form of human insight and the most important of the sciences. His influence extended outside the realm of medicine, however. He became involved in government and served as chairman of the finance committee of the Reichstag, the German parliament.

In 1869 Virchow cofounded the German Anthropological Society, and in the years that followed he devoted considerable energy to anthropological research. He studied the physical characteristics of the Germans, and after performing a nationwide survey of schoolchildren, he announced that there was no pure German race; the Germans were a mixture of different physical and ethnic types. During the 1880s Virchow played an important role in establishing two anthropological institutions, the Berlin Ethnological* Museum and the Museum of German Folklore.

*ethnological relating to ethnology, the study of the division of humans into races and their origin, distribution, relations, and characteristics

One of the founders of modern evolutionary biology, the British naturalist* Alfred Russel Wallace made important contributions in natural history, geography, biology, and ethnography*. His most notable achievement was the development of a theory of evolution based on natural selection*, an idea that he developed independently of Charles DARWIN. In addition to his contributions in natural sci-

Alfred Russel
WALLACE
1823–1913
NATURAL HISTORY

On a trip to Southeast Asia, Alfred Russel Wallace developed Wallace's Line to separate the mammals of the Malay Archipelago into two species. He claimed that species found east of this imaginary line were closely related to mammals of Australia and those found west of the line to mammals in Asia.

*naturalist one who studies objects in their natural settings

*ethnography branch of anthropology dealing with the scientific description of different cultures

*natural selection theory that within a given species, individuals with characteristics best adapted to the environment survive and successfully produce more offspring than other individuals, resulting in changes in the species over time

ence, Wallace was also a supporter of many social issues, including women's rights.

Early Life and Work. Born in Wales, Wallace was the eighth of nine children. His family suffered from constant economic setbacks when he was a child, forcing his parents to live in an inexpensive, but picturesque, rural area of Wales. Wallace spent his first five years in the Welsh countryside before he moved to Hertford, where he attended school. He studied French, Latin, geography, mathematics, and history, but his intellectual development was more the result of his extensive reading of travelogues, biographies, classics, and other works.

In 1837 Wallace went to London to live temporarily with his older brother John, with whom he worked as a carpenter. He attended lectures at the London institute known as the "Hall of Science," and became acquainted with the ideas of the Welsh social reformer Robert Owen and of other religious thinkers. The following year Wallace became an apprentice to his brother William, a land surveyor. It was around this time that Wallace first began to experience the lure of nature, but he did not actively pursue his interest until 1841. The purchase of a book on botany–to help begin an herb collection–marked the beginning of Wallace's scientific career. His interests in botanical explorations and reading continued to grow from this point forward.

When the surveying business began to diminish in 1843, Wallace was forced to find other work. He became a teacher at the Collegiate School in Leicester, England, where he taught English, arithmetic, surveying, and drawing. During this time Wallace read many books on the natural sciences, including works by Alexander von HUMBOLDT, Thomas Malthus, Charles DARWIN, Charles Lyell, and Robert Chambers. These books greatly influenced his intellectual development, as did his explorations in the forests around Leicester with his new friend Henry Walter BATES.

Following his brother William's death in 1845, Wallace returned briefly to surveying, but he continued reading, collecting plant and animal specimens, and corresponding with Bates. That same year he read the anonymously published, controversial book on evolution by Robert Chambers, *Vestiges of the National History of Creation,* and became convinced that species arise through natural laws rather than by the hand of God. Wallace persuaded Bates to accept this view also and the two set out to collect information on the variation and evolution of species.

Expedition to South America. In 1848 Wallace and Bates set off for South America. That same year they reached Pará, Brazil, and immediately began exploring portions of the Amazon basin. To increase the area they covered, the enthusiastic naturalists set out on independent expeditions. In 1850 they separated permanently, each concentrating on a different part of the Amazon region.

Wallace was impressed by the grandeur of the forest, the variety and beauty of the butterflies and birds, and his meetings with the indigenous peoples. He recounted his experiences in *A Narrative of Travels on the Amazon and Rio Negro,* published in 1853. Wallace set out to return to England in 1852, but his ship sank and most of the plants, animals, and objects he had painstakingly collected for later sale were lost at sea. While he did not publicly declare his views on evolution at the time, his ideas were reflected in his writings on the geographical distribution of monkeys, birds, and insects, and in his references to the "adaptation of animals to their food, their habits, and the localities in which they are found." Wallace rejected the traditional explanations for such phenomena, saying that naturalists were seeking new explanations for the variations in species. He believed that evolution was the right explanation, but he wisely said little about this until later in his career.

Expedition to Southeast Asia. Since Wallace's trip to South America did not resolve the question of how species evolve, he decided to make another expedition—this time to the Malay Archipelago (group of islands) in Southeast Asia. With support from the Royal Geographical Society in London, Wallace set sail in 1854 on an expedition that would last eight years and cover about 15,000 miles. He traveled to many islands, collecting biological specimens for his own research and for sale, and writing various scientific articles based on his findings.

Wallace gathered about 127,000 specimens, enabling him to publish scientific papers on a range of topics. These works alone would have established him as one of the great English naturalists of his time, but it was his classic natural history and travel book—*The Malay Archipelago,* published in 1869—that earned him an international reputation and lasting fame. Many people consider this work to be one of the finest scientific travel books ever written.

From the time he arrived in the Malay region, Wallace gathered precise data on groups of animals in order to determine their geographic distribution and to explain their origins through evolution. In 1855 he wrote a paper titled "On the Law Which Has Regulated the Introduction of New Species," in which he presented a persuasive argument on the same topic. The paper, which he based on accepted scientific facts and personal observations from his travels, clearly marked Wallace as a proto-evolutionist.

Ideas on Evolution. In his 1858 paper "On the Tendency of Varieties to Depart Indefinitely From the Original Type," Wallace formulated the principle of natural selection, the mechanism by which new species evolve. It was this paper that marked him as a codiscoverer with Charles Darwin of the mechanism of natural selection to explain evolution. Wallace sent the paper to Darwin and it was simultaneously published with Darwin's own paper on the same topic. Many English scientists, including the geologist Charles Lyell and the botanist Joseph Hooker, read and were impressed by his work.

Wallace continued to publish profusely on the topic, supporting his ideas with original and forceful arguments. In 1876 he wrote

Wallace and Darwin

In 1858 Charles Lyell and Joseph Hooker submitted Wallace's paper and Darwin's essay on natural selection to the Linnean Society of London. They emphasized that Darwin had formulated the idea before Wallace and had already amassed much supporting data but had not yet published his papers. Wallace, then in Malaysia, was not consulted about these arrangements and did not learn about the presentation until after the papers were published. Later, however, he said that the arrangements were quite fair. Although Wallace and Darwin had developed the theory independently, Darwin, already a much more well known naturalist, received most of the credit.

Wallace, Alfred Russel

Turning Back the Clock

Wallace's ideas about human evolution put him at odds with Darwin and many other scientists of the day. By attempting to reconcile science with religious and social views, Wallace appeared to step away from the strict scientific method when it came to explaining human evolution. Speaking of Wallace's rejection of natural selection as explaining human evolution, Darwin remarked, "I hope you have not murdered too completely your own and my child," referring to their theory of evolution by natural selection.

*genetics branch of biology that deals with heredity

*eugenics study of improving human heredity by means of genetic control

*vivisection practice of dissecting or cutting into the body of a living animal for the purpose of scientific investigation

Geographical Distribution of Animals, summarizing current knowledge on the subject; and in 1880 he published *Island Life,* applying evolutionary concepts to animals and plants found on islands. He gave many lectures on the topic, both in England and in the United States.

Around the 1860s, Wallace began to use the idea of mimicry, first proposed by his traveling companion Bates, to support evolution. Bates suggested that relatively scarce and unprotected species might resemble other species that are protected by their strong smell and bad taste. To this Wallace added that a species may have two or more very different forms, and each one may mimic, or copy, a different model. He also observed that these protective resemblances depended on the usefulness of physical characteristics, the need for protective concealment, the variability of color, and the fact that concealment can most easily be obtained through color changes.

Wallace's ideas on human evolution underwent significant change. Before 1862 he considered humans to be animals with a close kinship with other primates, such as apes and monkeys. This view changed in the early 1860s, when he accepted religious ideas about God and spiritual beings and began to believe that the idea of natural selection could not adequately explain all aspects of human development. He argued instead that natural selection did not apply to humans because of their superior intellect. This attempt to reconcile science with religious beliefs shocked many of Wallace's fellow scientists, especially Darwin.

Other Contributions. Wallace's research on the geographical distribution of animals in the Malay Archipelago led to the important discovery that a distinct geographical boundary separates the animal species of Southeast Asia and Australia. This boundary became known as the Wallace Line and its exact placement has shifted many times since it was first proposed by Wallace as new data has accumulated. Wallace also presented advanced views on the cause of the ice ages and their impact on species. His experience as a surveyor helped him make important geological observations in South America and in Southeast Asia. He also presented opinions on astronomy and genetics*.

In addition to his scientific work, Wallace pursued many social and political interests. He strongly opposed vaccination, eugenics*, and vivisection*, and was a supporter of women's rights. He was also involved in Spiritualism, a movement that emphasized the possibility of communicating with the dead. Although some of Wallace's views on religion, Spiritualism, and other nonscientific issues tended to diminish his reputation among his peers, he received many honors. He was awarded medals by the Royal Society, the Linnean Society, and the Royal Geographic Society; received honorary doctorates from the Universities of Dublin and Oxford; and was elected to the Royal Society. Wallace died in Broadstone, England, at the age of 91.

August Paul von Wassermann was a pioneer in the field of biochemical* diagnosis and therapy. As director of the renowned Kaiser Wilhelm Institute in Berlin, he investigated the use of blood serum* to determine the presence of such diseases as cholera and tuberculosis. He is best known for developing the Wassermann test for the diagnosis of syphilis, a sexually transmitted disease.

The son of a nobleman who served as banker for the royal court of Bavaria, Wassermann was born in Bamberg. He studied medicine at the Universities of Erlangen, Vienna, and Munich and received his M.D. from the University of Strasbourg in 1888. Three years after graduating he began to work at the hygiene institute in Berlin headed by the famous German bacteriologist* Robert KOCH. Later that year, he followed Koch to the Institute for Infectious Diseases, where his research focused on problems related to cholera and diphtheria*.

Wassermann was eventually promoted to the position of director of the institute's clinical division, and in 1906 he became director of the division of experimental therapy and serum research. He left the institute in 1913 to take over as director of the Institute for Experimental Therapy at the Kaiser Wilhelm Society for the Advancement of Science in Berlin. However, when World War I broke out the following year, his research came to a halt.

During the war Wassermann supervised epidemic control on the Eastern Front and later served as director of the Office of Hygiene and Bacteriology for the Prussian Ministry of War. When the war ended in 1918, he returned to his institute, which had been renamed the Kaiser Wilhelm Institute for Experimental Therapy and Biochemistry. In 1924 Wassermann began to show symptoms of a renal* disease, from which he died the following year.

Wassermann's earliest research and writing dealt with cholera immunity and the antitoxin (agent that is capable of counteracting the effects of a specific disease-causing toxin) for diphtheria. He showed that many people have diphtheria antitoxin in their blood serum and that such people have increased resistance to diphtheria infection. He also studied the bonds between toxins and antitoxins. His results showed that matter from the brain of a healthy animal could neutralize the toxin that causes tetanus*.

By 1900 Wassermann had become increasingly interested in studying complement, a substance in normal serum that destroys harmful bacteria and other materials. He was interested in uncovering whether complement could be used to determine the presence of disease antigens* or antibodies*. If so, he believed that it could be used as the basis of diagnostic tests to detect infectious diseases.

Working with colleagues, Wassermann researched the possibility of using complement to locate antibodies in tuberculosis patients. In 1906 he achieved a breakthrough on another front: using complement therapy to diagnose syphilis in humans. Called the Wassermann test, this method is still widely used as a diagnostic tool. In other research, he sought unsuccessfully to find a way to treat cancer through the blood-

August Paul von
WASSERMANN
1866–1925
IMMUNOLOGY, SEROLOGY

*biochemical referring to biochemistry, the science that deals with chemical compounds and processes occurring in living organisms

*serum fluid in the blood that carries substances that provide immunity against disease

*bacteriologist specialist who studies microscopic organisms called bacteria that can cause infection and disease

*diphtheria infectious disease caused by a bacterium and characterized by inflammation of the heart and nervous system

*renal of or relating to the kidneys

*tetanus infectious disease marked by contractions of the voluntary muscles; also known as lockjaw

*antigen substance that stimulates the production of antibodies, substances in the blood that help fight or counteract a specific disease toxin

*antibody protein produced by the immune system to neutralize the presence of a foreign protein in the body

stream. Late in his life he focused his research on using complement to diagnose tuberculosis.

August
WEISMANN
1834–1914
ZOOLOGY, GENETICS

*genetics branch of biology that deals with heredity

*naturalist one who studies objects in their natural settings

*natural selection theory that within a given species, individuals with characteristics best adapted to the environment survive and successfully produce more offspring than other individuals, resulting in changes in the species over time

*embryology branch of biology that deals with embryos, organisms from the first division of the fertilized egg through the early stages of development before birth or hatching

*crustacean class of animals that typically have a body covered with a hard shell or crust, such as lobsters, shrimp, and crabs

*chromosome threadlike structure in the cell that contains the DNA (genes) that transmit unique genetic information

*DNA deoxyribonucleic acid, the material in chromosomes that carries genetic information from ancestor to offspring

August Weismann is best known for his work on heredity. His theory of the germ plasm (a hereditary material) represented a significant contribution to early genetics*. He was also a supporter of the English naturalist* Charles DARWIN's theory of evolution (historical development of a species) by natural selection*.

Life and Career. Born in Frankfurt, Germany, Weismann demonstrated an early interest in nature, gathering beetles and butterflies, breeding caterpillars, and assembling an impressive collection of plants. He attended school in Frankfurt, where he excelled in physics, chemistry, and botany, and later enrolled at the University of Göttingen. Although he had hoped to become a chemist, he followed the advice of his father and a family friend who thought he should have a practical means of earning a living and studied medicine instead.

After earning his medical degree in 1856, Weismann continued his scientific researches while working as an assistant in a hospital. Two years later he began to practice medicine in Frankfurt, and shortly thereafter he revived his childhood interest in zoology. Early in 1861 he spent a few months at the University of Giessen, where he became interested in studies of insects.

Weismann practiced medicine again for a short time in Frankfurt, and from 1861 to 1863 he was the private physician of the Archduke Stephan of Austria. Meanwhile, he continued his studies of insects and pursued scientific researches in his spare time. In 1863 he finally gave up the practice of medicine to pursue his interest in zoology at the University of Freiburg, where he later taught anatomy and zoology. Weismann remained at Freiburg for the rest of his career.

Research and Theories. Between 1862 and 1866 Weismann wrote six papers on insects and another on heart muscle. During this time, however, his eyesight began to trouble him and he was unable to use a microscope for ten years, yet he continued his research and studies.

From his study of insects and their embryology*, he turned to small crustaceans* and other animals, including Hydrozoa, a class of marine organisms. In the mid-1880s, while studying the primitive germ cells of Hydrozoa, Weismann concluded that the germ cells of animals contain a substance, germ plasm, that is preserved and passed on from one generation to the next. He extended this finding further and developed his theory of germ plasm to explain heredity and development. The idea has undergone much modification and has been given greater specificity with the discovery of the role of chromosomes*, genes, and DNA*. Although Weismann was not the first to propose this idea, he was the first to develop it into a coherent explanation of inheritance and bring it into agreement with new understanding of the cell.

In the years that followed, Weismann revised his concept of germ plasm and using new research, developed his theory further. By 1885 he had located the germ plasm within the cell nucleus. He realized that when the germ plasm from two parents is combined in a fertilized egg, the amount of hereditary substance would increase in each generation unless it was reduced at some stage. Using the idea of cell division, he explained that as the cell nucleus divides, each offspring nucleus would receive only half the germ plasm present in the original nucleus.

Weismann next debated the question of whether acquired traits were heritable. He cut off the tails of a group of mice and observed that their offspring had tails, concluding that acquired traits are not inherited unless they affect the germ plasm. Using this discovery to further develop his theory, he proposed that certain invisibly small units in the germ plasm—which he called "biophors"—did not mix freely as did certain other hereditary factors. He then theorized the existence of larger hereditary units—called "determinants"—as the bearers of hereditary traits. With this discovery, Weismann's theory of the continuity of germ plasm was more complete.

In Support of Darwin. An early supporter of Darwin's theory of evolution, Weismann claimed that natural selection alone could explain the formation of different varieties and species of plants and animals. In 1894 he gave a lecture in which he explained the role of natural selection in both the progressive development of some variations and the disappearance of useless organs.

Weismann believed that the theory of natural selection was adequate to explain phenomena beyond what Darwin had intended. Using principles based on his own theory of germ plasm, he defended Darwin's work, extended it, and expressed his own concepts in new terms. Weismann eventually came to see natural selection as occurring on many levels. He concluded that there were fluctuations in nourishment and in the conditions of life even among the biophors and determinants in the germ plasm, and that natural selection determined their chances to reach development and expression in an individual.

Later Life. Weismann was an impressive teacher, and for decades he drew a steady stream of students from many countries to his laboratory at the University of Freiburg. He was also the first director of the university's zoological institute and museum.

Retiring in 1912, Weismann devoted his time to writing an overview of his ideas. After the outbreak of World War I, he became ill and also deeply unhappy because members of his family were on both sides of the conflict. A member of various scientific societies, including the Royal Society of London and the American Philosophical Society, Weismann was also the recipient of many honors and awards. In 1908 he received the Darwin Medal from the Linnean Society in London along with a citation that read: "Professor Weismann has played a brilliant part in the development of Darwinian theory, and is indeed

August Weismann is best known for his opposition to the principle that acquired traits can be inherited from one generation to the next and for his germ plasm theory.

the protagonist of that theory in its purest form. . . ." By the time of his death in 1914, he had gained recognition as one of the world's leading zoologists.

Alexander WILSON

1766–1813

ORNITHOLOGY

The son of a smuggler and weaver, Alexander Wilson had no scientific background or training. Still, in the last several years of his life, he almost single-handedly founded the field of ornithology, the scientific study of birds, in America.

Wilson was born in Paisley, Scotland. He was a bright student but was forced to end his formal schooling at age ten to help support his family. Three years later he became a weaver's apprentice, and he spent several years traveling across Scotland peddling cloth. A gifted amateur poet, he wrote a poem that became popular but was attributed to the great Scottish poet Robert Burns. One of the poems Wilson wrote landed him in legal trouble and forced him to leave Scotland for America. He settled near Philadelphia, Pennsylvania, and took up a career as a teacher.

Wilson developed a keen interest in birds, stimulated by the huge flocks of ducks and geese he observed near his home. After a time he began to sketch birds brought to him by his students, gradually developing his drawing skills. At age 40 he abandoned teaching and set out to scientifically classify and draw in color all of the birds of America. He planned to author a ten-volume work on the subject, and in 1808 he found a Philadelphia publisher who agreed to launch the first volume. The publisher agreed to continue publishing the series if Wilson could line up 200 subscribers.

Between 1808 and 1813, Wilson traveled the length and breadth of the United States, observing and collecting specimens and landing customers for his book. He not only drew his subjects with exacting detail but also familiarized himself with the scientific literature of each species. His text and paintings worked together to make his work *Ornithology* a masterpiece. In all, he described and painted more than 250 species of birds and added 48 new species to those known to exist in the United States. Some scholars have suggested that the work of the great American ornithologist John James AUDUBON was inspired by Audubon's first exposure to Wilson's book. Wilson died in Philadelphia at the age of 47.

Friedrich WÖHLER

1800–1882

CHEMISTRY

The German chemist Friedrich Wöhler was the first to synthetically produce an organic compound (urea) from inorganic substances. He also developed a method for preparing metallic aluminum that eventually was developed into an industrial process for producing aluminum.

The son of a court official and leading citizen of Frankfurt, Wöhler was born in the town of Eschersheim near Frankfurt. From an early age, he had a passionate interest in chemistry and in collecting minerals. After attending public school and the Frankfurt Gymnasium, he studied at the Universities of Marburg and Heidelberg, and received his degree in medicine from the latter in 1823.

While at Heidelberg, Wöhler became friends with Leopold Gmelin, one of the most prominent chemists in Germany, who encouraged Wöhler to pursue chemistry. After earning his medical degree, Wöhler went to Stockholm, Sweden, to study with Jöns Jacob Berzelius, the leading chemist in Europe. Wöhler studied with Berzelius for nearly a year, and the two became close friends. During his life, Wöhler translated some of Berzelius's most influential works, including reports and textbooks.

Research in Organic Chemistry. Returning to Germany in 1825, Wöhler began teaching chemistry at an industrial school in Berlin. It was at this school that he made his two most important discoveries. In 1828, while experimenting with the inorganic compound ammonium cyanate, he was able to synthesize, or artificially create, urea. Until this time, scientists had considered urea a product of animal origin, a substance produced in the kidneys. Wöhler's achievement helped dispel older established notions about a special "life force" necessary for the production of organic materials and living things. He followed this synthesis with several others. His work was regularly cited and became a standard reference for scientists who were working to develop a chemical explanation for the origin of life.

While in Berlin, Wöhler met the chemist Justus von LIEBIG, and the two became lifelong friends and colleagues, working together on many studies and experiments. The most important and best-known product of this collaboration involved the study of the oil of bitter almonds. Wöhler and Liebig established the existence of a substance, composed of three elements, that remains stable and constant from one chemical compound to another. Their work marked an early serious attempt to understand the structure of organic compounds. Moreover, many of the compounds they prepared in the course of their experiments became important in the future development of the field of organic chemistry.

Scientific Writing and Other Accomplishments. After about 1840 Wöhler and Liebig continued to publish papers jointly, but they did no more major investigations together. This was due primarily to Wöhler's hectic schedule. Earlier in 1836 Wöhler had accepted a position as professor of chemistry at the University of Göttingen, where he remained for the rest of his life. In addition to his work there, he directed the university's laboratories, served as inspector general of all apothecaries* in the German state of Hannover, and translated chemistry texts and papers.

Notwithstanding these responsibilities, Wöhler managed to produce a steady stream of interesting papers. Always fascinated by geological samples that friends and former students sent to him from around the world, he published some 50 papers on minerals and meteorites. He also continued to pursue his interest in organic chemistry, and working with the French chemist Henri Saint-Claire Deville and

*apothecary individual trained to make up the drugs necessary to fill prescriptions; also called pharmacist or druggist

185

the German scientist Heinrich Buff, he isolated and extracted various chemical compounds.

Evaluating Wöhler's Work. In the mid-1800s inorganic chemistry was a stable and unchanging field. Most scientists simply collected data and prepared new compounds, and their interests dwelt in the materials themselves: rocks, crystals, or chemicals. In this respect, Wöhler was a man of the time; there was hardly a metal for which Wöhler did not prepare new compounds, and he collected large quantities of data.

Had Wöhler used emerging theories to guide his research, he might have accomplished more in organic chemistry. However, many of his papers were either on topics already absorbed into current theories or were too far advanced to affect current ideas. Like other chemists of the time, Wöhler spent time on substances of biological or medicinal interest, which because of the complexity of the molecules, failed to provide clear results.

Wöhler was a popular and outstanding teacher, attracting students from the world over to the University of Göttingen. Later in his career he was less interested in laboratory research, preferring to deliver lectures and leave the experimentation to his assistants, who also helped instruct his students. He gave his students great freedom in choosing problems to investigate, and permitted them to publish the results of their studies under their own names, a practice that was rather unusual for the time. Wöhler was an honorary member of many scientific societies and the recipient of numerous awards. He died in Göttingen at the age of 82.

Caspar Friedrich
WOLFF

1734–1794

BIOLOGY

physiology science that deals with the functions of living organisms and their parts

The German biologist Caspar Wolff was the first scientist to disprove the widely accepted theory of preformation, according to which all organisms begin as invisible, miniature, and fully formed in the egg or sperm and that their development involves merely growth and expansion without any fundamental changes in form or structure. Wolff's work showed that development is a complex process that involves many important stages between the time of conception and the time of birth.

The son of a tailor, Wolff was born in Berlin. He studied medicine at the Berlin Medical-Surgical College and obtained his doctorate at the University of Halle, despite strong criticism of his doctoral dissertation by the prominent scientists Albrecht von HALLER and Charles BONNET. It was the first of several setbacks for Wolff, who was trying to establish his scientific career. He was refused a post at the St. Petersburg Academy of Sciences in Russia, and later attempted unsuccessfully to gain a position as lecturer at Berlin's Medical-Surgical College.

In 1761 Wolff became a field doctor in the Prussian army, and he lectured on anatomy at the Breslau Military Hospital. He returned to Berlin two years later as a private lecturer in anatomy, physiology*, and medicine. At this time he restated the theory of generation that was the subject of his doctoral thesis and responded to the earlier criticism of the work by Bonnet and Haller, further decreasing his chances of a professorship. In 1766, three years after moving to Berlin, Wolff finally received an invitation to join the St. Petersburg Academy, where he conducted the research that led to his most important discoveries.

Wolff closely studied plants and their growth, which gave him new insight into the processes of development. He determined that plant growth occurs only at the ends of certain organs, known as the growing point. He observed the gradual formation of leaf layers in cabbages and chestnut trees, and he discovered that the blossom of any plant is simply a modified leaf. This discovery would form the basis of Johann GOETHE's theory of metamorphosis, which states that all the organs of a plant result from the transformation of leaves.

In addition to plants, Wolff also studied the development of animals. He traced the development of the heart and blood vessels in chick embryos*. He also studied the formation of blood and the development of the extremities (wings and feet), the intestines, and the kidneys. By examining the intestines, he established that different organs form from different layers of tissue in the embryo. This laid the foundation for the theory that all of the organs of an embryo develop from three basic types of tissue layers. Wolff's work in this area contributed significantly to the growth of the field of embryology.

Wolff's work showed conclusively that organisms are not preformed, but actually begin life as a mass of cells that form tissues that in turn change form and develop into an adult organism. He tried to explain the process by which organs develop. He believed that all life originates in a liquid substance in which bubbles or globules form. He argued that some force allows vital juices or nutrients to enter a plant or embryo. To Wolff, nutrition, growth, and development were the results of this essential force combined with an ability to solidify. He felt that these two factors explained not only individual differences in development between organisms, but also the differences between plants and animals.

Wolff later abandoned his theories of organ development and his ideas about essential forces and the ability to solidify. He replaced them with the belief that "the formation of organic bodies in general is caused by one natural force" that makes up part of the animal or plant. However, he did not agree with the animists* that this force was intelligent and acted according to a divine plan. He even went so far as to say that the soul (anima) is merely "an extract of the brain and brain matter." He claimed that the soul is born with and inhabits the body but does not exist before the beginning of life.

Wolff explored many other areas in addition to plant and animal development. His anatomical research included a study of the muscles of the heart and the connective tissue. One subject that particularly fascinated Wolff was the study of human monstrosities. He collected specimens that he stored in the St. Petersburg Academy's anatomical cabinet. He was apparently working on the preparation of a major treatise on the theory of monstrous births that would set forth his ideas on the subject. However, he died of a sudden brain hemorrhage before finishing the work. He was 60 years old.

*embryo organism from the first division of the fertilized egg through the early stages of development until birth or hatching

*animist one who believes that the vital principle of organic development is immaterial spiri

GLOSSARY

A

alchemy medieval form of chemical science, especially one that sought to turn base metals into gold or silver or transform something common into something special

analogy form of reasoning based on the assumption that if two things are alike in some respects, then they are alike in all other respects as well

anesthetic substance that causes loss of sensation with or without loss of consciousness

animist one who believes that the vital principle of organic development is immaterial spirit

anthropological related to the study of human beings, especially in relation to origins and physical and cultural characteristics

anthropology study of human beings, especially in relation to origins and physical and cultural characteristics

antibody protein produced by the immune system to neutralize the presence of a foreign protein in the body

antigen substance that stimulates the production of antibodies, substances in the blood that help fight or counteract a specific disease toxin

apothecary individual trained to make up the drugs necessary to fill prescriptions; also called pharmacist or druggist

asphyxiation death caused by lack of oxygen

atrophy wasting away of tissues or organs

audiology scientific study of hearing

B

bacillus rod-shaped bacterium

bacteriologist specialist who studies microscopic organisms called bacteria that can cause infection and disease

bacteriology science that deals with bacteria, microscopic organisms that can cause infection and disease

bile substance produced by the liver

biochemical referring to biochemistry, the science that deals with chemical compounds and processes occurring in living organisms

C

cadaver dead body, especially one intended for anatomical dissection

cardiac of or relating to the heart

cardiovascular relating to the heart and blood vessels

cauterize to seal and numb a wound by burning with high heat

centrifuge device used to separate materials of different density by spinning them at high speeds

chemotherapy treatment of disease by means of chemicals that have a specific effect on certain disease-producing organisms

chromosome threadlike structure in the cell that contains the DNA (genes) that transmit unique genetic information

cosmology study of the origin, history, and structure of the universe

cranial of or relating to the skull (cranium)

creationist one who believes that the world and all living things were created by God as described in the Bible

crustacean class of animals that typically have a body covered with a hard shell or crust, such as lobsters, shrimp, and crabs

crystallography study of the properties of crystals

culture to grow microorganisms, such as bacteria or tissue, in a specially prepared nutrient substance for scientific study

cytology branch of biology that deals with the structure, function, and life history of cells

cytoplasm organic and inorganic substances outside the cell's nuclear membrane

D

dietetics science of applying the principles of nutrition to diet

differentiated referring to differentiation, the process whereby cells, tissues, and structures are specialized to perform certain functions

diphtheria infectious disease caused by a bacterium and characterized by inflammation of the heart and nervous system

diuretic tending to increase the discharge of urine

DNA deoxyribonucleic acid, the material in chromosomes that carries genetic information from ancestor to offspring

E

embryo organism from the first division of the fertilized egg through the early stages of development until birth or hatching

embryology branch of biology that deals with embryos, organisms from the first division of the fertilized egg through the early stages of development before birth or hatching

empirical based on or derived from observation and experiment

entomology scientific study of insects

epidermis outer layer of the skin

ether light, volatile liquid used mainly as solvent and anesthetic

ethnography branch of anthropology dealing with the scientific description of different cultures

ethnological relating to ethnology, the study of the division of humans into races and their origin, distribution, relations, and characteristics

eugenics study of improving human heredity by means of genetic control

evolution historical development of a biological group such as a species

evolutionist one who studies evolution, the historical development of a biological group such as a species

F

fermentation process of change in organic substances in which microorganisms called enzymes cause compounds such as carbohydrates to break down into alcohol or acids

flagella whiplike structure used by certain organisms to move through a fluid medium, such as water or blood

forensic referring to the use of science in criminal and legal investigations

G

gastric of or relating to the digestive system

genetics branch of biology that deals with heredity

genus category of biological classification; class, kind, or group of organisms that share common characteristics; *pl.* genera

geomagnetism of or relating to the earth's magnetic field

geophysical of or relating to geophysics, the scientific study of the physics of the earth, including weather, magnetism, volcanoes, earthquakes, and ocean structure

gladiator in ancient Rome, a person engaged in a fight to the death for the sake of public entertainment

gout disease marked by painful inflammation of the joints

H

hematology study of the formation, structure, and diseases of the blood

herbalist person who collects or deals in herbs, especially medicinal herbs

heresy belief that is contradictory to church doctrine

histological relating to histology, the branch of anatomy that deals with the minute structure of animal and plant tissues, observable only through a microscope

histology branch of anatomy that deals with the minute structure of animal and plant tissues, observable only through a microscope

homology relationship characterized by similarity in structure and evolutionary origin

humanist referring to humanism, a cultural and philosophical movement to revive ancient Greek and Roman works and to value individuals' capacity for reason and dignity during their earthly life

hybrid offspring produced by crossing two or more varieties or species of plants or animals

hybridization process of creating a hybrid, an offspring produced by crossing two or more varieties or species of plants or animals

hybridize to produce an offspring by crossing two or more varieties or species of plants or animals

hydrodynamics scientific study of the motion of liquids

I

immunology science that deals with the immune system, which protects the body from foreign substances, cells, and tissue by causing the body to produce substances to counteract the infectious materials

inoculation introduction of a disease agent into an animal or plant to produce a mild form of the disease and render the organism immune

internist physician specializing in internal medicine

invertebrate animal without a backbone

L

lesion wound or injury

M

malignant showing abnormal growth and a tendency to spread throughout the body

mechanics science that studies how energy and force affect objects

medieval relating to the Middle Ages in Europe, a period from about 500 to 1500

metabolism set of chemical reactions in organisms that convert food into energy and tissue

metaphysics branch of philosophy that deals with the fundamental principles or ultimate nature of existence

meteorology science that deals with the atmosphere, especially the weather and weather predictions; also known as atmospheric science

microbe microscopic organism

microbiologist scientist who studies microscopic life-forms, such as bacteria and viruses

microbiology study of tiny organisms that can only be observed through a microscope

microorganism tiny living thing that generally can be seen clearly only through a microscope

Middle Ages period between ancient and modern times in western Europe, generally considered to be from the A.D. 500s to the 1500s

mineralogy study of the properties of minerals

mitosis separation and replication of chromosomes that takes place prior to cell division

mollusk marine animal with a shell of one or more pieces enclosing a soft body

morphology branch of biology that deals with the form and structure of plants and animals

mutation genetic change, which when transmitted to offspring, results in heritable variations

N

natural history systematic study of animals and plants, especially in their natural settings

natural philosophy set of theories or ideas about the natural world; theoretical basis for research in the natural sciences

natural selection theory that within a given species, individuals with characteristics best adapted to the environment survive and successfully produce more offspring than other individuals, resulting in changes in the species over time

naturalist one who studies objects in their natural settings

neural of or relating to the nerves or nervous system

O

obstetrical referring to obstetrics, the branch of medicine dealing with pregnancy and childbirth

obstetrics branch of medicine dealing with pregnancy and childbirth

ophthalmology medical specialty focusing on the structure and function of the eye, as well as diseases of the eye and their treatment

orography study of the physical geography of mountains and mountain ranges

P

paleontologist one who studies extinct or prehistoric life, usually through the examination of fossils

paleontology study of extinct or prehistoric life, usually through the examination of fossils

pancreas gland that controls the production of insulin and produces the juices (chemicals) that enable the body to digest and absorb fats

pancreatic of or relating to the pancreas, the gland that produces the juices (chemicals) that enable the body to digest and absorb fats

parasitic relating to a parasite, an organism that lives on or within another organism from whose body it obtains nutrients

pathologist one who specializes in pathology, the study of diseases and their effects on organisms

pathology study of diseases and their effects on organisms

pharmacology science that deals with the preparation, uses, and effects of drugs

phosphorescence property of some organisms to give off a natural glow or light

physiological of or relating to physiology, the science that deals with the functions of living organisms and their parts

physiologist one who specializes in physiology, the science that deals with the functions of living organisms and their parts

physiology science that deals with the functions of living organisms and their parts

placenta flattened organ in pregnant mammals that connects the fetus to the maternal uterus and facilitates the exchange of nutrients

plague contagious, widespread, and often fatal disease

polarize to cause light to vibrate in a pattern

pomology scientific study and cultivation of fruit

posthumous occurring after the death of an individual

protozoa group of one-celled microorganisms

psychoanalysis method of treating emotional disorders in which the patient is encouraged to talk freely about personal experiences

putrefaction decay of living matter

Q

quarantine to isolate someone who suffers from or has been exposed to a contagious disease, in the hope of limiting the spread of the disease

R

rabies disease of the nervous system usually transmitted to humans through the bite of infected animals, often dogs

radical favoring extreme changes or reform

receptor specialized organ or cell that is sensitive to and responds to certain stimulating agents

Renaissance period that marked the beginnings of modern science and the rebirth of interest in classical art and literature that occurred in Europe from the late 1300s through the 1500s

renal of or relating to the kidneys

rigor mortis stiffness of the body after death

S

satire literary work that uses humor or wit to make fun of a person or idea

sepsis toxic condition resulting from the spread of infectious bacteria

serfdom form of slavery in which medieval European peasants were bound to work on the lands owned by aristocrats

sericulturist one who practices sericulture, the process of raising silkworms for the manufacture of silk

serology study of the properties and reactions of serums, clear watery fluids in the blood that carry the substances that provide immunity against diseases

serum fluid in the blood that carries substances that provide immunity against disease

spermatozoon male reproductive cell; *pl.* spermatozoa

spore single-celled, environmentally resistant body produced by plants and some microorganisms and capable of development into a new individual directly or after mixing with another spore

suffrage right to vote

suture division between the bony plates of the skull

synthesize to create artificially

T

taxonomic relating to taxonomy, the orderly classification of plants and animals into groups and subgroups according to their relationships

taxonomy orderly classification of plants and animals into groups and subgroups according to their relationships

tetanus infectious disease marked by contractions of the voluntary muscles; also known as lockjaw

theological referring to theology, the study of religion

theology study of religion

tourniquet tight bandage that restricts the flow of blood

toxicologist one who specializes in toxicology, the science that deals with the effects, detection, and antidotes of poisons

toxicology science that deals with the effects, detection, and antidotes of poisons

typhus bacterial disease transmitted by body lice that causes severe fever, headache, and delirium

U

undifferentiated not specialized

V

vagus nerve either of a pair of nerves that arise in the brain and supply the organs with nerve fibers

ventricle muscular chamber of the heart

vertebrate animal with a backbone

vesicle fluid-filled cavity in the body

viniculture cultivation of grapes

vivisection practice of dissecting or cutting into the body of a living animal for the purpose of scientific investigation

SUGGESTED READINGS

History

Asimov, Isaac. *Asimov's Chronology of Science and Discovery*. New York: HarperCollins, 1994.

———. *A Short History of Biology*. New York: Doubleday, 1980.

Bowler, Peter J. *Evolution: The History of an Idea*. Berkeley: University of California Press, 1989.

Brooks, John Langdon. *Just Before the Origin: Alfred Russel Wallace's Theory of Evolution*. New York: Columbia University Press, 1984.

Cohen, Bernard I. *Album of Science: From Leonardo to Lavoisier, 1450–1800*. New York: Charles Scribner's Sons, 1980.

Cole, Francis J. *History of Comparative Anatomy: From Aristotle to the Eighteenth Century*. New York: Dover, 1975.

Coleman, William. *Biology in the Nineteenth Century: Problems of Form, Function, and Transformation*. New York: Cambridge University Press, 1978.

Corsi, Pietro. *The Age of Lamarck: Evolutionary Theories in France, 1790–1830*. Berkeley: University of California Press, 1988.

Crombie, A.C. *The History of Science from Augustine to Galileo*. New York: Dover, 1995.

Farber, Paul L. *The Emergence of Ornithology as a Scientific Discipline, 1760–1850*. Boston: D. Reidel, 1982.

Hall, Marie Boas. *The Scientific Renaissance, 1450–1630*. New York: Dover, 1994.

Hall, Thomas S. *History of General Physiology, 600 B.C. to A.D. 1900*. 2 vols. Chicago: University of Chicago Press, 1969.

Haller, John S., Jr. *Outcasts from Evolution: Scientific Attitudes of Racial Inferiority, 1859–1900*. Urbana: University of Illinois Press, 1971.

Horder, T.J., J.A. Witkowski, and C.C. Wylie, eds. *A History of Embryology*. New York: Cambridge University Press, 1985.

Keeney, Elizabeth. *The Botanizers: Amateur Scientists in Nineteenth-Century America*. Chapel Hill: University of North Carolina Press, 1992.

Leicester, Henry M. *Development of Biochemical Concepts from Ancient to Modern Times*. Cambridge, Mass.: Harvard University Press, 1974.

Lennox, James G. *Aristotle's Philosophy of Biology: Studies in the Origins of Life Sciences*. New York: Cambridge University Press, 2001.

Locy, William A. *The Growth of Biology: Zoology from Aristotle to Cuvier, Botany from Theophrastus to Hofmeister, Physiology from Harvey to Claude Bernard*. New York: H. Holt and Company, 1925.

Magner, Lois N. *A History of the Life Sciences*. New York: Marcel Dekker, 1994.

Mayor, Adrienne. *The First Fossil Hunters: Paleontology in Greek and Roman Times*. Princeton, N.J.: Princeton University Press, 2000.

Olby, Robert. *Origins of Mendelism*. Chicago: University of Chicago Press, 1985.

Persaud, T.V.N. *Early History of Human Anatomy, from Antiquity to the Beginning of the Modern Era*. Springfield, Ill.: C.C. Thomas Publishers, 1984.

Porter, Roy, ed. *The Cambridge Illustrated History of Medicine*. New York: Cambridge University Press, 1996.

Rothschuh, Karl E. *History of Physiology.* Translated and edited by Guenter B. Risse. Huntington, N.Y.: Krieger, 1973.

Rudwick, Martin J.S. *The Meaning of Fossils: Episodes in the History of Paleontology.* Chicago: University of Chicago Press, 1985.

Sachs, Julius von. *History of Botany, 1530–1860.* Oxford, England: Clarendon Press, 1890.

Smith, Roger C. *Smith's Guide to the Literature of the Life Sciences.* Minneapolis, Minn.: Burgess, 1980.

Stresemann, Erwin. *Ornithology from Aristotle to the Present.* Edited by G. William Cottrell. Translated by Hans J. and Cathleen Epstein. Cambridge, Mass.: Harvard University Press, 1975.

Biographies

Abbott, David, ed. *The Biographical Dictionary of Scientists: Biologists.* New York: Peter Bedrick Books, 1984.

Ackerknecht, Erwin H. *Rudolf Virchow: Doctor, Statesman, Anthropologist.* Madison: University of Wisconsin Press, 1953.

Asimov, Isaac. *Asimov's Biographical Encyclopedia of Science and Technology: The Lives and Achievements of 1510 Great Scientists from Ancient Times to the Present Chronologically Arranged.* Garden City, N.Y.: Doubleday, 1982.

Brock, Thomas D. *Robert Koch: A Life in Medicine and Bacteriology.* Washington, D.C.: ASM Press, 1999.

Brock, William H. *Justus von Liebig: The Chemical Gatekeeper.* New York: Cambridge University Press, 1997.

Darwin, Charles. *The Autobiography of Charles Darwin.* Edited by Francis Darwin. New York: Prometheus Books, 2000.

Debré, Patrice. *Louis Pasteur.* Translated by Elborg Foster. Baltimore, Md.: Johns Hopkins University Press, 1998.

Desmond, Adrian. *Huxley: From Devil's Disciple to Evolution's High Priest.* Reading, Mass.: Addison-Wesley, 1997.

Desmond, Adrian, and James Moore. *Darwin.* New York: Warner Books, 1991.

Dupree, A. Hunter. *Asa Gray, American Botanist, Friend of Darwin.* Baltimore, Md.: Johns Hopkins University Press, 1988.

Fisher, Richard B. *Joseph Lister, 1827–1912.* New York: Stein and Day, 1977.

Frank, Robert G., Jr. *Harvey and the Oxford Physiologists.* Berkeley: University of California Press, 1980.

Gillispie, Charles C., ed. *The Dictionary of Scientific Biography.* 18 vols. New York: Charles Scribner's Sons, 1970–1980.

Harvey, Joy. *Almost a Man of Genius: Clémence Royer, Feminism, and Nineteenth-Century Science.* New Brunswick, N.J.: Rutgers University Press, 1997.

Holmes, Frederick. *Claude Bernard and Animal Chemistry: The Emergence of a Scientist.* Cambridge, Mass.: Harvard University Press, 1974.

Jordanova, L.J. *Lamarck.* New York: Oxford University Press, 1984.

Kastner, Joseph. *John James Audubon.* New York: H.N. Abrams, 1992.

King-Hele, Desmond. *Erasmus Darwin: A Life of Unequalled Achievement.* London: DLM, 1999.

Koerner, Lisbet. *Linnaeus: Nature and Nation.* Cambridge, Mass.: Harvard University Press, 1999.

Ogilvie, Marilyn, and Roy Porter, eds. *The Biographical Dictionary of Scientists.* Third edition. New York: Oxford University Press, 2000.

Profitt, Pamela, ed. *Notable Women Scientists.* Farmington Hills, Mich.: Gale Group, 1999.

Roger, Jacques. *Buffon: A Life in Natural History.* Translated by Sarah Lucille Bonnefoi. Edited by L. Pearce Williams. Ithaca, N.Y.: Cornell University Press, 1997.

Secord, James A. *Victorian Sensation: The Extraordinary Publication, Reception, and Secret Authorship of* Vestiges of the Natural History of Creation. Chicago: University of Chicago Press, 2000.

Shearer, Benjamin F., and Barbara S. Shearer, eds. *Notable Women in the Life Sciences: A Biographical Dictionary.* Westport, Conn.: Greenwood Press, 1996.

Smith, Linda Wasmer. *Louis Pasteur: Disease Fighter.* Springfield, N.J.: Enslow Publishers, 1997.

Talbott, John Harold. *A Biographical History of Medicine: Excerpts and Essays on the Men and Their Work.* New York: Grune & Stratton, 1970.

Tyler-Whittle, Michael Sydney. *The Plant Hunters: Being an Examination of Collecting with an Account of the Careers and the Methods of a Number of Those who have Searched the World for Wild Plants.* New York: Lyons & Burford, 1997.

Warner, Deborah Jean. *Graceanna Lewis, Scientist and Humanitarian.* Washington, D.C.: Smithsonian Institution Press, 1979.

Williams, John R. *The Life of Goethe: A Critical Biography.* Malden, Mass.: Blackwell Publishers, 1998.

Yount, Lisa. *Antoni van Leeuwenhoek: First to See Microscopic Life.* Springfield, N.J.: Enslow Publishers, 1996.

On-line Resources

American Museum of Natural History. *Web site generated by the museum that provides educational resources, exhibition information, and links to the museum's research library and* Natural History *magazine archives.*

http://www.amnh.org

Catalog of the Scientific Community in the Sixteenth and Seventeenth Centuries, Rice University, Texas. *Contains a catalog of 631 biographies of scientists from the sixteenth and seventeenth centuries.*

http://es.rice.edu/ES/humsoc/Galileo/Catalog/catalog.html

History of Science Society at Washington University. *Provides description of organization, links to publications, professional links, a database of subject matter, reading lists, and academic links.*

http://depts.washington.edu/hssexec

International Society for the History, Philosophy, and Social Studies of Biology. *Official web site for the organization, containing newsletters, research in the history of science, educational resources, and links to other relevant web sites.*

http://www.phil.vt.edu/ishpssb

Institute and Museum of History of Science in Florence, Italy. *Provides information about museum and its library, access to on-line exhibitions, description of research activities and publications, listing of events and news, and links to related web sites.*

http://galileo.imss.firenze.it

Internet History of Science Sourcebook. *Provides links to numerous web sites with information covering the history of science from ancient Egypt to the current day. Links to sites providing on-line manuscripts and original texts are provided as well.*

http://www.fordham.edu/halsall/science/sciencesbook.html

MedWeb at Emory University. *Provides links to various web sites that contain information about the history of medicine.*

http://www.medweb.emory.edu/MedWeb

Museum of the History of Science, Oxford. *Provides information about the museum, listing of events, access to on-line exhibits and collections database, archive of on-line newsletters, information about the museum library, and links to other history of science web sites.*

http://www.mhs.ox.ac.uk/

Zoological Record, BIOSIS and the Zoological Society of London, Biographies of Biologists. *Provides links to numerous web sites with biographical information about important figures in the history of biology.*

http://www.york.biosis.org/zrdocs/zoolinfo/biograph.htm

PHOTO CREDITS

INDEX

Page numbers in **boldface** refer to the main entry on a subject.

Page numbers in *italics* refer to illustrations, figures, and tables.

A

Acetic acid, 150
Acetic fermentation, 145
Acid crystals, 143
Acoustics, 82
Acquired characteristics, inheritance of
  Jean Lamarck and, 102, 106, 107
  August Weismann and, 183
Agassiz, Alexander, 1–3
Agassiz, Elizabeth Cabot Cary, 1–3
Agassiz, Jean Louis Rodolphe, 1–3
Aging, 133
Agricultural chemistry, 117
Air, analysis of
  Stephen Hales and, 73
  Hippocrates and, 85
"Airs," 80
Airs, Waters, Places (Hippocrates), 86
Albertus Magnus, Saint (Albert the Great), xi, 3, 9
Alchemy, 97
Almonds, 185
Aluminum, 184
Amazon, insects of, 14–15
Ammonium cyanate, 185
Ammonium paratartrate, 144
Amputation, 122
Anatome plantarum (Malpighi), 127
Anatomy
  Aristotle's study of, 8–9

comparative anatomy, 114
  Galen and, 60, 61
  Albrecht von Haller and, 75
  Thomas Henry Huxley and, 90
  Ibn Sīnā and, 97
Anatomy, scientists of
  Giovanni Alfonso Borelli, **29–31**
  Realdo Colombo, **38–39**
  Girolamo Fabrici, **55–57**
  Luigi Galvani, **62–63**
  William Harvey, **76–81**
  Friedrich Gustav Jacob Henle, **83–84**
  Paul Langerhans, **107–108**
  Leonardo da Vinci, **109–114**
  Marcello Malpighi, **126–127**
  Johannes Müller, **134–136**
  Andreas Vesalius, **172–175**
The Anatomy of Plants (Nehemiah Grew), xii, 69
Anima, 165
Animal chemistry, 117
Animal classification. *See also* Taxonomy
  Aristotle and, 7
  Carl Linnaeus and, 119
Animalcules
  Antoni van Leeuwenhoek and, 108
  Lazzaro Spallanzani and, 162
"Animalculists," "ovists" *vs.,* 109
Animal magnetism, 131–132
Animism
  Georg Ernst Stahl and, 165
  Caspar Wolff and, 187
Annals of Chemistry and Pharmacology, xiii, 117
"Anna O.", 34

Anthrax
  Heinrich Koch and, 99–101
  Louis Pasteur and, 147, 148
Anthropology
  Élie Metchnikoff and, 133
Anthropology, scientists of
  Karl Ernst von Baer, **11–12**
  Clémence Royer, **154–155**
  Rudolf Carl Virchow, **175–177**
Antibodies
  Paul Ehrlich and, 53
  August Paul von Wassermann and, 181
Antigens
  Paul Ehrlich and, 53
  August Paul von Wassermann and, 181
Antiseptics
  Joseph Lister and, 120, 122–124
  Ignaz Semmelweis and, 159–160
Antitoxins
  Emil von Behring and, 17
  August Paul von Wassermann and, 181
Aorta, 114
Apes, 50
Aphids
  parthenogenesis and, 28
  Nettie Maria Stevens and, 166
Apollonius of Perga, 30
Archetypes, 64
Archive of Pathological Anatomy and Physiology and of Clinical Medicine, 175–176
Aristotle, **4–9**, *5*
  Albertus Magnus as translator of, 3
  and William Harvey, 78

199

Index

Index

M

Index

Index